CITIZENSHIP AND DEMOCRACY

A CASE FOR PROPORTIONAL REPRESENTATION

CITIZENSHIP
AND
DEMOCRACY

A CASE FOR PROPORTIONAL REPRESENTATION

NICK LOENEN

Dundurn Press
Toronto • Oxford

Editor: Doris Cowan
Designer: Sebastian Vasile
Printer: Best Book Manufacturers

Canadian Cataloguing in Publication Data

Loenen, Nick
    Citizenship and democracy

(Towards the new millennium series)
Includes bibliographical references.
ISBN 1-55002-280-6

1. Proportional representation – Canada.   2. British Columbia. Legislative Assembly – Reform.   3. Canada. Parliament – Reform   I. Title.   II. Series.

JL167. L63 1997   328.3'347'0971   C96-932421-9

1   2   3   4   5   BJ   01   00   99   98   97

The publisher wishes to acknowledge the generous assistance of the **Canada Council,** the **Book Publishing Industry Development Program** of the **Department of Canadian Heritage,** and the **Ontario Arts Council.**

Printed and bound in Canada.

Printed on recycled paper.

Dundurn Press
2181 Queen Street East
Suite 301
Toronto, Ontario, Canada
M4E 1E5

Dundurn Press
73 Lime Walk
Headington, Oxford
England
OX3 7AD

Dundurn Press
250 Sonwil Drive
Buffalo, NY
U.S.A. 14225

TABLE OF CONTENTS

ACKNOWLEDGEMENTS

WHEN AND WHERE did this work start? Where is the start of anything? When and where does a person begin? This study is my work, but the seeds were sown long ago. Perhaps by a mother who instilled self-confidence, and a father who was educated without the benefit of much schooling. He fought an oppressive social order to establish workers' rights, and resisted National Socialism so that persons might be free. Perhaps it started with my maternal grandfather, a day labourer who in the 1890s walked with a wheelbarrow from Nieuw Loosdrecht to Amsterdam (thirty-five kilometres as the crow flies) to purchase books. He and his friends in the Young Men's Christian Society would study the books he brought back and debate the meaning of existence. Where is the beginning of anything? Did the idea for this book start during my five years on the back bench, as I grew more and more aware with each passing year that all decisions of importance are made outside the legislature, and that power is concentrated exclusively at the top?

This study owes much to the inspiration that came from my parents and grandfather, and from many others. Much of the work is based on a master's degree thesis, which took shape under the professional and watchful eye of my adviser, Paul Tennant, and benefited from the helpful suggestions of other members of UBC's Political Science faculty, especially Ken Carty and Alan Cairns.

Marilyn Zuidhof-Loenen and Jeff Loenen helped with the initial editing of the manuscript, which Doris Cowan of Dundurn Press polished into a most readable text. George Gibault, who combines practical political instinct with a love of history and political philosophy, offered penetrating commentary. Their enthusiastic support and helpful suggestions were much appreciated. My research was also generously assisted by the library staff at UBC and the legislative library in Victoria.

Finally, without my wife Jayne's tolerance for my strange, unsociable working habits, this work would not exist. I am grateful to all of these persons, and many not mentioned, for being part of my life. They all helped shape this project.

BREAKOUT TO DEMOCRACY

by Patrick Boyer, Q.C.

T HE REAL LIMITATIONS of Canadian political practices and institutions of government lie not only in their often paltry and confused outcomes, but more profoundly in the inherent incapacity
of the structure as it currently exists to deliver anything close to what a
modern, democratic, pluralistic society requires.

It is in that context that this book provides a masterly "systems
analysis" of a major flaw in the relationship between what we as
Canadian citizens expect from our democratic institutions and procedures, and what they actually deliver to us.

Nick Loenen not only examines the perverse shortcomings of the
voting system, but he does so in the context of Canadian political culture and democratic values. The result is a book that provides not only
information, but understanding.

Voting systems are an integral component in the equation of our
political democracy: freedom of expression *plus* the right to vote *plus*
the availability of choice between parties *plus* a fair and free election
process *equals* a representative legislature and accountable government. Right? Not necessarily.

This "equation" of democracy leads to different outcomes, depending, as with any equation, upon the variables – such as which voting
system is introduced into it. If all other elements of free and fair democratic elections are held constant, but we remove one kind of voting
system (such as our so-called "first-past-the-post" plan) and replace it
with another (such as the proportional voting method), the results will
be different.

A voting system which proportionately allocates votes among candidates in a way that more accurately reflects the actual weight of voting preferences expressed by the electorate has tremendous importance to any political society which considers itself, as we Canadians do, to be democratic.

Citizenship and Democracy makes clear, however, that a much richer harvest awaits us with the use of a saner voting system. More than just better numbers, there is also the potential for a dramatic *qualitative* improvement in the nature of democracy and accountability in Canada.

Why battle over fairness about where the constituency boundaries are drawn, or fight for the right to vote, or establish qualifying legal criteria for candidates who run for public office, or impose campaign spending limits, or worry about electoral broadcasting rules – if simultaneously we employ such a blunt system for calculating voting outcomes that it trivializes and even mocks these other refinements in our democratic electoral system?

The true nature of Canada's voting system is certainly not just an academic or theoretical topic. The outcomes of many recent Canada-wide and provincial elections would have been different – and consequently the make-up of the legislatures and the nature of the political agenda and legislative programs would also have displayed a more varied complexion – if proportional representation rules had been in operation.

Nor is this a tired old topic from the past. New Zealand has just completed in late 1996 its first election using a multi-member proportional representation system. Immediately after the last Canadian general election in 1993, voices for electoral reform again called out in favour of proportional representation here, too, since it would have produced a more balanced House of Commons by more accurately reflecting the percentage of popular vote each party actually received.

Under present Canadian electoral laws, it is enough just to get one more vote than anybody else. In a field of many candidates, therefore, the winner's edge over the others may only require 30 or 40 percent of the ballots cast, not even close to a majority. Yet the fundamental tenet of democracy is: the majority decides.

Since this is true, and since dissatisfaction with the working of our political system has been such a dominant undercurrent in our culture and public life for some time now, you may well ask: Why has this subject not even shown up yet on the public radar screen?

Usually we do, in fact, hear an outcry just after most elections, when the distorting power of the existing system — where a simple plurality at the constituency level translates into a lopsided majority of seats in the legislature – has once again shocked the sensibilities of Canadians. That is when the crude nature of Canadian voting outcomes is most dramatically on display, and when the topic is good for an editorial or two, or perhaps a "Commentary" on CBC radio by a political scientist. Then this sudden quest for a more mature democratic system again fades away, like other one-day wonders.

Clearly a more sustained battle is required to win the day for vibrant citizenship, robust democracy, and political accountability. It is a battle that requires a clear plan, and a process of public education. That is where Nick Loenen and *Citizenship and Democracy* enter the arena.

This new book on proportional representation, in making the all-important link between citizenship and democracy, serves as a fresh rallying point for all of us committed to transforming Canada into an authentic democracy. It provides all the ideas and arguments needed for a sustained effort between elections to mobilize sufficient support for our democratic modernization.

It will not be an easy battle to win. Our own political history proves that. Prior to the Parti Québécois coming to power in Quebec in 1976, its members had gathered at endless week-end policy meetings to thoroughly debate and democratically vote upon the many planks in their electoral platform – including proportional representation. Not only did the grass roots of the party want it, for the sake of fundamental democratization of Quebec's electoral system, but so too did the leader of the Parti Québécois, René Lévesque. When the party came to power, however, and the leader himself was keen to implement this change in the electoral system, he suddenly met new resistance from his caucus and even members of the cabinet. Perhaps the old system wasn't so bad after all, these newly elected office holders now reasoned, since it had served to elect them. Why change?

Thus even with a clearly enunciated policy favouring proportional representation, endorsed in the electoral mandate given to the party and its platform by the voters and supported from the very top by the leader himself, the initiative ran into two insurmountable obstacles: the weight of the status quo and the opportunism of those suddenly converted to favouring the rules by which they had come to power. As a result, Quebec today continues to be quite indistinct from all other provinces, at least in this sharing of the common Canadian voting system of first-past-the-post.

Is this example unique? Unfortunately not. When Jean Chrétien campaigned for the leadership of the Liberal Party in 1984, he said in Brandon, Manitoba, on 9 May, that bringing in a system of proportional representation would be "one of my first acts as prime minister." The federal election system had to be reformed, he pledged, to end western alienation. Jean Chrétien lost that particular leadership race to John Turner, but won another one a few years later and did go on to become prime minister in 1993. Somewhere along the line between Brandon and 24 Sussex Drive, though, his pledge for proportional representation got lost.

This is more than a partisan question, as these two examples demonstrate. It is a political problem and an institutional challenge of the first order: how do you bring about a fundamental political reform when those with the real control of the political system, the public agenda, and the majority of votes in the legislature have decided against it?

What can you do when they have come to favour the rules by which they gained their majority in the legislature, even though they came into office pledged to change those very rules?

The truth is that our notion of an "electoral mandate" as given by voters to the party winning the most seats to implement its program is largely a convenient constitutional fiction. To overcome this institutional and political hurdle, to generate a clear and specific mandate from which no government could comfortably hide, a political sky-hook may be needed, such as a binding referendum on the question of proportional representation.

It is possible, of course, that in such a referendum the considered vote of Canadians might determine that we should not switch to proportional representation and in fact ought to continue with the present voting system. After all, it is a system that does produce stability at the level of the legislature, even if this is at the cost of reflecting imperfectly (and sometimes actually distorting) the electorate's voting-booth verdict. Canadians would no doubt be told in any referendum debate that, based upon examples in other countries, proportional representation might ensure a mirror image of the balloting choices of the electorate – but it would come at the price of creating a legislature with many parties, and many small parties, and therefore instability at that level. The House of Commons, or the provincial legislature, would be admirably democratic in its representation of the different voices and views in Canadian society, but it would be a very difficult place (we would be led to believe) to actually get anything done. Better to "stick with the devil we know."

This line of reasoning – which in our past has often been invoked to reject the idea of proportional representation by accepting the pragmatic benefit of first-past-the-post even with its acknowledged faults – is usually sealed with the argument that here in Canada we don't want to have unstable parliaments like those in Italy or France or other countries with proportional representation.

Since we've not tried it here, though, this argument is only conjecture. What we have tried, for sure, is the present system. We certainly know it well. Unquestionably it scores very high as a difficult place to actually get anything done.

The difficulty in Canadian politics is that we never think things through very far, and almost never to their logical conclusion or necessary implication. A referendum on the ballot question "Do you approve of changing to a voting system based upon proportional representation?" with a short but intensive prereferendum campaign period during which the pros and cons were publicly and throughly debated, would no doubt serve us well in thinking through collectively the realities of our inherited system of representative democracy.

A referendum has another role, as a check on arbitrary use of political power by incumbents, in this matter of changing the voting system. For instance, in looking at our history, one might at first blush say there has been something of a trend *away from* proportional representation. In places where we've had it, proportional representation is now gone. The plot, however, is thicker.

In western Canada, departures from the old simple-plurality system had been made in British Columbia, Alberta, and Manitoba. Some of these experiments may not have been as rigorous as the new voting system now called for in this book by Nick Loenen, yet nevertheless they do remind us that alternative voting systems are hardly alien to the Canadian experience.

British Columbia, for example, with the provincial elections of 1952 and 1953, had in operation a preferential or alternative ballot on which the voter marked the names of candidates in order of preference. It was under this system that the Social Credit Party came to power in 1952 with one seat more than the CCF. The province returned to the simple plurality system for the 1956 election, and the system has stayed the same since.

In Alberta a combination of systems was in force from 1926 to 1959, with the preferential or alternative ballot being used in rural single-member districts, and the single transferable vote in the two multi-member districts of Edmonton and Calgary. Elections since 1959, however, have been conducted in Alberta on the straight plurality system, with the province divided into single-member districts.

When the Manitoba Law Reform Commission tentatively recommended in 1978 that the plurality system be replaced for provincial elections by a single transferable vote system in the multi-member ridings and an alternative vote system in the single-member rural ridings, the proposal rang with certain familiarity. For, like Alberta, Manitoba had also used a combination of preferential and single transferable ballots in the past. From 1920 to 1945, voters in the City of Winnipeg had a scheme of proportional representation. Each electoral district was entitled to elect 10 members to the legislature and voters had a single transferable ballot. For the elections of 1949 and 1953, Winnipeg's representation was expanded to 12, with the city subdivided into three electoral districts, each of which elected four members. St. Boniface was also established during this period as a two-member district. Proportional representation was continued in all four multi-member districts. In rural Manitoba the preferential or alternative ballot was employed in single-member districts in the three elections of 1927, 1932, and 1936. Starting in 1958 the voting in both rural and urban ridings reverted entirely to a plurality vote in single-member constituencies.

The municipal election system of some larger cities in Western Canada, too, was a part of this pattern, with proportional representation being adopted in Winnipeg, Calgary, Edmonton, and Vancouver in the 1930s. Much earlier, under the Ontario provincial Election Act of 1885, the City of Toronto was converted into a three-member constituency for elections to the legislature, which resulted in a type of proportional representation from the city.

Now for the vital lesson: not one of these shifts from proportional representation back to simple plurality voting systems came about as the result of a publicly supported referendum. They were made, instead, by elected representatives, who either favoured changing rules to enhance their incumbency or who had themselves been elected by the first-past-the-post system (members of provincial legislatures), voting to change the municipal electoral system.

Indeed, the rule was that any change away from proportional representation at the municipal level in Alberta had to be approved by local electors in a plebiscite. That seemed like a sufficient restraint on abuse of the power of incumbency. In the case of Calgary, however, an expedient was found to circumvent this direct democracy check on the system. In 1973 Calgary City Council passed a resolution requesting provincial legislation that would let the city change its voting procedures without going through a plebiscite. On June 6, 1974, the Municipal Elections Act was amended to permit the Calgary City Council and Calgary school boards, which were also using proportional balloting to pass their by-laws and resolutions, to discontinue use of that voting system without any longer having to submit the matter first to the electors for their assent through balloting. Then on June 24, 1974, Calgary Council used its new power to repeal the bylaw which had provided for proportional representation.

It was thus by a provincial-municipal juggernaut combination of incumbent office holders that the accountability mechanism of local democracy and the responsiveness of a politically refined voting system were both set aside. Such are the lessons from our history that we do well to remember today in preparing our battle plan for a democratic breakout. Our past teaches us about the virtual necessity of having a national binding referendum to bring in a system of proportional voting to elect members of Parliament, or province-wide referendums to do so at the provincial level.

The situation in Canada's legislatures today certainly demands a fresh look at proportional representation. No matter what some may smugly say about the 'instability' of other countries' parliaments, no matter the cynicism which might be suggested by our own history in moving away from proportional representation in those instances where we had it, we have a duty now to move forward. The degree of partyism in Parliament and the legislatures by this final decade of the twentieth century makes a sham of our pretence of having effective, democratic, representative democracy.

Nick Loenen's timely and well-crafted book, which explores the relationship between citizenship and democracy through the particular lens of our country's voting system, sets out for all to see the possibilities for a real democratic breakout. Cleanly delineated, in the pages that follow, is a route to achieve our real potential as Canadians, to energize our legislatures, and to create a political system that is robustly democratic and definitely more accountable.

Nick Loenen's lucid analysis and sharp yet balanced critique of the behavioural and philosophic imperatives that drive Canadians is, in many respects, like a map and compass to help us get past the shoals that so frequently impede, sometimes even ruin, our authentic life journey – both as individual citizens and as a collective society – in the dynamic culture of our times.

Written by a thoughtful, widely read and highly practical person, Nick Loenen's book is all the more authentic and credible because he has served as an elected representative at both the municipal and provincial levels. So, like all of us who have been there, he has seen the real flaws of the electoral and parliamentary system. Like many of us, too, he continues to defend, while seeking to reform, that system – because at the end of the day we know that it is potentially our greatest bulwark in curbing excesses of power and balancing the diversity of our common Canadian community.

So much of what passes for public debate in Canada is focused on our "problems," so little on how we can change underlying conditions so those problems themselves will no longer arise. This book is a welcome exception.

INTRODUCTION

One trend must be reversed. That is the inclination ... to relegate decision making to the executive, to give cabinet the job of making decisions. Out of reach of the people, closeted away from the majority of the people's representatives, they run things their own way. This limitation of the powers, this narrowing of the citizen's power base, this deification of the few is unfortunate at the best of times. As a politician who has been both a Minister and a backbencher, I can express my concern firsthand![1]

PUBLIC DISCONTENT WITH government and politicians has increased over the last two decades, is greater in Canada than in the U.S., and is greater here than most places world-wide.[2] Canadians think government is not responsive to them or their needs. We are supposed to be a representative democracy; elected members are supposed to speak and act for their constituents; but instead elected members are held captive by party interests, and between elections citizens have no control over the political elite. The noted Canadian journalist, historian, and author, Peter C. Newman, has described the changing Canadian attitude toward government as moving from deference to defiance. Canada is among the world's most fortunate countries, yet there is anger in the streets. Government institutions, designed mostly in the nineteenth century, are failing, and cannot meet the needs of a Canada poised to enter the twenty-first century.

National unity is under severe threat. The Quebec referendum on separation held on 30 October 1995 took Canada to the brink of unprecedented political, economic, and social chaos. Former Prime Minister Pierre Elliott Trudeau's vision, of one nation united by centralized political power and more government services at the federal level in Ottawa, is more distant than ever. Separatism, both in Quebec and in the West, is fuelled by the opposite impulse of decentralization.

Disappointed with what they perceive as a lack of responsiveness in the federal institutions, both Quebec and the West want to bring government closer to home. The rise of the Reform Party of Canada, and the wide support for democratic reforms such as *recall, referendum* and *initiative* are evidence of the distrust Canadians harbour for the traditional political institutions. A succession of unpopular measures – the North American Free Trade Agreement, the Goods and Services Tax, and especially the almost universal support of the Charlottetown Accord by the political elite against the wishes of the people – have left Canadians suspicious about the responsiveness of their political institutions.

National unity is threatened by economic as well as political forces. Our fiscal mismanagement is a disgrace. Economically, Canada is falling behind. Forty years ago, when my family arrived here from Holland, 22 cents Canadian equalled one guilder; today these currencies are at par. Canadian purchasing power has dropped dramatically relative to the important Japanese yen and most European currencies. Canadian government indebtedness is unprecedented. The social costs of government debt are enormous. Government appetite for debt servicing increases the cost of borrowing, including capital for residential mortgages and business investment. The strong purchasing power of offshore money drives real estate prices out of reach for our own young families. For many, home ownership is an unattainable dream. Reckless government overspending, which started under Trudeau, jeopardizes the universality of social programs. A federal government that is broke cannot maintain national unity. Businesses that are over-taxed cannot provide jobs. Canada's economic and political predicament must result in the creation of a new form of federalism.

A new federalism must go beyond a new division of powers between the federal and provincial governments. The old institutions have failed us, and must be discarded. Canada must become a democracy with institutions that are truly representative and responsible. Politically, Canada is living a lie. We think we are democratic, but we are not. We think the majority rules, but it does not. We think laws are made by the people's representatives in Parliament and the provincial legislatures, but the reality is otherwise. We think MPs and MLAs speak for the citizens they represent. They do not. We think Parliament and the legislatures are watchdogs holding governments responsible. They are not. We think that our voting system, by conjuring up parliamentary and legislative majorities where none exist among the people, provides strong government able to guard the public interest. Yet academic, comparative studies prove what any casual observer can see: that we have weak governments that frequently sacrifice the public good for short-term political gain. People regularly express the belief that government is out of touch. Public policy related to the growth of government, overspending, mounting debt, high taxation, family breakdown, control of violent crime, constitutional matters, refugee claimants, aboriginal issues, the state of education, social programs, fisheries, special interest groups, and handouts to business – in all these areas and more, government action is frequently out of tune with the citizens' concerns. The growing disparity between public expectations about our political culture and the actual political practices must be bridged to restore public trust in our governing institutions, giving government the legitimacy it now lacks.

My generation has bankrupted Canada, and mortgaged the future of our own children. It is not something to be proud of. In fact, it is shortsighted, selfish, and immoral. Is this what we the citizens personally wanted, or do we have a political system that breeds irresponsibility for political gain? I submit that the latter is the case. In particular, this study argues for a root-and-branch change to our voting system. Many observers have noted the undemocratic results that our voting system typically produces, but few have studied the impact our voting system has on the distribution of power between cabinet and the legislature, or how that lopsided distribution of power has rendered the concept of responsible government a myth, robbed the people's representatives of their independence, and eroded the concept of citizenship. Without a strong concept of citizenship and public-spiritedness, political parties are reduced to election machines, and governing to an endless brokering of sectional, private, and special interests.

This study recommends that our present *single member plurality* (SMP)[3] voting system be replaced with the *single transferable vote* (STV). Taking the British Columbia electorate and legislature as an example, it considers the defects of SMP, and suggests how STV, in contrast, opens the possibility of new forms of political behaviour. A change in voting system to STV would not automatically solve every defect and all failings of our present political institutions, but it has the potential to give voters more choice, to control their elected representatives, waste fewer votes, bring greater political diversity into Parliament and the legislatures, lessen party discipline, weaken the power of the prime minister and the premiers, increase the power of Parliament and the legislatures, restore responsible government, render government more responsive to changing public demands, enhance the role of political parties in the formation of public policies, deliver a more efficient government, connect government to the people, foster a political culture of democratic participation, and enhance citizenship.

This study suggests institutional change to increase the likelihood that when government acts, the citizens have spoken, and when the citizens speak, the government acts. This study is about limiting the misuse of government power, and increasing citizens' power of choice, which is so necessary for human freedom. Thomas Hobbes, the seventeenth-century British political philosopher, titled his work on government *Leviathan* after that mystical, large and powerful sea-monster. Government is big, with enormous coercive powers. Paradoxically, such power is the condition of our freedom: without law, there would be anarchy, chaos, and barbarism. But the balance between freedom and oppression is almost impossible to maintain, and the power so essential to preserve freedom often destroys it. The twentieth century has been more violent than any previous time in history. It has witnessed oppression, terror, and death inflicted on millions, not because it lacked government, but because the Leviathan of government ran amok. Why should any of this concern the peaceful citizens of Canada and British Columbia? Are we about to succumb to totalitarianism? No, but neither are we a shining example of democracy. Consider the following.

Item 1: Late in the evening of Saturday, 6 February 1988, the then premier of British Columbia, Bill Vander Zalm, returned from a holiday in Hawaii. Speaking to the press a few minutes after he stepped off the plane, he announced that funding for all abortions would be discontinued. The next day his caucus entered a two-day meeting. Funding for abortions was not an item on the agenda, but, in response to a question, the premier told his caucus that government policy was as stated by the premier at the airport; end of discussion. On Monday, 8 February, cabinet met and by order-in-council amended the provisions of the Medical Services Plan to effect the policy. CBC Vancouver asked, by way of phone-in poll: "Should the government pay for abortions that result from rape and incest?" The answer: 2,901 said yes; 496 no. On 6 March, two polls showed 66 percent of the citizens opposed the government's new policy.[4] The B.C. Supreme Court ruled against the government on 7 March, on technical grounds, suggesting that if the government insisted on this policy, there were better ways of doing it.[5]

Item 2: On 12 September 1994, Quebec elected a government committed to taking Quebec out of the Canadian federation. The separatist Parti Québécois received 44.7 percent of the popular vote and 77 seats. The Liberals received almost the same popular vote, 44.3 percent, but only 47 seats. The premier-designate, Jacques Parizeau, claimed to have a mandate to set in motion the process leading to sovereignty for Quebec.[6] Opinion polls at this time consistently showed support for sovereignty in Quebec at 40 percent.

These items show a premier and a premier-designate committed to using the powers of office to implement a policy not supported by a majority of the citizens.[7] Parizeau went on to use not only all the powers of his office but also the considerable ability of a provincial legislature, including its propaganda arsenal, to take Quebec out of the Canadian federation. In a representative democracy government action is supposed to reflect what the people, acting as citizens, would have done had they made the decision themselves. If our governmental institutions are meant to ensure that the citizens' will prevails, then the two items cited are instances of institutional breakdown. The contrary could be argued. In this view, the judicial branch of government stopped Premier Vander Zalm, and the people stopped the Parti Québécois in the referendum. The government as a whole did not fail; in fact, these instances show that the institutional checks and balances work. The reply to that is twofold: first, can there be satisfaction with a system that takes us to the edge of the precipice, and causes so much unrest and confusion, particularly in the instance of Quebec? Second, the parts of government that are the subject of this work, namely the legislature and the electoral system, did fail. They failed to ensure that the citizens' will would prevail. What is true in these two instances holds equally for a vast array of government activities. What structural arrangements allow such failure?

In Item 1 the breakdown occurred because the Westminster parliamentary model[8] gives too much power to the first minister (prime minister or premier),[9] and in Item 2 the breakdown was due to a voting system that artificially generates majorities in the legislature where none exist among the people.[10] Our voting system typically awards government to a minority. For example, the legendary W.A.C. Bennett, who ruled as premier of B.C. for two decades, never enjoyed majority support. Each of the two items points to an area where representative democracy is endangered in our present system of government. First, government accountability is weak; and second, the composition of Parliament and the legislatures is not representative. The two problems are related; correcting the second holds the potential to remedy the first. The best way to prevent misuse of government power is to enlarge choice for people. A voting system that favours parties must be changed for one that favours citizens.

This study attempts to show that giving citizens more choice at election time, and more accurately translating the voters' preferences into seats, would concentrate power less in cabinet, and more in Parliament and the legislatures. A proportional voting system would do both – give citizens more choice,[11] and translate voters' preferences into seats more accurately.[12] This study therefore recommends replacing the present *single member plurality* (SMP) voting system with a form of proportional representation, namely the *single transferable vote* (STV)[13] in multi-member districts.

Much discontent with government exists because citizens feel powerless. The system does not respond to them. It is no wonder. Typically, our voting system gives government to a minority. We do not have a democracy. On almost every election night the majority of voters get neither the local representative nor the government they voted for. How democratic is that? Further, the system induces many not to vote for their first preference, but to vote strategically. The unresponsiveness of our system does not stop there; there is more. Those few voters whose choice does make it to the legislature are still not represented. All decisions of importance are made outside the legislature. Cabinet has too much power, rendering the people's representatives almost impotent. We get to vote for representatives who lack power, therefore *we* have no power. Having a voice in Parliament or the legislature is meaningless when Parliament and the legislature themselves have no voice. In addition, after voting day our representatives' allegiance is to the party, not the people.

The lack of accountability and responsiveness in government can be resolved by changing the voting system so as to give citizens more choice. The limited choice offered voters under our present system stifles political diversity and meaningful participation. Increasingly, people are experiencing, and have come to expect, greater diversity, for example in consumer goods, life-styles, education, entertainment, and multiculturalism. Our essentially nineteenth-century political institutions cannot meet modern demands. In education we see a blossoming of diversity, charter schools, independent schools, Montessori schools, schools for the gifted and those with special needs, a catering to consumer demands, a trust that people know what is best. Television channels proliferate, and cater increasingly to smaller, specialized audiences. The futurist Alvin Toffler, in his *Third Wave,* convincingly shows the trend toward a socially fractured society. We should not aim to reverse this trend, but to accommodate it. The yearning for greater diversity is ubiquitous, and accommodated everywhere – except in politics.

Our political institutions are out of step with the times; they limit choice, and inhibit diversity. Single member plurality (SMP) voting systems are unkind to minorities, except to the largest minority.[14] In an increasingly pluralistic society this is intolerable, and is a significant contributing factor to the widespread lack of trust in anything political. Government should be as pluralistic as the citizens it serves.[15] Attaining that goal requires substantial institutional change.

The material is presented as follows. Chapter 1 considers ideas about democratic theory, citizenship, and political participation. In particular, it suggests that increased participation will result in a more cohesive political community, and that it will be a cohesion that comes not from uniformity but from a shared commitment to a participatory process.

Chapter 2 considers three questions about the function and composition of the legislature. First, what do theorists in democracy and representative government teach? Second, what are the attitudes and expressed desires of the people? Third, what can be learned from recent court rulings? Analysis of these three areas strongly suggests that the legislature's composition should accurately represent the political diversity present in society, and that the legislature must have a significant role in law-making.

Chapter 3 is a study of the relationship between the B.C. cabinet and the legislature. SMP, combined with party discipline, weakens responsible government. The legislature has no power to hold government responsible, and it has no significant role in law-making. All decisions of importance are made outside its walls.

Chapter 4 examines the purpose of political parties. In particular, it concludes that under our voting system parties are mere election machines; they concentrate power at the top, and have no role in developing public policy.

The impotence of Parliament and the legislatures has not gone unnoticed. Many corrective measures have been proposed, such as direct democracy (recall, referendum and initiative), and parliamentary reforms (free votes, fixed election dates, and a more meaningful role for standing committees). These are discussed in Chapter 5, and are judged to be helpful but essentially inadequate. Chapter 6 introduces proportional representation generally, and STV in particular. It also suggests a B.C. electoral map using STV.

Chapter 7 considers the likely consequences of changing the voting system from SMP to STV, particularly on the functioning of the legislature and its relation to the cabinet. It concludes that such a legislature would more closely meet the requirements of democratic ideals. The chapter closes with a brief consideration of the possibility of implementation, given political realities and historical experience with electoral reform.

This is not a subject of merely academic interest. It is possible for citizens to participate more meaningfully in politics, to assume responsibility for public policies, and experience a greater sense of ownership over their government. Participation is important, both on an individual level and in the interests of maintaining a free social order. It is in ruling and being ruled that persons exercise their highest human capacities. By nature we are destined to live in community. Not everyone can be a ruler, but all should participate; not everyone can have their way, but all should have a say. Persons are less fully developed and satisfied to the degree they are excluded from political life. Participation must extend beyond voting in periodic elections. Alexis de Tocqueville warned that if between elections most public policy decisions are made for people, they will lose the ability to make choices at election time.

> It is in vain to summon a people, who have been ren-
> dered so dependent on the central power, to choose from
> time to time the representatives of that power; this rare
> and brief exercise of their free choice, however important
> it may be, will not prevent them from gradually losing the
> faculties of thinking, feeling, and acting for themselves,
> and thus gradually falling below the level of humanity.[16]

Citizens' participation is essential to the maintainance of a free social order. This, paradoxically, is especially true for democracies. Many observers, particularly de Tocqueville, note that the liberal democratic tradition breeds individualism: people turn in upon themselves, and few will bother to take an interest in public issues. Citizenship is undermined, and democracy left open to a new form of despotism; not the despotism of tyranny and oppression, but an "immense tutelary power"[17] – the vast bureaucratic state. People keep demanding more services. Their horizon has shrunk; it stops at their own immediate self-interest. The appetite for private benefits from the public purse destroys citizenship and freedom. For de Tocqueville, the only defence is a political culture of participation. That alone will broaden the limited horizon of individualism. To foster citizenship and preserve freedom, politics must be structured to promote commitment to common responsibilities, justice for all, and a society built on cooperation and consensus rather than the pursuit of private gain. In addition, social order depends on respect for law, respect implies assent, and assent requires participation. Proportional systems of representation are not sufficient, but they are necessary for fuller participation, an enlarged sense of citizenship, and the legitimizing of government authority.

Thinkers from Aristotle to Alexis de Tocqueville warn that democracy depends on informed, virtuous citizens, capable of participation and judgment. For J.S. Mill, the principal aim of good government is the improvement of people themselves, an improvement towards the concept of citizenship. He considered a proportional system the best means to that end.[18] The Norwegian scholar S. Rokkan viewed the spread of PR as the final stage in a process of increasing public participation, and thus the natural successor to suffrage reform. He describes Norwegian parishes that retain an SMP system as "pre-political." SMP gave way in Denmark in 1856, and by 1920 Great Britain was the exception in Europe.[19] When will Canada and British Columbia follow New Zealand's recent example, shed their colonial past and enter the modern, democratic political era?

The quest for PR is the manifestation of a desire for meaningful participation in the institution of government, such that the people's practice of citizenship will be enhanced and their essential humanity enlarged. It is based on a high view of human nature. Such is the motive that informs this study.

DEMOCRACY

If liberty and equality, as is thought by some, are chiefly to be found in democracy, they will be best attained when all persons alike share in the government to the utmost.[1]

F OR CANADIANS, DEMOCRACY means the right to vote: the citizens' right to select their rulers. How would you feel if after you slipped your vote into the ballot box someone removed it and destroyed it? You would have lost your democratic right. Yet that is what happens to most Canadians at most elections. Under our voting system most Canadians on election night do not get either the local candidate or the government they voted for. If we could start all over and devise a new voting system, would we select one that wastes most votes, gives government to a minority, and results in an adversarial, inefficient governmental system where all decisions of importance are made outside Parliament and outside the provincial legislatures? Not likely. It would offend our sense of democracy. Yet that is how our voting system works. Why are we not offended by what we have? Because most Canadians have never considered that our voting system could be other than what it is.

As we reflect on changing the voting system, it is important to consider what ends a voting system should achieve. Form must follow function. Most would agree that a voting system should achieve the ideals of democracy. But what are they?

Deeply held common beliefs, beliefs that are shared by all and seldom questioned, are the most difficult to describe and define. Such is the case with our belief in democracy. To most of us, democracy is good and important. Twice this century, Canada sent the flower of its youth to war to defend democracy. But what is democracy? Democracy refers, in part, to a particular system of social organization, a process for arriving at group decisions. For the purposes of this study, the focus is on that process. For now we need to set aside questions of substance, such as the concern that has dominated much of the twentieth century, namely, whether democracy aims at an equal distribution of goods, or at libertarianism.

When considered as a system for making group decisions, democracy in its most literal sense means "rule by the people." Pericles, largely responsible for Athenian democracy, told the people of Athens, "We are called a democracy because the government is in the hands of the many and not of the few."[2] Aristotle, as quoted above, put it even more strongly. His democratic ideal was to include all citizens in the ruling function. Note how different the contemporary Canadian concept is from classical democracy. In our version of democracy, a minority of citizens every four or five years selects the captain of our ship of state, who then orders everyone off the bridge for the duration of the voyage.

Classical democracy embodies the notion of self-rule, based on the belief that in an imperfect world – beset by ignorance, greed, rampant self-interest, abuse of power, prejudice, propaganda, public lies and mass manipulation – decision-making powers, particularly the coercive powers of government, are most effectively channelled to serving the public good when such power is shared among the many, rather than given to the few. Bertrand Russell wrote: "All history shows that, as might be expected, minorities cannot be trusted to care for the interests of majorities."[3] United States President Theodore Roosevelt stated, "The majority of the plain people will ... make fewer mistakes in governing themselves than a smaller body of men in trying to govern them."[4] But in addition to protecting the interests of all concerned, and ensuring few mistakes will be made, this chapter suggests, self-rule improves people, particularly by enlarging their sense of citizenship.

The democratic ideal is self-rule. However, this immediately raises a practical problem. Society is made up of many selves. Not everyone agrees on political ends. There are ideological differences, practical divisions, and competing visions at war within any society. What is the will of the people, and how is it to be determined? It is often internally inconsistent and contradictory: for instance, people may want more government services, but also lower taxes. Before the self can rule, that self must have some identity and consistency. We speak of this as the public interest and the public good, or the good of all. A people can rule itself only when there is a measure of agreement about what the public interest is. The voting system must make order out of chaos, and allow the public good to emerge. Therefore, before considering changes to our voting system to attain self-rule, it is necessary to ask if self-rule by the people can adequately promote and protect the public good, or the good of all. If self-rule is a recipe for chaos, it should be dismissed.

CLASSICAL LIBERALISM, SELF-INTEREST, AND THE PUBLIC GOOD

CLASSICAL LIBERALISM, AND most political thinking today, holds that the public good is best served by allowing everyone to pursue their own self-interest. It understands all political good as private good. Classical liberalism in the tradition of Hobbes, Locke, and Jefferson sees government, and most institutions in society, in terms of a contractual relationship. Autonomous individuals have calculated that it is in their interest to institute government and submit to its coercive powers. It is government by the consent of the governed. In this view, government is based on a contract made by citizens. The function of citizenship is both to create and to participate in government. The French and American revolutions gave content to what citizenship means in the liberal tradition.

By contrast, modern Canadian notions of citizenship are hopelessly ambiguous. Until 1947 there were no Canadian citizens, only British subjects residing in Canada. Subjects are not citizens, they neither create nor participate in government. Their function is to obey government. The term "subject" harks back to a social order based not on contract between citizens of equal worth but on a hierarchical order understood as rooted in the natural, God-ordained order. Canadian institutions of government are formally monarchical with ultimate power residing in the Crown, and the resulting distribution of power in our governing institutions is hierarchical, not diffused. Canadians have never popularly approved their constitution and order of government; in practice they are still subjects. But popular expectations have changed, rendering our governmental institutions increasingly unfit for the times. Today, popular Canadian concepts of citizenship are shaped by the liberal tradition from south of the border. That tradition places ultimate power with the people, and has organized governing institutions such that power is shared and diffused. No wonder distrust of government by Canadians is on the rise. It is fed by the disjunction between governing institutions designed to serve subjects and the popular conception by which Canadians think of themselves as citizens, and no longer subjects.

The liberal tradition leaves no doubt as to who is in charge. Individuals may retain their right to bear arms to protect themselves against government, should it overstep its boundaries. It is this argument that motivates resistance to gun control in the U.S. today. Classical liberalism sees government primarily as a vehicle for obtaining private benefits, particularly a list of individual rights, and the protection of private property. In addition, individuals are free to do whatever does not impinge on the freedom of others. There is a hesitancy to allow limitations on personal freedom for the common good. From this follows a general support for free economic enterprise without restrictions on trade. The state should interfere as little as possible with the freedom of individuals; the least government is the best government. In this view, private initiative, reward for individual effort, and personal self-interest are the great motivators for progress in science, medicine, business, technology, and the arts; government is well advised to not frustrate such motivators.

It is useful to refer to this tradition as *classical* liberalism, since it bears no resemblance to the federal Liberal party policies under prime ministers such as MacKenzie King, Pearson, and Trudeau. In our century the Liberals, lusting for power and responding to the needs of the Great Depression, abandoned their principles, forgot their philosophical roots, and turned into proud architects of the welfare state. As the former New Democratic B.C. premier Dave Barrett often remarks: the convenience of being a Liberal is that you don't always have to be one. Today, as the welfare state is coming to an end and neo-conservatism seems to have some staying power, many have turned to classical liberalism for inspiration.

Placing greater responsibility on private persons is a necessary corrective, even though it will be painful. Classical liberalism unleashed the creative talents, initiative, drive and energy of private persons, bringing unprecedented prosperity, hope, freedom from want, and relief from disease to more people than ever before. It has defended the worth and significance of each person, offered protection for minorities, and has the potential to curtail the stifling growth of government. But other aspects of classical liberalism need to be questioned. Today, as Canada faces national disintegration, governments that are broke, and major constitutional change, our people must recommit to a public good that goes beyond narrow self-interest. A democracy built on classical liberalism cannot provide inspiration for a vision of shared interests, public spirit, citizenship, and community. It is important to be lucid on why that must be so.

Classical liberalism provides the conceptual underpinnings for the political culture and institutions of the western democracies. This is particularly true of the United States of America. The U.S. Declaration of Independence is a manifesto proclaiming the supremacy of the individual, and the American government was instituted and mandated to serve the individual's inalienable right to the pursuit of personal happiness. Others, particularly Marxists and socialists, have rejected self-interest as a reliable guide to public interest. They correctly observe that a political community is more than the sum of its parts, but they underrate the role of private persons, and wrongly expect coercive state power to build public-spiritedness and public virtue. The decline and colossal failure of these totalitarian attempts, particularly after the collapse of the Soviet Union in 1991, suggests to some observers that classical liberalism, free enterprise, and capitalism have won, that all debate about ideology is superfluous, and that economic efficiency driven by technology will produce one universal form of government for all people the world over. The Reform Party of Canada's Preston Manning promotes a variant of this position. He considers politics to be primarily a process, which aims at discovering the common sense of the common people. If the process is perfected, it will unite people from across all the traditional political divides.[5]

Declarations about the death of ideology, like pronouncements about the death of God, seem premature. Just as spirituality has made a recovery over the past thirty years, because the search for meaning is an integral part of being human, so debate about the proper ends of government is not about to cease. And for the same reason. The search for a just social order is an inherently human activity. Adam and Eve's humanity consisted of being in charge of the Garden; that was their task in life, as it is ours. As long as greed, prejudice, injustice, world hunger, war, disease, and environmental destruction continue to exist, that task remains. Politics has historically been, and must continue to be, concerned with questions of right and wrong. Political divisions are rooted in different answers to questions regarding the political good. Such questions cannot be resolved by technology or process alone. The Reform Party of Canada's journey from populism to a narrow, well-defined policy agenda illustrates this truth. Manning's dream to bridge political divides by means of process alone is unrealistic. If, however, he persists, he may alienate even his own constituency, which is less committed to "letting the people speak," and more committed to seeing its decidedly neo-conservative agenda implemented.[6]

More particularly, Canadians are confronted by vast social and economic changes that necessitate on-going reflection about the purposes of governing institutions. National governments are weakening while international regulatory agencies are becoming more powerful, and linguistic and cultural divisions deepening; all of this fosters the trend to bring much of government as close to people as possible. Domestically, our institutions are failing us. The welfare state, which was created during the economic growth and expansion following World War II to provide unprecedented social benefits and security, is now crumbling. This retrenchment is driven less by ideology than by economic necessity. Short-term political gain induced governments over the past twenty years to immorally mortgage future generations. Just at the time that our national line of credit is drying up, our fiscal problems are compounded by an ominous shift in population from tax-payers toward tax-takers. There are currently, for every pensioner, seven persons in the Canadian work force. Thirty years from now, when the biggest bulge of baby-boomers hits retirement age, that number will drop to just two.

Such a drastic shift from providers to recipients of public benefits will precipitate much debate about the proper ends of government.

But there is more. It is widely acknowledged that Canada's economic growth will be sluggish in the foreseeable future. Under such conditions, as the noted author, researcher, and theorist Peter Drucker has found, the gap between rich and poor will widen. His research shows that regardless of economic order, whether planned or free-market, and regardless of social order, whether liberal-democratic, socialist, or dictatorial, in growing, expanding economies the gap between rich and poor narrows, while in shrinking or sluggish economies the gap grows.[7] The prospect of growing disparity in Canada between rich and poor will also ignite discussion about the proper and just role of government.

Human nature and intractable public policy issues ensure that the debate about political ideology will continue, but classical liberalism is itself burdened by inner contradictions. It sees government as a means to exclusively individualistic and private ends, which is a weak foundation for building citizenship, civic participation, and public virtue. Its theoretical justification for political community is feeble at best. Such contradictions are evident in our practice. Businesses, from the chartered banks on down, are anything but interested in free, unregulated markets, in spite of their rhetoric. To name but one example, there are no greater boosters of free enterprise than the dairy farmers of the Fraser Valley. While gladly accepting the generous benefits of government-enforced agricultural supply management, they fiercely defend a free market for everyone – that is, everyone else. Such contradictory behaviour is more than common hypocrisy. Rather, it is inherent in a public system that celebrates maximizing private benefits.

When the definition of *citizens* is reduced to nothing more than *rational, self-interested individuals,* the public good must of necessity be shortchanged. Private benefits, from welfare programs to farm subsidies, come at little or no cost to the recipient, but their cumulative effect on society is substantial, to the point of being detrimental. It is always rational for self-interested persons to support politicians and government programs that promise more private benefits from the public purse. But the political order, unlike the economic order, is not a market. The economic order is self-correcting, in that every benefit has a commensurate cost to the recipient. The political order lacks such a market mechanism. In the political order the cost of private benefits is spread over a large segment of the population. Under such conditions, rational self-interest defeats the public interest. Duty to self destroys duty to others. This explains why the ever-increasing encroachment of the welfare state on the private sphere has hardly been slowed even in countries supposedly committed to a limited state. The rational enticement to an ever-growing list of private entitlements subverts the alleged commitment to a limited state.

Classical liberalism – free-enterprise theory – is burdened by inner contradictions. It does not accurately describe the social-political-economic order of Western democracies, and its account of the human situation is only partially true. It was a flawed description from the start. The flaws are perhaps best seen in John Locke's attempt to justify private property. It is an instructive example of how not to do it. John Locke's seventeenth-century England was undergoing rapid change. Subsistence farming was on the way out, and agriculture was turning into a business. The medieval social order based on privilege and status was making room for a market economy based on merit and contract. In particular, new economic opportunities demanded the enclosure of the commons. From the earliest times, most of the land had been held in common, and could be used by anyone to graze livestock. No one needed permission to fish the streams for food or cut wood in the forests for fuel. The enclosing of land for exclusive private use meant that sheep herds could be enlarged, the wool industry expanded, and private fortunes enriched. John Locke set about to find a rationale for the enclosures and the new social relations that followed. His *Second Treatise* asks how a private person can come to own that which the Creator made for the good of all.[8] If the earth was made for the benefit and use of all people, by what right can anyone put a fence around any part of it and claim exclusive, private ownership? Our current concern about aboriginal land claims shows Locke's question to be of enduring interest. Locke's answer is instructive because it shows an inherent weakness of classical liberalism.

Locke starts his defence of private property with the premise that each person has ownership of his own body, mind, and being. Next, Locke says that if we mix what we own with whatever is given in common, that which is so mixed is thereby taken out of the commons. To illustrate this, Locke asks his seventeenth-century readers to cast their minds across the ocean, to observe there in the wilds of America how the Indians live. The deer that roam the plains belong to no one in particular, until some Indian hunter gives chase. The fruit upon the tree belongs to no one in particular until someone exerts himself, and climbs the tree to pick it. Chasing game or picking fruit has the effect of mixing one's labour, which one owns, with what is given in common, and such mixing removes that item from the commons, and makes it justifiably private property. For example, by tilling soil, a man acquires ownership of that soil.

To justify large private holdings, Locke argues that when a servant mixes his labour with what exists in common, ownership is vested not in the servant but in the servant's master. Locke, not totally deprived of a social conscience, contends that reason and God suggest limits to the acquisition of private property. One should not acquire more than one can use for oneself, or acquire more than can be used before it spoils. These limits prevent us from depriving others, and wasting what God has provided for good use. But happily, Locke notes an escape from such confining limitations on human acquisitiveness. Resources acquired by mixing labour, whether one's own or that of one's servant, may be converted into money. And money has the singular advantage of neither spoiling nor ever being too plentiful for one's use.

CITIZENS: PRIVATE PERSONS WITH PUBLIC DUTIES

IT IS IMPORTANT to note that Locke's description of Native ways in the wilds of America is distorted. No Indian of the time acted as a lone individual. To be a hunter was to be authorized to act in the interests of the tribe by assuming the public duties that accompanied a tribal position. Indian men did not hunt game or harvest a crop only to return to the tribe with a message for their women, children, and old folk that if they, too, wished to eat they must hunt and harvest for themselves. On the contrary, for Indian hunters the fruit of their labour was communal, not private property. Concern for the well-being of others was inherent in the condition of being a hunter; a private person was endowed with public duties.

It is essential to recognize that every form of social order requires the endowment of private persons with public duties. John Locke's universe, like much of classical liberalism, and free enterprise theory today, is too simplistic. It is a universe that consists of individuals stripped of social relationships and public duties. It is an artificial, unreal universe, denying the essence of any social order, which is the endowment of private persons with public duties. Is it ever the case that a person is truly an individual, an entirely private person?

In our time and place, much political talk is cast in terms of the individual. We are told government exists to protect the rights of the individual, to maximize opportunity for the individual, and to promote private initiative. Such undue focus on the individual is as foreign to reality as the communist's claim that human existence finds complete fulfilment in serving the state. Neither the private person nor the collectivity exhausts the fullness of life. To avoid either extreme, it is imperative to develop among democratic peoples a strong sense of citizenship. To reach agreement about the public good, Canada and British Columbia's political communities need citizens, persons who are strong, free, diverse, and unique – but endowed with a sense of public duty.

Citizens are persons in a particular kind of relationship, and they have a context. They are more than individuals but less than comrades; their existence extends beyond their own person, but their specificity is not absorbed by the collectivity. Truly separate individuals don't exist. Of course, individual persons do exist. But persons are always more than just individual. Persons invariably exist in a variety of relationships and contexts. For example, upon waking in the morning, typically, my first awareness is of my wife, Jayne, which makes me a spouse, until I go downstairs and meet persons who are children, making me a parent, and so the day goes. Driving to work, obeying traffic lights and stop signs, we function as a citizens. At work I may be an employer or an employee, a consumer or a producer, a teacher or a student. After work, in our leisure time activities we may add to all of these relationships by entering any number of voluntary organizations, and finally, we stand in relationship to God, the source of life.[9]

Persons are always, from their very birth, in relationships. It is the condition of being human: there is no choice in the matter, and there is no escape from it. We may think ourselves to be an island of our own, but our inescapable human condition is that we are all part of the main. Robinson Crusoe is fiction, and the much vaunted individual an abstraction. But relationships are real, they are the stuff of human existence, they are the bricks and mortar through which individual persons, societies, and communities attain their identity, actualize themselves, and find fulfilment.

In classical liberalism, public duty results from a hypothetical contract predicated on self-interest. The contract is an instrument to attain private benefits, and may be cancelled when the benefits stop. Yet public duty, in the sense of civility, regard for others, does not derive from a contract, and its end is not, in the first instance, to yield private benefits. Social relationships and public duty are organic, they are part of what it means to be human. To refuse to embrace and respond to the call of public duty and citizenship is to diminish and impoverish not our pocketbook, but our humanity; it is to be sub-human, to miss our potential. As Solzhenitsyn has argued so beautifully, a society that reduces all social relationships to contract and legal terms has lost civility, decency, and its soul.[10] A social order based exclusively on the rights of man has difficulty evoking man's responsibility to society. The social fabric disintegrates, resulting in deep social problems, addictions, crime, AIDS, welfare problems, abortion on demand, and unloved and abandoned children. The soil of contract is too barren for civic duty.

A deepened, renewed Canadian political experience must start from the reality that politics is by nature communal, not individual. Without the communal, political institutions that serve the public good, and perhaps Canadian unity itself, will escape us. If there is no communal dimension to politics there is little need for persons to assume public duties, except as determined by contract.

Behaviour determined by contract can be altered at will. In contrast, behaviour that is rooted in our humanness is not open to endless experimentation. As fish must remain in water to be free, so human freedom exists within the parameters of conduct appropriate to humans. Each unique social relationship, organically embedded in the nature of reality, conditions human behaviour. For example, the particular obligations one has to a neighbour depend on who that neighbour is: a spouse, the neighbour's spouse, the plumber, a policeman, an employer, etc. Each relationship demands certain forms of appropriate behaviour from the participants. Such demands for behavioural appropriateness are intrinsic to the nature of the relationship. For example, the relationship of parent to child has some implications for behaviour that have universal application. Categories such as friend, spouse, employer, employee, citizen, student, teacher, judge, criminal, parent, child are not empty containers to be filled with whatever the human will decides. Here, as in so much of life, we do well to listen to nature, and observe how people actually relate to each other in social contexts.

For the purposes of this discussion, which aims to discover the way that leads to the public good, we need to understand the behaviour appropriate to citizens. If it is true that citizenship is the means by which private persons assume public duties, we need to investigate what those duties are, how they relate to democracy as self-rule, and how the institutional, structural arrangements of government enable persons to be citizens.

Benjamin Barber in his excellent study defines citizen as follows: "The citizen is the individual who has learned how to make civic judgments and who can evaluate goods in public terms."[11] Citizenship comes to its fullest expression when private persons participate in the legislative function of government, and when such participation itself engenders an enlarged sense of public responsibility. To illustrate how the public good can be arrived at, not through the motivation of self-interest but through an enriched form of citizenship and participation in a democratic form of group decision-making, I wish to draw on some personal, practical experiences, not from politics but from industrial relations.

DEMOCRATIC PARTICIPATION, CITIZENSHIP, AND THE PUBLIC GOOD

LIKE MANY OTHERS, I have experimented with the principle of including in the decision-making process all those affected by a decision. Influenced by progressive management theories and Abraham Maslow's theory of human needs, I consciously applied this principle to the organization of construction workers building houses. Being in charge of a construction crew, I would start the day by asking the workers what they thought we should do that day. Some workers, not being accustomed to such democracy in the workplace, rejected any invitation to participate in what they considered the exclusive domain of management. They rejected responsibility. But others rose to the challenge, and slowly the group as a whole started to participate. Soon the benefits became obvious. For example, on Monday the crew might be asked to decide when they considered their project would be ready for the roofers. Suppose, after some compromising, they decided that the construction would be ready for the roofers by Wednesday evening. Since it was their decision, the crew was more likely to ensure that the objective would be met, even if it required extra effort. If that decision had been made exclusively by management, the extra effort needed to meet the objective would have met with considerable resistance. Not having participated in the decision, the workers would feel no responsibility for its successful implementation. Often the democratic way is the most efficient way.

But the benefits of such a participatory process go beyond securing more efficient production and an improved bottom line. When the workers were included in the management function, their jobs were enhanced. They went beyond merely following orders; additional human capacities were enlisted, and these persons' sense of self-worth increased. They were not asked merely to carry lumber and pound nails, and their human capacity for exercising judgment and assuming responsibility was enlarged. Their participation and responsibility for the entire enterprise grew, making their job experience more creative and satisfying. Their reward for work went beyond merely collecting a pay cheque; it included pride in a job well done. They attained a greater measure of self-actualization, becoming what they were capable of becoming. In the process their horizons broadened, and participation meant assuming some responsibility for the project as a whole. Their immediate, narrow self-interest – the need to collect a pay cheque – became more directly linked in their own minds and experience with the performance of the whole crew, and the success of the project. The result was a deepened sense of responsibility and duty to the work group.

This should not be cynically dismissed as merely a sophisticated form of enlightened self-interest. It was an expanded experience of what it means to be human, an enlarged sense of being in charge, having dominion, exercising stewardship. All human activity strives for self-determination; it is a movement from servitude to freedom, a process of attaining the full range of human potential. Such self-determination need not be self-serving and egotistically self-centred.

There is a lesson to be learned from this simple example. If heeded, it could help restore trust in government, endow private persons with public duties, and enrich our concept of citizenship. The democratic process, if only we would practise it, is inclusive; power is shared, and those affected by a government decision are included in the decision-making process. Government decisions are the decisions of the citizens. A democratic form of government provides for citizen participation.

The participation of citizens in the ruling function is of a certain kind. Persons participating as citizens exercise judgment that aims at, and is informed by, the public good. The construction workers' participation was meaningful once they assumed common responsibilities. At that point, the crew became a team, and the good of all turned into a personal concern. To be a citizen is to be endowed by society with a public duty. One no longer acts as a private person. In the extreme instance of war, when taking life may be justified, private persons may do so only in their capacity as citizens. The actions, judgments, and behaviour of citizens are circumscribed by the public good. This truth is reflected in the public's distaste for politicians who attempt to use public office for private gain.

The process of participation must itself serve a purpose. In our example, worker participation led to greater efficiency, but that was not all, nor was it the primary goal. Workers realized a greater degree of personal potential, and their capacities as human beings were more fully attained. The work experience did not reduce, but expanded, these workers as persons. Similarly, a democratic system of politics and government should enhance the role people play in politics, expanding that role from private individual to citizen, from a client of government to a participant. This elucidates a further truth – that the system can be self-sustaining. Participation endows private persons with public duties, and such participation increasingly qualifies them for the task. People come to see citizenship not only as an entitlement to rights, but also as an opportunity to participate in public duties.

An enlarged notion of citizenship is particularly significant for its potential to redirect current neo-conservative politics from narrow, mean-spirited self-interest towards a politics that is generously public-spirited. The normative motive for greater participation is to enlist from among citizens their higher human capacities for sound judgment, for assuming responsibility, for shouldering willingly the common burdens that promote the common good, and to thus attain a measure of self-actualization, that is, to achieve the highest and best that humanity is capable of. The democratic process has the potential to overcome private and sectional interests so that the common good can be upheld, and in the process make community and citizenship more rewarding and satisfying.

Classical liberalism thrives on conflict. Our politics and form of government are adversarial. We think, too often, of politics as a zero-sum game. If Quebec wins, others must lose, a gain for the environment is a loss for the economy, a benefit for Natives must be an expense for others, praise for the opposition must detract from government. But self-governing citizens have the potential to experience community as a win-win for all. If self-rule discloses political community, politics becomes more than zero-sum, and the payoff is unexpected new benefits. Adversarial government must give way to cooperative and consensual forms of government. That takes a different system of decision-making, a different attitude, but also a different vocabulary. To speak of individuals is to highlight differences, to focus on our separateness, but to speak of citizens is to focus on what we have in common, and the equality citizenship bestows.

Citizens have equal status without losing their uniqueness. Citizens are equal, but not the same. Citizenship bridges, but does not eliminate, differences among people based on ability, income, gender, education, ethnicity, race, religion, age, and more. Democratic, self-governing citizens do not abandon or suppress their differences, whether political or otherwise. Instead, democracy provides institutional arrangements that allow differences to serve the common good. Citizens do not deny their individuality and unique personal characteristics; democracy does not seek unity through uniformity, rather, democracy is a process that accommodates diversity. Socialism and communism impose, by force, an unattainable egalitarianism. In contrast, democratic citizenship protects every person's individuality for the sake of the whole. Citizenship is the means by which the strengths of individual persons are made useful to the political community.

Classical liberalism understands politics as a means to an end. For democratic citizens politics is both a means and an end. The end is a deepened, enriched experience of what it means to be human. Citizenship becomes a calling, a task, an office through which private persons attain a greater measure of self-actualization. Individuals shaped by classical liberalism think government diminishes them, and therefore fear government (in the U.S. they carry arms). In contrast, citizens participate in government to be fulfilled.

Many observers, Rousseau, de Tocqueville, and J.S. Mill among them, maintain that people learn to consider, appreciate, and be informed by the public good and the interests of the community to the degree that they practise community service and participate in democratic decision-making processes. Rousseau believed that participation serves to educate the citizen, who learns to take into account wider matters than his own immediate private interests. If one is to gain cooperation from others, one learns that private and public interests are linked. For de Tocqueville, participation should start at the local level, and for that reason he would decentralize administrative decisions. Mill argues for an active, public-spirited character as the mainstay of democracy, and institutional arrangements that foster such character traits. Democracy as self-rule and citizenship are mutually reinforcing, and the whole becomes self-sustaining. To vitalize Canadian citizenship requires a more active democracy, and a dynamic democracy, in turn, results from a more vibrant citizenship. De Tocqueville wrote:

> I maintain that the most powerful and perhaps the only means that we still possess in interesting men in the welfare of their country is to make them partakers in the government ... civic zeal seems to me to be inseparable from the exercise of political right.[12]

The quest for a more democratic voting system and a form of government that fosters participation is a quest for a deepened and enriched citizenship, an attempt to more fully inspire private persons with a sense of public duty.

Citizenship is learned on the job, through practice. But in addition, there is a second source of instruction. Carole Pateman cites a number of studies that confirm what we would expect: people learn about, and are socialized into, participatory democracy when surrounded by other social relationships that exhibit democratic authority structures.[13] Experiences in the home, school, and workplace about the nature of authority can help or hinder political democracy. For us, the trends in the home, school, and workplace are unmistakable. Long gone are the days when it was acceptable to say "Children should be seen and not heard," when students sat in straight rows and spoke only when spoken to, when workers tipped their caps to say, "Yes, boss, no, boss." Our society has seen an explosion of democracy everywhere except in our governing institutions. Our British voting system and parliamentary form of government date back to 1885, and remain essentially unchanged. As will be shown, the system violates modern values and expectations.

Consider the changes new attitudes have brought to the workplace. In industrial relations progress has been enormous. In B.C. in just twenty years we have moved from antagonistic, adversarial relations to a large degree of cooperation, from open enmity between labour and management to some respect and partnership. If anyone has doubts about the inherent benefits of a more consensual approach, consider the bottom-line results for industrial relations. In B.C., average annual worker days lost to strikes and lockouts was 1,563,171 for the years 1972–1976. During the last five years for which data is available, 1989–1993, this dropped to 431,936.[14] Considering that the average annual work force more than doubled between these periods, the improvement is astounding. Today's worker enjoys a large measure of independence and self-determination. Fellow workers, including management, often are more partners than competitors.

These new patterns of partnership are particularly evident and surprisingly fruitful in workplaces where employees benefit from employee stock ownership plans (ESOPs). Studies in the U.S. indicate the following with regard to employee stock ownership plans:[15]

- Companies with ESOPs are 1.5 times as profitable
- Companies with ESOPs have twice the annual productivity growth
- Firms in which a majority of employees own a majority of the stock generate three times as many new jobs
- As employees gain interest in their work and company, their quality of life increases
- Employees are more receptive to productivity improving technology when they share in the benefits
- Firms with profit-based plans have less turnover, absenteeism, supervision and improved quality and service.

In the workplace the trend of historical development is unmistakable – the movement is from serfs to workers to partners. Traditional notions of leadership are challenged. Instead of issuing orders, successful managers today resemble a coach building a team by drawing out the best in each participant. As Pateman notes, there is a mutually advantageous relationship between the various authority structures within a given society. For example, unlike Great Britain, countries with proportional representation systems of government have been among the first to experiment with workplace democracy. During the fifties and sixties, while Canada suffered from strikes, lockouts, and antagonistic labour relations – the British disease – Germany and other Western European countries were the first to pioneer co-operative labour relations. They placed worker representatives on boards of directors, and pursued conciliation, consensus, principles of partnership, co-determination, and profit-sharing. All the while their economies outperformed the British, and our own. Patterns of authority and decision-making in the home, school, and workplace have evolved towards participation and partnership. Today, our society is ripe for governmental structures that foster citizenship. The old hierarchical relationships of power and dominance in politics are no longer tenable.

In spite of so much pressure from nongovernmental social structures, there are those who think the average person will reject responsibility in governing, has little to contribute, is uninformed, has no feelings for the common good, and is pitifully ill-equipped to exercise sound judgment on important matters of state. In this view democracy is vastly overrated. Such arguments are difficult to counter. There are good reasons for suggesting that no one knows, because democracy, even representative democracy, has never been tried in large-scale settings. The U.S., the country generally considered most democratic of all, is not democratic in the sense argued for here. U.S. voter participation is very low, particularly among the lower classes. Government does not speak for them. The system still allows for too much concentration of power in the delivery of local benefits. In addition, political rulers are not a typical cross-section of American society. The political elite represents the milieu it is drawn from, the country's best educated and wealthiest class, and it shares their values and concerns. Currently, it takes at least six million dollars to gain a U.S. Senate seat. Such a representative mismatch is an inadequate instrument for self-rule by the people. The U.S. example has more to teach us about democracy. Self-rule by citizens has the potential to promote and be shaped by considerations of the common good; in contrast, U.S. politics is notoriously and primarily a contest between competing, special, sectional, even private interests. It is a paragon of the politics of brokerage, a prime example of using public institutions for private ends. U.S. politics is a gigantic, perpetual bargaining session, where all relationships are reduced to contract. In the U.S. system of government, nothing happens unless there is something in it for every participant (tellingly called "stakeholders").

To criticize U.S. culture is always fraught with difficulties. A nation so powerful and prosperous must be doing something right. It seems churlish to find fault. Perhaps one should simply state that the U.S. system of government does not encompass one's own vision of what a community of public-spirited citizens is capable of. Those who question whether people are truly capable of self-rule often turn to classical liberalism because it takes people as they are, egocentric and self-serving. There is no appeal to the higher, nobler human motives. In contrast, the argument for democratic self-rule of citizens is an appeal to what people could be, if given a chance. We shall not leave the world a better place unless we challenge what is, and appeal to what is best and noblest in the human spirit. History is an unfolding process; change should be channelled, not resisted. To not allow for growth in human development, to frustrate what is striving to be born, is (in the words of Laurence van der Post) to quench the spirit. Preventing the human personality from attaining its potential is a crime against humanity. Thomas Jefferson did not despair of people's ability to govern wisely. He wrote:

> I know of no safe depository of the ultimate power of
> the society but the people themselves, and if we think

> them not enlightened enough to exercise their control
> with a wholesome discretion, the remedy is not to take
> it from them, but to inform their discretion.[16]

In summary, in spite of the liberal tradition's unquestioned accomplishments – relieving human want and misery, recognizing the worth of individual persons, insisting that government be accountable to the people, and protecting minority rights – it fails to give a philosophical basis for political community, and its notion of citizenship is reduced, thin, and barren. Starting with duty to self, it is unable to reach duty towards others apart from contract. Social relationships conceived as a contract are primarily seen as dispensers of private goods. In contrast, organic social relationships are embedded in the nature of reality; they partake of our natural, normal, human condition, and are not primarily self-serving. They escape the limitations of contract, for they are not bound by what is but anticipate what could be, and hold promise for an enlarged notion of citizenship derived not from contract, but from what it means to be human.

Citizenship, the assuming by private persons of public duties, is an inescapable part of being human. If that citizenship is to take root and grow in Canada, more democratic forms of government will be required. Canadian political culture asks little of its citizens, and so it receives little. Democracy as self-rule and citizenship as the acceptance of public duties are social structures that go hand in hand. Turning private persons into public servants demands government that promotes democratic self-rule.

The question this chapter started with can now be answered. Is self-rule by private persons an adequate protection of the public good? Logically, even contract theories of political obligation need not have exclusively private, self-serving goals. As Charles Taylor observes, "I must decide and select my goals, doesn't mean, I must select as goal me."[17] Although that is logically true, in practice, the contract notion of classical liberalism has produced a political culture that too often decides public policy issues after calculating an economic cost-benefit analysis for the several participants. For example, Prime Minister Chrétien's eleventh-hour appeal for Quebec to stay within Canada, prior to the 30 October 1995 referendum, was based on exclusively economic considerations. If loyalty to Canada does not extend beyond the pocketbook, then Canada is finished, and should never have been. Canada's entire history has been in defiance of the materialism, liberal individualism, and republican disregard for tradition that drive American culture. Moreover, the argument Chrétien used to quell Quebec separatism is an argument in favour of Western separatism. If Quebec should stay in Canada because it is economically rewarding, the Western provinces, being net economic contributors, should leave. If contract is all we have, there can be no reservoir of goodwill, no allegiance to values beyond cash, to keep Canada united.

The argument for Canadian nationalism must be based on a commitment to public institutions that are so organized as to allow Canada's citizens and their diverse linguistic, regional, cultural, and religious communities to attain full self-expression for the enrichment of the whole. Society is more than economics, and prior to government. These two principles are fundamental. The first guards against reducing social relationships to contract, and the second limits the power of government.

To rise above pocketbook politics and contain government within its proper limits requires a strong notion of citizenship, and that in turn requires democratic self-rule. Self-rule is the means by which the decisions of private individuals can be in tune with the requirements of the public good. Participation in government has the potential to lift people beyond their private horizon and make them citizens. It is not that we are currently bereft of any notion of citizenship, but that our present notion is too barren and impoverished. It is starved from lack of meaningful participation. Our politics is primarily focused on rights, not on duty, responsibility, and obligation. In a democracy the collective wisdom steers the ship of state. Instead of being banned from the bridge after the captain has been selected, all views, opinions, and interests should be permitted to exert pressure on the tiller in proportion to their numerical strength. Such participation itself will direct the particular views, ideologies, and interests to focus on the public good, or the good of all. A voting system that leads to maximum participation by all is the mechanism to harmonize the various voices and discordant notes.

Our present political institutions deprive Canadians of the experience of citizenship. This is most unfortunate, because our history and much of our political culture provide fertile ground for an enlarged notion of citizenship. Richard Gwyn, the noted journalist and commentator, considers Canada's survival dependent on a political culture based as much on social responsibility and civility as on individual rights.[18] He suggests Canadians must reconnect with their past if they are to cultivate such a political culture of public-mindedness. We are different from the U.S., and in that difference lies hope for Canada's future.

Our differences from the U.S. run deeper than is usually recognized. For example, under the influence of the United Empire Loyalists, Canada's institutions were framed with the deliberate intention of avoiding the democratic extremism of France and our revolutionary cousins to the south. Our institutions were not considered instruments of private pleasure or gain, but were mandated to foster peace, order, and good government. As a result, Canadian institutions are far from democratic, and our governments have been more active, interventionist, and communitarian than U.S. governments. Government activism to promote community led to the building of the transcontinental railway in the nineteenth century, and the establishment of universal health care in the twentieth. Our rural population may see gun control as an unwarranted government intrusion, but unlike U.S. citizens, Canadians do not argue against it on the basis of an inalienable right to defend themselves against their own government. We are more deferential to authority, and less influenced by classical liberalism than is the U.S.

Both in English and in French Canada our cultural taproots reach back, via pre-French Revolution Europe, to Christian, Greek, and Hebrew societies. For those cultures, government was not an instrument for material abundance, but a quest to exemplify right relations; it defined the good life in terms of quality, not quantity. Those earlier cultures searched for political virtue, but modern, liberal political philosophy searches for personal freedom. A political culture of personal freedom lacks the cement to build community. The late George Grant, Canadian nationalist and political philosopher, wrote that our society needs to remember and re-imagine the nature of political community from the remnants that remain deep in the Canadian collective conscience; and so we should. Then, using modern insight into the nature of democratic decision-making processes, our task will be to restructure government, starting with the voting system, to facilitate the highest form of citizenship humans are capable of.

Canada is uniquely situated to be a trend-setter for the English-speaking world, enlarging the concept of citizenship, and redesigning governmental structures to facilitate citizen participation. Our political culture fosters public institutions that serve the public good. Our history of citizenship developed gradually, pragmatically; we were held back by tradition and matured rather slowly. Canadian citizenship did not arrive with a burst of revolutionary, democratic fervour demanding power for the people. Canada avoided democratic extremism and the attendant individualism that weakens political community in the United States. We carry the seeds of public-spiritedness, but lack the organizational structures. Our history demands an enlarged role for citizens to serve the public good.

In addition, the fundamental characteristic of Canada is its diversity. In language, culture, and geography, Canada's broad diversity demands an equally broad and meaningful citizens' participation. The impetus for significant reform comes from the current political/economic difficulties, and the resulting widespread distrust in government.

The imperative of our history, our geography and our current situation is to foster citizens – people who assume public duties, and, motivated by the public good, participate in the ruling function. The widespread participation of such citizens in the ruling function is the essence of democracy. Democracy is rule by the many, not the few. When the many rule, their sense of citizenship is enlarged, politics is focused on public ends, and political obligation is internalized, rather than the product of contract.

As we reflect on a voting system suitable to Canada's needs, the democratic aims to achieve are self-rule and widespread participation, because that builds citizens, and citizens serve the public good.

REPRESENTATION

Every representative system – geographical, proportional, or other – is an instrument whose purpose is to make effective the participation of citizens in communities too large to permit each a direct voice in substantive affairs. No such system will be perfect; but the continuing effort to improve old forms and devise new ones so as to make representation more just and more effective is an enterprise no democracy can wisely abandon.[1]

A POLITICAL CULTURE OF participation, partnership, and public-spiritedness will require organizational changes to make new forms of political behaviour possible. Our present system, designed to prevent partnership, participation, and conciliation, fosters wasteful competition, and decision-making by the few rather than by the many. What system must we turn to? For some observers, democracy as direct self-rule is, except for limited, small-scale instances, an impossible dream. To them, large populations and the complexity of government demand representative democracy – others doing for people what they cannot do themselves. The American founding fathers entertained the idea of direct democracy, but in the Federalist Papers they reject it in favour of representative democracy, for two reasons: first, in direct democracy communication would take too long, making deliberation too difficult; and second, mobs might be swayed by momentary passion. Today, modern means of communication can overcome the objections of the first reason, while the second is probably overstated, and if not, can be minimized through cooling-off periods and constitutional protections. Even so, can we reasonably expect people today to devote the time and energy needed to decide all major public policy issues? Some form of representative democracy seems necessary, even if only as an interim measure, until technology allows a fuller experience of direct democracy.

Still others hold the opposite view, contending that social diversity today makes representative democracy impossible. Alvin Toffler, for instance, suggests that the increased diversity and pluralism of society, which he calls de-massification, leads to a lack of consensus. In the absence of a majority opinion on almost all issues of importance, representatives can no longer speak for the people. In that view, the mechanism of representative democracy, which is designed to allow majority opinions to prevail, is obsolete when there is no majority to represent. Toffler's preferred solution is direct democracy, but failing that he calls for representative systems that share power and include minorities, a democracy of minorities, and "... methods whose purpose is to reveal differences rather than paper them over with forced or faked majorities ..."[2]

Direct democracy, or democracy as self-rule, may not be fully possible or even desirable in every instance, but the image of people ruling themselves must be retained. We need not choose between representative democracy and direct democracy; a healthy mixture of the two is entirely possible. As long as we continue to elect people to govern for us, representative democracy should be fashioned, and continually improved, to meet the demands and ideals of democracy as self-rule. Toffler is correct that in the absence of a majority opinion about the public good, it will not do to have the voting system generate forced or faked majorities. Democracy as self-rule must be a constant goal to be worked toward – approximated, not abandoned. The Canadian form of representative democracy fails this test. It does not foster self-rule by citizens. It concentrates power. Our voting system, by design, restricts the range of political issues that will be represented, and it does not represent the majority. Moreover, it ensures that between elections citizens have no role in ruling, and that the legislatures and Parliament are cabinet-dominated. None of this need be so.

British parliamentary democracy is a highly developed, sophisticated form of social organization and system of governance. The various components are interrelated, but the kingpin is the voting system. By determining who is represented and how political power is distributed, it also determines the relationship of cabinet to Parliament. Voting systems define the rules by which electors choose those who will govern them. They stipulate who can vote, the number of constituencies and their boundaries, the number of seats assigned to each constituency and, most important, how votes are translated into seats. Voting systems are not objective, purely technical, mechanical, or value-free. Far from it. Each voting system is based on a specific set of values, and the various systems are based on significantly different views of the nature of representation, representative democracy, the role of political parties, and the crucial relationship between the legislature and the government.[3] Debates about the merits of different voting systems quickly centre on who and what ought to be represented, and the nature of representation itself. Theories of representation help disclose the democratic values we may wish to see reflected in a voting system.

THEORIES OF REPRESENTATION
THEORIES OF REPRESENTATION raise significant questions that most voters seldom think about. Pitkin, in an influential linguistic study, identifies many elements of representation.[4] These elements may be grouped in two categories, "structural" and "substantive." The structural element deals with who and what should be represented, that is, it considers the make-up of the legislature, while the substantive element emphasizes what it is a representative does. Pitkin repeatedly warns that both are necessary, and blames much confusion on theorists who hold any one element of representation as sufficient for the whole.[5]

STRUCTURAL REPRESENTATION
Hobbes had a very simple notion of representation; for him, every government represents its citizens, since all citizens are bound by government decisions. This may not be useful as it does not separate representative government from totalitarian forms of government, or any other. In this century, Joseph Schumpeter advanced a view influential among academics, politicians, and voters alike. He wrote:

> The democratic method is that institutional arrangement for arriving at political decisions in which individuals acquire the power to decide by means of a competitive struggle for the people's vote.[6]

In this view, when formal requirements for authorization and accountability are met, the outcome is representation. The formal requirements are free, competitive elections at regular intervals. This, essentially, is our system. Democracy arrives for one day every four or five years. Between elections there is no role for citizens. In our system democracy is defined as the power to select the ruling elite. Schumpeter's requirements are necessary, but are they sufficient for political representation? Others would want to specify more particularly both the composition and function of the popular assembly before it could be said to represent the people.

Under the influence of democratic ideals that shaped the American and French revolutions, theorists began to conceive of representative bodies as microcosms of the population. Comte de Mirabeau told the French Constituent Assembly in 1789, "… the representative body should at all times present a reduced picture of the people – their opinions, aspirations, and wishes, and that should bear the relative proportion to the original…".[7] Across the ocean, John Adams advanced the same concept.[8] In this view, for a legislature to be representative, it must consist of people who share the characteristics of the electorate and hold political convictions that are similar to theirs; and they must do so in the same proportion as those characteristics and convictions exist among the electorate. The legislature should "mirror," or be an accurate reflection of all the politically significant characteristics of the population in whose behalf it is to act. J.S. Mill was an ardent proponent of this view. To him, parliament should be an arena, "where every person in the country may count upon finding somebody who speaks his mind." Mill states further that, "In a really equal democracy, every or any section would be represented, not disproportionately, but proportionately."[9] This position may be referred to as descriptive representation.

In Mill's view, human nature is such that one's interests are best represented and protected by oneself, and if not oneself, at least someone very like oneself. The goal is self-rule. If physical restraints prevent actual direct democracy as in the original, the substitute should, in its composition and function, resemble the original. If all the eligible voters in British Columbia could meet to conduct governmental affairs, every stripe and shade of political persuasion would be represented; hence, for a legislature to be representative, it too should embody in its composition the politically significant diversity present among the voters. Only then, according to this view, can a legislature begin to express the will of the people, and be correctly described as representative of the people.

The specification "politically significant" is important. Descriptive representation need not imply that political representation must involve sociological representation, such as gender, age, income, religious affiliation, level of education, ethnicity, or occupation. Such sociological differences often do imply political differences, but they need not. Political interests often cross sociological categories.[10] It is the diversity of political interests that needs representation. Pitkin observes that the history of representative government is "… shaped by the changing demands for representation based on changing concepts of what are politically relevant features to be represented."[11] Human differences that reflect political differences change with changing times. For example, religion is less politically significant today than it used to be.

J.S. Mill does not see sociological representation as a prerequisite for political representation. In fact, he turned to a proportional system of representation partly because it would allow persons of exceptional talent, ability, and distinction to attract voter support. Mill's theory of representation is not a levelling device. However, sociological representation may carry political significance. For example, Mill also holds that it takes someone from the labour class to represent the interests of the labour class, presumably because belonging to the labour class is politically significant. Also, sociological characteristics carry symbolic significance, apart from any political importance. I may not share the political views of the middle-aged white males in the legislature, but if no middle-aged white males were ever elected, my identification with the legislature would be weakened. Therefore, a voting system that consistently limits elected office to certain segments of society could not be considered politically representative.[12]

This descriptive view of representation has a strong intuitive appeal. I have not found any contemporary scholars who take a strong opposing view to descriptive representation as applied to the composition of a legislature. Going back to scholars in history, we find that Edmund Burke opposed both universal manhood suffrage and voting districts of equal numerical size, because they would lead to personal representation. MPs would become agents for the people of their district, and be subservient to their will, instead of serving the national interest.[13] In this view, the representativeness of a popular assembly is measured by output – its actions, not its composition. It is helpful not to place all emphasis on composition alone. Representation is a multifaceted concept. Much has changed in society since Burke's talk about a natural aristocracy. Certainty about the knowledge, wisdom, and virtue of legislators has dwindled and the opinions of the people have gained greater respect. Burke had no doubt that the legislators' superior education, wisdom, and virtue would lead to sure knowledge of what is best. Mill was less sure, and therefore thought that all opinions should be represented in deliberations from which truth would emerge. But even Burke supported extending suffrage to Irish Catholics because their interests were not represented.[14] I support Vernon Bogdanor when he writes, "the best guarantee of justice in public dealings is the participation in their own government by the people most likely to suffer from injustice."[15] That is the purpose of ensuring that the legislature mirrors in composition the people it serves. Descriptive representation is a prerequisite for any voting system wishing to approximate democracy as self-rule.

Descriptive representation requires that every politically significant segment of the population is proportionally present in the legislature. To test our voting system against this criterion requires that we know what politically significant elements exist in our society today. Since society is in constant flux, and since agreement on this issue is difficult to attain, the best system would leave that decison to the free choice of the voters. The voting system should be such as to allow the greatest number of significant political interest groups to be represented if the citizens so choose. Chapter 6 will show how that is possible under the single transferable vote (STV), but for now it is sufficient to note that our present single member plurality (SMP) voting system restricts voters' selection to only a few of the ever-changing politically significant views that are present in society.

SMP prevents the full range of political diversity from being registered. SMP represents geographical territory; seats are assigned to a particular place. In this regard, too, SMP is out of step with the times. Increasingly, people's interests are not bound to any particular geographical area. The residents of the Peace River country may well share some political concerns that are different from those of the residents of West Vancouver, but what political uniqueness is attached to living on one side of Vancouver's Kingsway as opposed to living on the other side? The main provincial political issues are equally relevant, wherever one lives within the province. For example, in British Columbia some important issues are the economy, government overspending, the enormous debt, high taxation, health care, crime prevention, the question of whether or not to fund abortions, protecting the environment, fighting the federal government, welfare benefits, ICBC, gas and electric rates, WCB, education. People have different views on these issues, but their differences are mostly unrelated to where they live. Of course, other issues, such as Aboriginal land claims, highway construction, logging, mining and land-use questions generally, do have a much stronger local impact. It is also true that any issue, education for instance, has a local dimension, but the big decisions are made in the provincial capital.

Which are more important to citizens: provincial issues or local ones? The protest groups that converge on the lawns of the legislature are invariably drawn from all over the province. They seldom come from one riding to represent an issue peculiar to that riding. The notion that each of the 75 present B.C. ridings embodies a unique community of interest with some level of relevance for the people that live there is a hold-over from the horse-and-buggy days.[16] Six of the eight electoral boundary acts in Canada refer directly or indirectly to the importance of representing diverse communities of interest in the legislature. But for all that, actual definitions of what a community of interest consists of are elusive.[17] We change the boundaries and mingle the alleged communities of interest every six or seven years without precipitating identity crises among the voters.[18]

Society is changing. As Toffler has pointed out, Second Wave (industrial society) social structures aggregated people into ever larger masses, but Third Wave (information age) social structures are having the opposite effect: they "de-massify" people. The Third Wave has introduced a much greater diversity of interests. Society is becoming increasingly pluralistic. Electronic communication assists these tendencies by building communities of interest across vast distances. Today, people living three hundred kilometres from each other may well share interests more closely than persons three doors apart. The future described by Toffler sixteen years ago has arrived. Instead of assigning seats to a given territory, why not assign some legislative seats to women, to minorities, to highly educated people, to certain professions, to farmers, fisherman and loggers, or to those who pay the most taxes; why not seats for children, single parents, and the poor; and finally, why not a few seats for fish, fowl, and forests?

The point is, if the politically significant elements of our social diversity are to be represented, the territory-based single member plurality system cannot begin to do the job. It was designed to serve a two-party system, when people's lives hardly extended beyond the local village. Of course, no voting system can ensure that absolutely every politically relevant difference is represented, but the ideal can be attained more closely than SMP allows. As Mill predicted, our voting system prevents voters from using the ballot box to express opinions about most of the issues that matter to them. The full diversity of issues that are present in Canadian society finds no expression. The result is a Parliament and legislatures where too many politically significant groups are not represented. Under SMP one ballot must express all, votes cannot be transferred to candidates within one's own riding, or to candidates of other ridings. Hence, the voter's choice is extremely limited. Suppose some voter wishes to vote for a male with a university education, who belongs to the NDP, and this voter has just three policy concerns: a much tougher stand on crime, support for loggers as opposed to environmentalists, and more money for health care. Such a voter would not be atypical, but under SMP it is virtually impossible to successfully vote this list of concerns. First, there will be only one NDP candidate; there is a 50 percent chance that this candidate will be male, a somewhat better than 50 percent chance that he will be university educated, and much less than a 50 percent chance that he will share the voter's three policy concerns.

Second, if somehow one candidate matches this voter's concerns, that voter faces yet another difficulty. The chance of electing one's preferred candidate is less than 50 percent. Under SMP, typically between 35 and 45 percent of voters get the candidate they vote for. Our voting system is designed such that on election day the majority of voters waste their vote. Such results do not foster a culture of citizenship. Because SMP is structurally incapable of representing accurately a modern, pluralistic society, citizens who take their public duty seriously on election day are frustrated: they cannot express a responsible judgment. At best, their choice consists in selecting the least of evils, or the best of a bad bunch. Meaningful participation is inhibited, and the resulting government cannot be representative. Consider, as an example, the federal riding of New Westminster. Before 1993, New Westminster was held by New Democrat Dawna Black, an outspoken member of the left wing of her party. In 1993 New Westminster went to Paul Forsyth, a strong right-wing Reformer. What happened to New Westminster? There were no boundary changes, or massive demographic shifts. Did the voters shift from one extreme to the other? Not likely. Paul Forsyth won with less than 30 percent of the vote; he is no more representative of the people of New Westminster than Dawna Black was before him. Our governments are not representative. Outside of a two-party system, SMP cannot bring people's concerns into the legislature. Our voting system is unfit for the times. It need not be thus. The voting system should allow voters to grade all the competing issues.

To further illustrate how problematic representation becomes under SMP consider Reform Party innovations. Some Reform Party of Canada MPs have recently on their own initiative surveyed their constituents on controversial legislation such as gun control and then voted accordingly, even if they had to go against the caucus. This unusual action is in fulfilment of party policy to have elected members represent their constituents, and is well motivated. Yet it raises some questions. Whose views deserve representation, those who voted for the MP, those of the MP's party, or all constituents? Why should those who did not vote for the MP be considered? If the survey results of all constituents is different from those who voted for the MP, and the MP votes with the majority, the peculiar situation emerges where those who won the election are left unrepresented. Again, under SMP questions of representation are clouded and ambiguous. SMP elections do not establish a clear mandate on a particular platform between a particular group of people and a particular representative. This, too, need not be thus.

SUBSTANTIVE REPRESENTATION
Political representation involves more than formal requirements for authorization and accountability, or stipulations about who and what should determine the composition of the legislature. The legislature exists to *do* something. Representation has to be an activity, not just a condition. We must specify what that activity consists of: what is a political representative to do? For example, should representatives be guided by their own judgment, opinion, conscience, or that of their

constituents? Any vote in the legislature by a representative either cor-responds to how the constituents would have voted themselves, or it doesn't. If it doesn't, then surely those constituents are without repre-sentation. Some hold that it is nearly impossible to determine the wish-es of tens of thousands of people on any number of issues. Besides, government must provide leadership, too; the wishes of the people at the moment may not be in their best interest. Government is an instru-ment to arrive at wise decisions after careful deliberation and full con-sideration of all relevant information. Why revert to mob rule, allowing the ill-informed and least competent to dictate policy? In this view, lis-tening too closely to the people turns representatives into mere errand boys, while the importance of government requires qualified persons capable of sound, independent judgment. There are good arguments to support both of these seemingly irreconcilable positions – often referred to as the mandate/independence controversy.

Pitkin has shown that this controversy derives from an equivoca-tion embedded in the word *representation* itself. "The core meaning of 'representation' is making present in some sense what is nevertheless not literally present."[19] Those who insist that the people's opinions and wishes must count want to make present, in a meaningful way, what is not present. Those who insist that a representative must have discre-tion to act correctly point out that if the represented is itself present, no representation takes place. The represented must be absent in some meaningful sense. Pitkin suggests that representation is a careful, pru-dent balancing between these two extremes. Where a representative's actions bear no relationship to, or even contradict, the wishes and interests of the represented, no representation occurs. Similarly, where a representative must not act except on the explicit instructions of the represented, there too no representation takes place. The extremes are out of bounds. With this in mind, Pitkin offers this definition: "Representation means acting in the interest of the represented, in a manner responsive to them."[20]

The last part, "in a manner responsive to them," is significant, and also misunderstood.[21] It indicates that in a democracy representatives must explain themselves, especially when their view of the interests of the represented differs from the popular view. In particular, Pitkin looks for a network of institutional arrangements that allow citizens to express an opinion. She does not expect citizens to express an opinion on every issue, but the means should be in place for them in the event they have an opinion to express. In Canada this is best illustrated with reference to local governments, which have more effective mecha-nisms to solicit citizens' views than the senior governments. For exam-ple, zoning decisions involve a comprehensive public hearing at each stage of the process: the official community plan, the area plans, the rezoning applications, and the development permits. Affected residents must be informed by mail, signs and notices in the print media of stipulated size and frequency. In addition, local councils must consult voters on borrowings for capital expenditures above a certain monetary value, and are bound to follow their will as expressed through referenda. These are the kinds of institutional arrangements Pitkin is after. She is concerned that the output of the legislature serve the public interest, but that cannot be all; a benevolent dictator or despot might well serve the public interest.[22] Representative government, in this view, requires in addition a process that includes people in the decision-making.

Burke strongly defended the need for representatives to use their own best judgment, and held that individual voters or groups of voters may not always be, at all times, the best judges of their own real interest. But he also considered that where a representative consistently disagrees with the represented, the view of the people must prevail, since the people as a whole are best equipped to judge, over time, their own interest. Also, if the people's view is known beforehand on an important matter, that view should prevail.[23] Burke is often thought to have said that citizen input is unnecessary, but his position is more balanced.

The various aspects of representation considered suggest a progression – a range of conditions and requirements that are necessary if government is to be truly representative. Free, competitive elections, enabling the electorate to express a judgment on the performance of the representatives after the fact, are the most basic requirement, and some analysts consider them sufficient. Others insist that in addition the composition of the legislature must be prescribed to ensure that all politically relevant opinions and interests are present. The behaviour of the representatives may also need to be considered: what they do, and how they do it. Representation is a multifaceted concept. Where one places the emphasis depends on one's values and view of human nature, on the degree to which citizens' participation is considered desirable, and on the history of a people and their social homogeneity. If one is committed to classical democracy, i.e., self-rule and maximum participation to improve and develop the character of citizens,[24] then the full range of requirements seems desirable, particularly in a society with significant political diversity.

Few contemporary scholarly works overtly disagree with Pitkin's view of representation. However, many studies aim to measure responsiveness in terms of output – the services a representative delivers.[25] As a result of this attempt to measure responsiveness by means of quantifiable, empirical research data, there seems to be less emphasis on process, and perhaps an unstated acceptance that output is all that matters to the average voter, and that process in representative government need entail no more than periodic free and competitive elections. In contrast, Pitkin's concern with responsiveness is directed at process, not output. Output must serve the interests of the represented, but in a democracy, where government is, as much as possible, "in the hands of the many, not the few," the *manner* in which this is done is as important as *what* is being done. The process is as important as the end product. That I take to be Pitkin's point. It is one I endorse.

Defenders of our voting system argue that people have less concern for the process than the end result, the output of a government. Unfortunately, it is true that many persons have no interest in the democratic process as such. Concern with process is kindled only when their "bread and circuses" are cut off. Such behaviour indicates an impoverished view of government and citizenship. If government is primarily an instrument to dole out material plenty to the masses, then there is no qualitative difference between a dictatorship and a free society. Democracy and human freedom are ill served by empirical political-science studies that focus exclusively on output while neglecting process.

Whether one accepts the mandate or independence view of representation, or the Pitkin version of responsiveness, one essential ingredient is common to all: representatives must have the freedom and means to act for, and on behalf of, the represented. They must have as much power as the people would have were they present in person. Where allegiance to party or political leader takes precedence over the interests of the represented, representation is weakened. Where a political party, prime minister, premier, and cabinet diminish the independence of the representatives, the channel through which citizens are to engage in self-rule is obstructed. Where a representative is impotent, the represented are impotent. Parliament and the legislature must have a significant role if the people are to be heard. If the people cannot be heard through their representatives, representation – and hence democracy – is weakened. Parliament and the legislatures are the people's forum; it is the place where the people vicariously engage in self-rule.

In addition, if one supports the Pitkin view that representativeness implies responsive institutional arrangements, the legislature itself is the first institution to be assessed for responsiveness. Then the question is: when people have an opinion to express, can they express it through the legislature? How well the B.C. legislature measures up to these requirements of substantive representation is the subject of chapter three.

POPULAR DEMANDS

To TEST WHETHER representative government can be an avenue for a substantial degree of self-rule, requirements for the composition and function of the legislature derived from theories about representative government have been considered. But what do the people say? Voters may not be familiar with theories of representation but they do not therefore lack views on how their representatives and government should act, and their views are surprisingly similar to those of the theorists considered here. People express opinions in a variety of ways, including polls, the lobbying of special-interest groups, and their vote at each election.

ELECTIONS

Why do people vote? What are their intentions? Do voters vote for the local candidate, the party, or the party leader? Perhaps, they vote *for* nothing, but strategically, *against* something.[26] B.C.'s political culture is particularly infected by the latter. National election surveys show the leader and party to be far more significant factors for voters than local candidates.[27] If so, how are representatives to understand their role, and what is the function of the legislature to be? If votes for a representative are primarily expressions of support for the party leader and the party platform, then party discipline is a virtue, and a weak legislature most desirable. Every election is followed by statements from academics, journalists, and others, to the effect that "The people have spoken," and "You can't argue with democracy." All this gives rise to the view that government receives a mandate from the people on the basis of a platform. Since the people vote for the leader, the party, and its platform, no legislature should be in a position to thwart the will of the people. The people have a right to expect the government to deliver on its promises, and the government should be given the tools to do so. Defenders of SMP point to this as its virtue; it creates strong government, able to make decisions and implement its program. This is said to lead to accountability – the government is given the tools to do the job, and has no one to blame should it fail.[28]

However plausible such a view may appear, it would have more validity if prime ministers and premiers were elected directly, like U.S. presidents, or if voters had two ballots, one for the local candidate and one for electing the government. SMP focuses on local constituency representation. A modern political culture that relies on mass political parties and focuses on the leaders, not the local candidates, cannot achieve its aims through a single-member, riding-based system. That system was designed for times and conditions completely different from ours, when MPs enjoyed the independence necessary to serve local interests. Today, if a vote for the local candidate is in reality a vote for party and platform, then a list proportional representation system – in which voters choose from a list of candidates, ranking them in order of preference – that focuses on party and leader would be far more appropriate. Voter intention would find its way into the legislature, majorities would not be artificially manufactured, the role of the representative would be without ambiguity, and truthful claims about the meaning of an election would be possible.

The contention that, under SMP (single member plurality), government has a mandate from the people is suspect not only because the votes were actually cast for local candidates, but also, and this is the more important reason, because SMP allows minorities to elect government. In the provinces as in national politics, governments are typically not elected by the majority of the voters, but by the voting system. SMP translates votes into seats and produces a legislative majority where none existed among the voters. Our governments lack legitimacy; in most instances their mandate is questionable. For example, the current B.C. government won with 39 percent of the popular vote; fully 61 percent of the people did not support its leader, party, or platform. This is not an exception, but the rule. In 1903 parties first entered B.C. politics. In all except four of the twenty-five general elections held between 1903 and 1996, the government received less than a majority of the popular vote. The exceptions occurred in 1909 and 1912, during the wartime coalition of 1945, and in 1949. Also, it is possible for a party to go from opposition to a majority government despite receiving less of the popular vote than in the previous election; this happened to the British Columbia NDP in 1991.[29]

Governments that receive a legislative majority artificially manufactured from a minority of the votes cannot legitimately claim to be the people's choice, or the voice of the people. Representation under our system is ambiguous and problematic. To return to the example I gave in the Introduction, Vander Zalm was elected on a decidedly pro-life platform, so why was there public resistance to his abortion policy? He was only doing what he promised to do. Did Vander Zalm not win, did he not have a majority of the seats? In fact, because Vander Zalm's win was artificial, and not a true expression of the mind of the people, he, like most governments, lacked a clear mandate. Many who voted for Vander Zalm did not intend to endorse his pro-life stance. SMP is a crude instrument, not sufficiently refined to register accurately the mind of the electorate. When elections are fought on issues of substance, the results are unclear.

Most elections are not fought on policy platforms of any substance. SMP, combined with modern campaign strategies, induces parties to engage in politics of image, perception, and personality, instead of principle, policy, and platform.[30] Political strategists know that a platform with too much detail can be harmful to their election chances.[31] Discussion of policies leads people to make decisions; decisions that might go against the party position. Images, bereft of content, are much safer. Under our present system governments are not elected because of their policies. They receive a performance mandate, not a policy mandate. Did former B.C. premier W.A.C. Bennett have a mandate to buy B.C. Electric in 1956, or Dave Barrett to introduce the Agricultural Land Reserve in 1972? The assertion that in our system government is democratically chosen and mandated is contrary to fact on two counts: typically, the majority does not support the government, and elections are seldom about policies.[32] Whatever it is that people "say" at election time, elections are usually not expressions of confidence in the new government by a majority of the people. This, of course, does not stop every new government from claiming to be the voice of the people. Following the 1988 federal election, which was largely concerned with free trade between Canada and the U.S., Mulroney claimed to be asking for a mandate for free trade, and he won, but with only 43 percent of the popular vote. Given the fabrications, inventions, myths, and insincerity that permeate our political system, it should come as no surprise that trust in government is low.

POLLS AND SURVEYS

Deciphering the will of the people from election results under SMP is like reading chicken entrails, but polls and surveys are more meaningful. When people are asked, one fact stands out. There is widespread, deep cynicism about politicians and our political institutions.[33] Every year pollster Martin Goldfarb measures the level of trust and respect Canadians have for various professions. Laschinger reports that politicians are usually at or near the bottom of the Goldfarb list.[34] Similarly, the Lortie Royal Commission on Electoral Reform and Party Financing found that Canadians' level of trust and confidence in their political institutions is low, and declining over time; that cynical attitudes are more pronounced here than in the United States or the world at large. Lortie attributes the low level of public trust to three factors: one, the perceived control party leaders have over their supporters in Parliament; two, political parties that inadequately represent the population in all its diversity of interests; and three, political institutions that offer little opportunity for significant participation.[35] With reference to the first reason, Lortie reports a survey in which 78 percent of respondents agreed with the statement: "We would have better laws if Members of Parliament were allowed to vote freely rather than having to follow party lines."[36] A closely related survey tried to uncover whether people think the role of their representative is to be a trustee or an agent. A full 67 percent thought MPs should follow the views of the people in their riding.[37] MPs themselves have a different view. They see their role as primarily using their own good judgment.[38] The Reform Party of Canada's official position is to end party discipline to allow elected members to represent constituents' views.[39] In recent years most political parties talk about lessening party discipline. All this attests to a growing public sentiment that government should listen more effectively to the people. It is clear that people think government, and particularly their elected members, should be their mouthpiece, but that under our system their MPs do not get the message out. Also, those surveys support a descriptive view of represention, that is, people agree that the legislature should accurately mirror the political diversity as it exists out on the street. However, Lortie is mistaken in blaming the current unrepresentative nature of Parliament and the legislatures on political parties. It is the voting system that is the cause, not the parties.

One study that measured opinions about our voting system asked how respondents felt about a system that often awards a majority of seats, and hence the government, to a party that does not have a majority of the votes. In B.C. only 41 percent found this acceptable. The same study then asked respondents if they would favour a system of two votes, one to elect their local representative and one to elect the government. In B.C. 70 percent favoured such a two-vote system. The same study attributes both these responses to a desire for greater control by voters over their local representative.[40] Obviously, people do not think the system allows their will to filter through without distortion.

SPECIAL INTERESTS

A significant number of people also speak through special interest groups. The existence, prominence, and public support of interest groups in itself suggests that many people do not consider political action through one's elected local representative to be effective.

For example, the Canadian Advisory Council on the Status of Women is not concerned so much that party discipline and the relative powerlessness of Parliament frustrates responsiveness to their agenda[41]; their view is more radical: they believe men cannot represent women. Demands for gender equity in representation grow from the belief that differences between the sexes are significant enough to warrant women's being represented by "one of their own." Proponents claim that history shows men have failed to represent women's issues and interests, that women have been marginalized and disadvantaged, if not oppressed. In the past, they point out, women's property was taken without compensation, and their enfranchisement was ridiculed and opposed by men. In the present, women are paid less, suffer discrimination in employment and pension schemes, are disproportionately represented in menial jobs, and are objects of sexual harassment. Issues of particular concern to women include pay equity, spouse and child maintenance payments, pensions for homemakers, support for single-parent families, more equitable asset distribution upon divorce, and legislation pertaining to abortion and reproductive technology. The largest government expenditures are in health, education, and social services, and these departments, some claim, are concerned with issues that affect women more directly than men. All this is offered as proof that women cannot fairly be represented by men.[42] Many women are no longer content to support an outdated voting system that recognizes geographical interests but ignores human interests. The latter, in today's society, are deemed far more significant. Another study gives some evidence that such voices are representative of women generally. Blais and Gidengil found that "... women are less likely than men to find the present system of translating votes into seats acceptable."[43] A particularly bold suggestion demands that every riding have a male and a female seat, because "assimilation has failed, we need a strategy of separation."[44]

Lortie Commission research shows that women, ethno-cultural groups, visible minorities and Aboriginal people are all underrepresented in the House of Commons.[45] Progress towards gender equity for elected members is painfully slow. In federal elections, it may take another forty years.[46] The B.C. general election of 1991 elected 25 percent women MLAs, compared to only 13 percent in 1986 (the percentage was unchanged after the 1996 election). Whether this trend will be sustained remains to be seen. A recent study of B.C. party activists concludes that "British Columbia's extra-parliamentary parties remain predominantly male-dominated institutions."[47] To speed up gender equity, women's groups are calling for a proportional voting system.[48] The reason is simple; proportional systems accurately represent, in the legislature, the full diversity of issues and concerns, and changing social trends are responded to quickly. Numerous studies have shown that gender equity is much easier to attain under proportional systems than under SMP.[49]

So, what do the people say about representation? Election results tell very little. We do know that elections in Canada typically do not democratically mandate a government. This should make us cautious about assigning a dominant role to the cabinet. There may be good reasons why the cabinet should control and dominate Parliament and the legislatures, but the claim to a popular mandate is not one of them. People are distrustful of a system that gives too much power to the party leaders and puts the interests of the party ahead of the needs of the citizens. They want representatives who will speak for them. Significant groups of electors reject a voting system that results in a legislature that cannot accurately reflect the politically significant interests of the people, as they exist among the electorate – the interests of women, for example, who make up more than half the population. In this regard, popular opinion and significant political theorists agree. Their criticism of our system of representation is the same.

To these demands can be added calls for popular democracy, such as recall (which would allow voters to recall their representative from government if they were not satisfied with his performance) and initiative (which would allow private citizens to initiate legislation).[50] All such demands and sentiments of distrust have no significance except as evidence that people expect Parliament and the legislatures to have a considerable degree of power. Most people have little knowledge of and even less interest in the exact relationship between the cabinet and Parliament, but they are clear about their representative being their voice, and if that representative has no voice, they have no voice. In the eyes of some, people are equally without a voice if their representative is not "one of their own." The quest to end undue party discipline, the quest for popular democracy, the quest for gender equity, the quest for a system of representaton whereby every politically significant constituency throughout the country and province can find itself represented in Parliament and the legislature, are all quests for participation, power, clout, and influence. The expectation is that a person's vote will count, that people can make a difference, that they can participate meaningfully, that their interests will be protected. What else is democracy for? The desire to have "one of their own" is a desire for participation, for recognition, for entry into the game. Why? Because the legislature is considered to be a decision-making body, and as its name implies, a place where laws are made. To participate in the legislature, even vicariously through a representative, is to participate in substantial self-rule. The legislature is the people's forum, the ultimate depository of the people's power, and their sovereignty. At least, so it is thought.

THE CHARTER AND RECENT COURT RULINGS
THE CONCERN FOR meaningful participation by citizens in the legislative process, through their elected representatives, also underlies a number of recent court decisions related to section 3 of the Charter of Rights and Freedoms. In particular, these cases reveal a concern that citizens have equality of legislative power. They are therefore important to this study. As a bonus, the courts also introduced the concept of "effective representation." This concept caused one scholar to write: "To this reader, the Trojan Horse of the argument for proportional representation may be buried in these cases."[51]

61

Alan Cairns observes that the Charter has induced Canadians to think of themselves as citizens with rights.[52] One such right is the right to vote, as found in section 3.

> Every citizen of Canada has the right to vote in an election to the House of Commons or of a legislative assembly, and to be qualified for membership therein.

Three cases, one heard by the Supreme Court of Canada, have tried to understand the meaning of this section for electoral systems. In reviewing these cases it will be of particular interest to understand why the courts hold to the principle of voter equality, and to discuss whether section 3 requires representation of all political groups, particularly political constituencies that are not bound to a geographic location. If the latter is the case, SMP itself is in violation of a Charter right, and must be replaced by proportional representation.

British Columbia's electoral boundaries legislation was the first to be tested against section 3 in what came to be known as the Dixon case. Chief Justice McLachlin of the B.C. Supreme Court (as she then was) delivered her judgment on 18 April 1989.[53] The argument centred on the urban/rural split whereby some urban MLAs represented fifteen times the population of the least populous rural riding under the B.C. legislation then current. This suggests that the votes of some are fifteen times more powerful than the votes of others. McLachlin observed that "the purpose (of the right to vote) cannot be less than to guarantee to citizens their full democratic rights in the government of the country and the provinces." And "...the right to vote and participate in the democratic election of one's government is one of the most fundamental of the Charter rights."[54] Such a fundamental right must not be diluted for some citizens by giving greater weight to the vote of others. Therefore, to ensure equality of voting power, representation must be by population in equal numbers. The electoral system must protect the equal worth of each citizen. Without equality of voting power, the popular will cannot be determined.

> The essence of democracy is that the people rule. Anything less than direct, representative democracy risks attenuating the expression of the popular will and hence risks thwarting the purpose of democracy.[55]

However, the court found that absolute equality cannot ever be attained, and must also be tempered by historical and geographical considerations. In practice, the aim must be to attain relative equality. B.C.'s legislation was found to contravene section 3, because many of its electoral boundaries constituted "considerable" infringements, even of the right to relative equality of voting power.[56]

The court elaborated on why equality of voting power is so important. After observing that elected representatives have both a legislative and an ombudsman's role, the court wrote:

> In the legislative role, it is the majority of elected representatives who determine who forms the government and what laws are passed. In principle, the majority of elected representatives should represent the majority of the citizens entitled to vote. Otherwise, one runs the risk of rule by what is in fact a minority.[57]

Voting power resides in the capacity of a citizen's vote to make a difference in determining who forms the government and what laws are passed. That power must be equal for each citizen. (It is noteworthy that the court seems to be unaware that SMP regularly, consistently, and by design produces majority governments from a minority of the votes. Compromise of the principle of voter equality is an inherent feature of SMP, and is not restricted to the unequal populations of electoral districts. Even if all districts were precisely equal in population, governments under SMP would continue to be elected by minorities. If the court had looked at all the logical implications of its principle, our voting system in its entirety would have been judged to contravene section 3.)

The *Dixon* case found that geographical factors might warrant deviation from strict equality based on population, but subsequent cases broadened the rules to include nongeographical differences. Following *Dixon*, the Saskatchewan government referred its Electoral Boundaries Commission Act to the province's Court of Appeal for an opinion on its constitutionality.[58] The Court of Appeal interpreted section 3 as embodying principles very similar to those established in the *Dixon* case. "One person one vote" also means "a vote of equal worth." To give full effect to this Charter right, electoral laws must "strive to make each citizen's portion of sovereign power equal." This will lead to "fair and effective representation." In devising electoral boundaries the controlling and dominant principle is equality in the numbers of citizens each legislator represents. By way of explanation, the court wrote:

> This is so because most citizens can participate (in government) only as qualified voters through the election of legislators to represent them. ... Voters' rights merit constitutional safeguards in this way because the proportionate share of voting power enjoyed by each elect-

ed member of the Legislative Assembly. Any malappor-
tionment with respect to voter population, and the subsequent dilution of a person's vote, is reflected in the
exercise of power in the legislature. The array of powers enjoyed by the legislature are exercised through the
aforementioned voting scheme in our democracy.
Since these powers touch the lives of each and every
citizen in one way or another, the preservation and
growth of our democratic process is not furthered by
electoral practises which offend the worth of a person's
vote.[59]

The court held the legislation to contravene section 3. This was
appealed to the Supreme Court of Canada, which delivered a decision
on 6 June 1991, reversing the opinion of the Saskatchewan Court of
Appeal.[60] In this decision, the Court did not disagree with the Appeal
Court in any matter of principle, but found that in addition to equality
of voting power, section 3 also guarantees "the right to effective representation." This right derives from the nature of representative democracy whereby each citizen is entitled to be represented in government,
and "of having a voice in the deliberations of government."[61] Since "it is
more difficult to represent rural ridings than urban,"[62] a smaller population for rural ridings is justified. The right of citizens to participate in
governing is in practice more difficult for some than for others.
Allowances have to be made to ensure that the exercise of each citizen's portion of sovereignty can in practice be effectual. That is the
essence of effective representation.

This ruling would allow rural districts to have smaller populations.
But note the reasons. It seems that the Courts picture the process as
follows. Citizens have a right to participate, through their representatives, in governing. This requires communication and contact between
representative and the represented. In rural ridings such contact is
deemed to be more difficult than for urban ridings; hence deviation
from strict mathematical parity is justified for rural ridings. The court
asserts the popular myth that citizens participate in ruling between
elections.

That access to one's representative is more difficult in rural ridings
is a concern familiar to every electoral boundaries commission. But
these recent court cases go beyond the traditional concerns by broad-
ening the scope of factors that fall within the concept of effective representation.

Factors like geography, community history, community
interests and *minority representation* may need to be

taken into account to ensure that our legislative assemblies effectively represent the diversity of our social
mosaic. These are but examples of considerations
which may justify departure from absolute voter parity
in the pursuit of more effective representation; *the list
is not closed.*[63]

Some of these factors are territorial, and can be accommodated by SMP.
Others, such as minority representation, may require districts that are
not contiguous, and therefore, a proportional system of representation.
The logical consequence of this ruling must lead to PR, particularly
when the list of political "considerations" that potentially come within
the scope of effective representation is not closed.

In 1992, the Alberta government submitted its Electoral Boundaries
Commission Act to its Court of Appeal for an opinion on its constitutionality.[64] The Appeal Court found the Supreme Court's doctrine of
"effective representation" a "difficult" one, for two reasons. First, minority claims to effective representation might affect the tradition of sin-
gle-seat districts and contiguous boundaries. This court, at last, recognized the implications of the entitlement to effective representation of
non-geographical political interests, but unfortunately tried to distance
itself. Because, second, it held that whereas shared representation
might encourage mutual respect, to allow every group in society its
own member in the legislature might have the opposite effect. Clearly,
the concept of effective representation is far from resolved, and open to
further challenge. Public debate preceding the 1992 Charlottetown
Accord referendum questioned the assumption that the Senate should
represent place or territory. This challenge came particularly from
women, the disabled, visible minorities, and Aboriginal
representatives.[65] The court rulings reviewed here provide such groups
considerable encouragement to pursue their cause. If they do, the
courts will need to consider not just lines on a map and population
quotas but the far more interesting question of our electoral system's
efficacy in representing accurately a modern, diverse, pluralistic society whose citizens demand participation, and how such participation
can be effective where party discipline and an executive-dominated
Parliament deprive the citizens' representatives of the independence
necessary to be a representative.

For the purpose of this study it is important to note the reasoning
behind the judgments. The courts suggest that each citizen possesses
a portion of sovereign power which entitles him or her to participate
in governing, to have a voice, and to make a difference. This legislative or governing power is exercised through the citizen's representative. The act of exercising this legislative power is not restricted to

casting a ballot on election day once every four or five years. It is a continuous process requiring communication and contact between the representative and the represented. Citizens are entitled to ongoing participation. The implications of decisions about electoral boundaries reach into the legislature, affecting its day-to-day operations. Ensuring citizens the effective representation to which they are entitled is the representative's legislative role. The courts do not think it sufficient to vote for the captain, and to then be ordered off the bridge.

Professor Ken Carty of the University of British Columbia believes these court decisions fundamentally misunderstand the Parliamentary system.[66] The court rulings assume the British parliamentary system is democratic in the sense that sovereignty resides with the people, instead of the Crown, and that governmental decisions are made in Parliament. The court's misunderstanding is a reflection of the misunderstanding that exists on the street. The popular view, and that of the courts, is fed by the cultural influences that spill across the border from the American democracy. Our formal government institutions were imported from Britain for the express purpose of stopping at the border the excesses of the democratic zeal of the times. Now the question is: what will give way, the British institutions, or the popular view? And what role will the courts, encouraged by their new powers under the Charter, assume? The popular views are not about to disappear. Therefore our British institutions should be made more democratic. They need not be abandoned in favour of the American congressional system, but we need to rethink concepts, such as responsible government and sovereignty of the people, and practices, such as the riding-based voting system.

In summary, there is much agreement between what the theorists, the people and the courts say. The court's demand for effective representation is the same as Pitkin's understanding that political representation in a democracy requires the legislature to reflect proportionally in its composition the politically significant heterogeneity that exists within society, and institutional arrangements to facilitate responsiveness. Such requirements are no different from the people's desire for representatives who will take direction from the represented. All three viewpoints assign an important function to Parliament and the legislatures. They consider the legislature to be a forum where the people act through their representatives, where political factors are present in proportion to their electoral strength, and where such political factors have a voice, and can be heard. The people, the theorists, and the courts all assume that government is elected by the majority, and that the legislators make laws in the interest of their voters. In Canada such assumptions are wrong.

Because of our voting system, governments fail the most basic test of democratic representation: they are not elected by majorities, and the composition of Parliament and the legislatures does not reflect political diversity proportionally. Our voting system, designed for a two-party system when local community and place of residence circumscribed nearly all of a voter's existence, inhibits choice and diversity. It is unfit for the democratic temper of our time. It restricts democracy to a choice of rulers, on voting day, by the largest minority. The majority of citizens see their votes go to waste, and between elections democracy ceases altogether, because once the rulers are assured their faked majority they control Parliament and the legislatures.

Citizenship is not enhanced, or particularly uplifted, when on election day the majority of citizens receive for their efforts a local representative and a government they did not support. Their votes are wasted, their concerns, opinions and interests rejected, their slice of sovereignty frozen out; they are cut off from participation, not part of the team. Until the next election their experience of citizenship does not extend beyond paying taxes, extracted from them by a government they did not choose. Their condition is more like that of serf or subject than citizen; they endure taxation without representation. This is what alienates people from government. When one is not represented, government cannot be an extension of oneself, the means of democratic self-rule. Lacking a positive identification with government, most people turn against government. The opportunity to foster citizenship, civic pride, and identification with government as the embodiment of common purpose is squashed before it can germinate. It is a source of hope that the express wishes of the people and recent court decisions reject our voting system. In this regard, our governing institutions are far behind the times, and fall short of people's expectations.

Defenders of SMP suggest that elections should result in government. In this view, for a voting system to produce within the legislature a microcosmic representative image of the population, the politically diverse make-up of the country reflected in an elected body, is less important than that it produce a group sufficiently cohesive and stable to govern. In this view, the choice is between accurate representation and stable government. The burden of this study is to show why such a choice is not necessary. We should aim to have both accurate representation and stable government. Pitkin has shown that representation requires a careful balance between the composition of the legislature and its output. Defenders of SMP focus primarily on output, while proponents of PR usually focus on the composition of the legislature. A voting system fit for a representative democracy must answer both needs.

But even the output of SMP is questionable. The winner-take-all approach of SMP, which denies a role to anyone who did not win in an election, is best seen in the operation of Parliament and the legislatures. After the bitter competition of an election contest there is no reconciliation, no opportunity to practise the politics of inclusion. Our form of democracy does not lead to self-rule, because too many voters are excluded.

Chapter 3 considers the operation of the B.C. legislature. The distribution of power and the mode of decision-making are examined to determine whether they meet the requirements of substantive representation, so that governing may be "in a manner responsive to them [the citizens]." It concludes that under our cabinet-dominated parliamentary system legislators do not make the laws; that decisions about public policy are made outside the legislature; and that since legislators are beholden more to their parties than to their voters, their actions even when they have power to act will not be primarily in the interest of their voters.

THE LEGISLATURE

*Behind the familiar and reassuring facade
of the Parliament buildings in Ottawa lie
an unfair system of election, an inefficient
legislature, an autocratic and secretive
cabinet, a frustrated Opposition, and a
couple of reminders of our colonial and
undemocratic past. We can and must
devise a better system of government if we
hope to preserve democracy.[1]*

THIS STUDY CALLS into question the legislature's ability to hold the cabinet responsible, and it asserts that the legislature is inclined to surrender its legislative function to the cabinet, such that all decisions of importance are made not inside, but outside the legislature. This chapter aims to establish that this is so, and the likely reasons why it is so. Before beginning, it is important to note what this chapter is *not* about.

First, in the parliamentary system as opposed to a congressional system, the legislature does not often initiate, draft or propose legislation.[2] The cabinet meets in private, decides its policies, and then maintains a united front in presenting them to the legislature. Perhaps in a less complex, simpler era it was otherwise, but today the legislative function of the legislature consists in debating, amending and voting on bills (legislative proposals) and a budget put forward by the cabinet. This study does not question that process. To question that is to question the essence of the parliamentary system. This study wishes not to abolish the parliamentary system, but to remove obstacles to its proper functioning. Nor is this an appeal to return to an alleged "golden age" when much legislation is said to have originated from private member's bills.[3]

Second, many scholarly studies have tried to assess the relative influence and power of legislators within a given legislature, and also between legislatures. Such studies, empiricist and behaviourist in methodology, measure in minute detail what legislators actually do.[4] We learn what occupies their time, and perhaps what kind of influence they have: how much and in what areas. These studies search for causal relationship between a legislator's level of education, political socialization, and previous experience and the degree of influence he or she attains. Most of these findings are not particularly helpful for this study. Statements about individual legislators do not easily translate into statements about legislators as a collectivity, or the legislature as a whole. That certain legislators may be deemed to have more influence than others – because they speak more frequently, ask more questions and use more words, or are considered leaders by their peers – reveals little about the distribution of power between the cabinet and the legislature. To have influence in the legislature is not the same as having influence in government. This chapter considers the relationship that holds between the legislature and the cabinet, not the relationship between legislators.

RESPONSIBLE GOVERNMENT
POLITICS, ESPECIALLY GOVERNMENT, is about power. Everything in the legislature is animated by the appetite for power. Those who lack it want it; those who have it fight to maintain it. The framers of the American Constitution understood this well; they trusted no one with exclusive power. As a result, the congressional system shares power. In the American system, the legislative and the executive branch can both act within their respective fields, but not independently, as each needs the support of the other. In contrast, the parliamentary system does not require that power be shared. Rather, all power is given to the cabinet; it alone acts. Nor is there a separation of powers, the cabinet is part of the legislature. The task of overseeing the cabinet, of holding its actions up to public scrutiny, and of vetoing policies and laws that are not deemed to be in the public interest, rests in Canada primarily and in Britain entirely, with the legislature. In the parliamentary system government is said to be "responsible" because the cabinet must give an account of itself to the legislature. Upon losing the confidence of the legislature, the cabinet is removed. Confidence in the cabinet is tested by formal motions of confidence, majority support for any bills involving expenditure of public funds, and votes on ministerial estimates.[5]

Responsible government was introduced to Canada not by referendum or even by law, but by a simple dispatch from the Colonial Office in London. Lord Durham's report of 1838–39 recommended " ... administering the government on those principles which have been found perfectly efficacious in Great Britain:"[6] He meant a political system in which the cabinet is directly responsible to the legislature, and in which the ministers are members of the legislature. In 1848 Earl Grey, the colonial secretary, instructed Nova Scotia's lieutenant-governor, John Harvey, to ensure "...that any transfer which may take place of political power from the hands of one party in the province to those of another, is the result, not of an act of yours, but of the wishes of the people themselves."[7] From there responsible government spread to Canada (Ontario and Quebec), New Brunswick, Prince Edward Island, and Newfoundland. British Columbia adopted responsible government in 1871 upon joining Confederation.[8] In Australia, the first constitutional conference, held at Sidney in 1891, debated responsible government, which it described as a governor general and "...his advisors, such persons sitting in Parliament, and whose term of office shall depend upon their possessing the confidence of the house of representatives, expressed by the support of the majority."[9] Later, and much closer to home, Henry Angus instructed residents new to B.C. as follows:

> A minister ... may be dismissed at any time if he is distrusted by the representatives of the people in the Legislative Assembly. He is said to be a responsible minister because he is answerable to the legislature for his actions in office: and government carried on by responsible ministers is called responsible government.[10]

It is noteworthy that proponents of responsible government for the North American colonies spoke of it as self-government. Langstone's extensive study of the coming of responsible government to Canada uses the terms *responsible government* and *self-government* interchangeably. In their technical use these terms cannot be interchanged. Responsible government is government by cabinet in behalf of the Crown, enforced by an oath of allegiance to the Crown. The role of the legislature is to approve, or withhold approval from, the actions of cabinet. The term *self-government* is more appropriately applied to the congressional system, which allows the people's representatives to be lawmakers. That responsible government was described as self-government might indicate that the classical concept of democracy as self-rule was present at the birth of responsible government in Canada. For example, Earl Grey concludes his dispatch with these words: "... it is neither possible nor desirable to carry on government of any of the British Provinces in North America in opposition to the opinion of the inhabitants." This being the nineteenth century, "inhabitants" for Grey, meant the men (not the women) of the local ruling class. But that aside, the principle holds: laws are useless if not acceptable to the people. To this day, the democratic principle that the legislature exists to express the wishes of the people co-exists uncomfortably with the practice of parliamentary government, which vests sovereignty in the Crown, not the people. Pitkin does not choose between responsible and congressional government. She stipulates only that the process be such as to permit the people's views to be heard, and to influence law-making. The aim of this study is to show how responsible government can be made to work as it was intended, that is, to enable the legislature to hold cabinet accountable. The argument is that the result will largely satisfy Pitkin's requirements without the need to adopt the congressional system.

THE LEGISLATURE IN PRACTICE

THE FORMAL REQUIREMENTS of responsible government are meticulously observed in the B.C. legislature, but sadly, they do not have their intended effect. Cabinet is so powerful that the legislature is rendered nearly impotent to oversee, scrutinize, or veto the legislative agenda. A cursory look at the B.C. *Journals* will quickly establish that the cabinet is never denied legislation it wants. With majority governments, all government bills pass, as do all ministerial estimates and every budget. In every election since 1956, single member plurality (SMP) has artificially generated legislative majorities out of a minority of votes. Such legislative majorities have ensured the legislature's compliance with whatever legislation, budgets, and estimates the cabinet placed before it – without exception. What power to veto, what power to call to account, what power to dismiss is there, if in practice these alleged powers are never exercised? A power on paper that is never used is no power at all.[11] An Australian describes law-making in the parliamentary system as follows: "Once the point of Legislation is reached, it is usually assumed the battle is over. The theoretical sanctions of withdrawal of confidence, amendment, or rejection of government measures, in practice, are most unlikely to be used."[12]

Power is with the cabinet, and the legislature is the arena where it exercises its power. That power cannot be used arbitrarily, or kept completely behind closed doors. Legislation and the budget must be placed before the legislature, in a prescribed, open, public process. No doubt the process itself influences the behaviour of the cabinet.[13] The legislature may not be able to stop or significantly amend legislation, but it is a forum to expose government measures to full public scrutiny. The legislature draws public attention to government action. This is a formidable weapon because governments are sensitive to public opinion. The legislature is used by the opposition to mobilize public opinion against the government. The cabinet and the opposition both know the unofficial rules. These rules do not permit the legislature to deliberate meaningfully, reflect on the great issues of the day, and then find agreement in a mutually satisfactory solution. On the contrary, the legislature is an adversarial public forum where the combatants battle for public opinion. Their instrument is propaganda, the projection of images, "spinning" stories, and "packaging" their leaders.[14] The goal is to win the ultimate prize – power. The objective is not to deliberate, but to discredit, not to build consensus, but to attack, not to support, but to tarnish the credibility and image of the opponents. The primary venue for this contest is the legislature.

The formal process of putting legislation through the legislature need not be an exclusively negative experience for the cabinet. The process is used as a marketing tool, a stage from which to "sell" the cabinet's agenda, to legitimize the cabinet's agenda in the public mind, and to build acceptance and consensus among the diverse interests in society. The process is also used as a shield to dodge opposition attacks. The cabinet controls the orders of the day, and the select standing committees' agendas. The latter provide a fertile field to "bury," indefinitely, embarrassing issues and questions.[15] The cabinet uses the legislature to market-test its legislation for public response. If the response is unfavourable the legislation is left to "die" on the order paper. In summary, the legislature's procedures, designed to prevent arbitrary use of power, may be used by a cabinet to its advantage, while always risking unfavourable public exposure. But the legislature's role in formulating the legislative agenda is minimal, and its ability to veto virtually nonexistent. The legislature is an arena where a contest takes place. This contest is not a debate about law or public policies, but a battle in which the object is the destruction of the credibility of one's opponents in the public mind. As a result, some question if the institution should appropriately be called a legislature at all.[16]

Some may object that this characterization of the legislature is excessively unsympathetic, and that useful debate does take place. J.S. Mill, for example, conceived of the legislature as a deliberative body.[17] And Carl Schmitt traces in detail how parliamentary government is founded on liberalism's belief that truth flows from the free competition of ideas.[18] In this view, parliamentary rule is justified by open debate leading to truth. Is the legislature not a place for open, unfettered debate? Do the MLAs not fill several volumes of Hansard each year? Does the clash of ideas in open, public debate not represent the essence of the legislature and the finest tradition of liberalism?[19]

Again, practice and theory are two different things. True debate and deliberation consist of persons taking turns speaking while others listen. In the legislature everyone speaks, but no one listens. Any comparison between speeches in local government and those in the B.C. legislature reveals the superior level of debate at the local government level, though the subject matter may be less significant. In the legislature, unlike local government, all minds are decided before the speeches begin. There is no need or desire for genuine debate. Former Prime Minister Lester Pearson comments in his memoirs on his reluctance to speak in the House of Commons:

> The main reason ... was that much of the debating seemed artificial, a kind of play-acting. The words were for the record, not uttered in hope that they would change the minds of anyone. Minds were, with very few exceptions, already convinced.

Philip Givens, a federal Liberal backbencher, has this perspective:

> The vast majority of Canadians think the House of Commons is a place where speeches are made and listened to. What actually happens is that at the end of question period every day the House flushes out like a toilet bowl – members leave, cabinet ministers leave, the press gallery empties, and you get up to talk to 240 empty seats... nothing is accomplished by debate... I don't know why we don't have the US Congress idea – if you want to get something on the record, you put it there and you don't have to spout it to empty seats.[20]

Words spoken in the legislature, particularly by the opposition, may be very critical of the cabinet's legislation, and hence generate negative publicity. But talk in the legislature is seldom debate and rarely contributes to the formulation of public policy. B.C. voters should not think their representative goes to Victoria to participate in law-making, even if only negatively, through a veto. Minds are made up in advance: for the most part the government side will support whatever the cabinet presents, and the opposition will attack it. The opposition's influence is limited to instigating negative publicity. The cabinet proposes laws, taxes, and spending of public funds, and a compliant legislature invariably approves. I do not contend that the legislature is without any influence, and that cabinet power is totally arbitrary. The legislature can arouse public opinion, which is at times a powerful weapon. Nor do I argue that cabinet should not be able to propose legislation exclusively. That would be an argument for the congressional system. My point is that all decisions of importance are made outside the legislature. In practice, the legislature will not overturn such decisions once they are made. The proper and internal role of the legislature, which is to exercise veto power to amend and/or refuse legislation, has been abdicated. In practice, it exists only at the outside limits of public tolerance for acts proposed by cabinet, and not always then.

Under our voting system, winners take all. The result is adversarial politics. Government, particularly the premier, erroneously thinks it has a mandate to rule with near dictatorial powers, eliminating the opposition from any positive role. As such, it is a most unproductive, inefficient system. Successive governments undo the legislation of their predecessors. The first major legislation of the Harcourt administration was to abolish the Vander Zalm labour code and replace it with one more friendly to their own partisan supporters. In Ontario, Premier Mike Harris wasted no time in reversing most of the Rae adminstration's social policies. Wild swings in public policy every five years are wasteful, generate public cynicism, and do not reflect the wishes of the electorate. B.C. politics is far more polarized than B.C. voters. It is imperative that the voting system be changed.

Former Premier Dave Barrett in his memoirs expresses deep regret at not having involved the people and the opposition more meaningfully in the process of developing and implementing public policy. He writes:

> On reflection, I think our administration should have worried problems through with the public a bit more. Any government that attempts to ram through a piece of legislation, even good legislation, runs the risk of having the idea shot down because people feel left out of the system. I regret that as leader I didn't use the talents of a significantly greater number of people in the legislature, both government and opposition. If we had used committees more extensively, we could have tapped into the considerable skills of opposition members.[21]

CAUCUS, PARTY, AND ELECTED MEMBERS

AS NOTED, MINDS are virtually always closed before the speeches begin. Closed minds are a function of the party caucuses, which are fuelled by the desire for power. Intraparty differences, in all but exceptional circumstances, remain behind closed doors. Caucus is the chief link through which party discipline is administered. More positively, caucus may also provide an opportunity for policy input. It is difficult to measure how much this really happens. If my own experience is typical, it happens rarely. Former MP Patrick Boyer reports that frequently caucus was not asked to give approval to government bills before they were introduced – as the party had pledged they would be – during the Mulroney administration.[22] Under Premier Vander Zalm, ministers would apprise caucus of legislation at the caucus meeting immediately before tabling the subject legislation in the legislature.[23] Prior notice was rare, and delay of tabling to allow more discussion even more so. The purpose of these caucus briefing sessions was less to discuss the merits of the proposed legislation than to anticipate how the opposition might react, to plot strategy, and to ensure members would all "sing from the same hymn book."[24]

In a former, simpler era, caucus was the means by which the cabinet kept abreast of public opinion. Caucus members were an important link between the electorate and the government. Modern means of communication, public opinion surveys, and polling have changed all that. Today a premier is in direct communication with the people. Each morning the previous evening's polls, surveys, and mass media tell the premier the mind of the province.

> ... if a Prime Minister has an Alan Gregg or a Michael Adams or anyone else sitting at his elbow, bending his ear, interpreting the facts and saying, 'Prime Minister, this is what the people are seeing and saying and thinking and feeling', then you don't want to bother listening to this distorted prism of a national caucus trying, in a garbled fashion, to explain what the people are thinking – let alone the House of Commons. It is not efficient.[25]

As early as 1938, Bertrand Russell, writing about the impact of mass communication on politics, observed, "The result has been to diminish the importance of the representative and increase that of the leader. Parliaments are no longer effective intermediaries between voters and governments."[26]

Today a government caucus member's primary role in the legislative process is to vote as instructed by the caucus whip, and to sell the government package in and outside of the legislature. Goddard, in assessing the role of caucus, concludes, "...decision-making appears to be undivided and concentrated at the top in B.C. given the weakness of the legislative assembly, and the legislative committee system of the Province."[27] It is commonly observed that within their respective jurisdictions the first minister within the parliamentary system has more power than a U.S. president.[28] When was the last time a prime minister or premier had trouble getting a budget approved?[29] Yet near-deadlock is a regular feature of the congressional system. Eugene Forsey writes, "The Prime Minister used to be described as 'the first among equals' in cabinet... This is no longer so. He is now incomparably more powerful than any of his colleagues."[30] Why are first ministers so powerful? Their power derives from the strength political parties gained after universal suffrage, and a voting system that manufactures faked majorities.

It was not always so. Sir John A. Macdonald, faced with a Parliament of largely independent MPs, relied on patronage to get his legislative program through the Commons. To him, Canada could not be governed without patronage.[31] Macdonald had to buy caucus loyalty with government largesse. For example, as with all his legislation, before tabling his numerous CPR relief bills, Macdonald would in each instance first secure support in cabinet and caucus. Such delays frequently brought the great railroad project to the brink of bankruptcy. Patronage greased the wheels of Parliament. Federal politics still centres on balancing the various interests of Canda's vast and disparate regions, but with one important difference. Macdonald's supporters in Parliament enjoyed sufficient independence to readily shift their allegiance, as many did at crucial moments. Modern prime ministers need not worry about support in Parliament; it is taken for granted. Party discipline has replaced patronage, and emasculated Parliament. Parliament is now terminally compliant; it shows few signs of life. Parliament, like the provincial legislatures, is superfluous to the development and implementation of public policy. One important study concludes, "Representative democracy in Canada is so dominated by political parties that some experts believe the party discipline exerted on most votes in our House of Commons and provincial legislatures is the tightest in the democratic world."[32] In Macdonald's day, MPs were consulted and could refuse; today MPs are simply told how they must vote. Party discipline is even more contemptuous of democracy than the patronage system was, but both are unworthy of a democracy. We need a voting system that fosters cooperation. Parliament has worked on patronage and party discipline. Now it must be made to work on partnership.

Canadian party discipline is certainly more severe than in Britain. Thatcher advised Trudeau she could not guarantee her backbenchers would vote to pass a unilaterally imposed federal constitutional package. As Peter McCormick has observed, "Had the situation been reversed, the warning would have been both unnecessary and inaccurate."[33] The citizens' representatives are "trained seals" to be manipulated by their parties. This derogatory, but eminently appropriate term first entered the Parliamentary lexicon on 15 May 1956. It was used by George Drew to describe the Liberal backbench in the famous "pipeline debate," and has been repeated in every session of every legislature since.[34] Elected members are beholden. It is virtually impossible to get elected as an independent.[35] The members are controlled by the party leaders.

Provincially, a party in power is controlled by the premier's office. This office influences nomination meetings, the flow of party funds, the party conventions, and hence the shelf-life of individual MLAs. In addition, a premier's ability to reward or punish includes the vast array of appointments he has the power to bestow. He can appoint cabinet ministers, parliamentary secretaries, directors of the boards of numerous Crown corporations, the caucus chair, House leader, speaker, deputy speaker, chair of Committee of the Whole, government whip, deputy government whip, chairs and membership of select standing committees, and task forces of all kinds. Also, the B.C. premier makes in excess of three thousand appointments to the boards of hospitals, colleges, and regulatory commissions and official bodies of all kinds. Such appointments are highly coveted, for the pay, the prestige, or both. The premier's office reaches far and wide, a fact any freshman MLA quickly learns. To obtain benefits for his constituency, an MLA cannot afford to cross anyone in the premier's office. Even under thrifty Vander Zalm, the premier's office employed nearly one hundred persons. Real power is not in the legislature, or even in the cabinet, but in the premier's office. Don Johnston, a former MP and cabinet minister, writes:

> The imposition of party discipline in the House of Commons has eroded the value of the institution. It has turned intelligent, vigorous, creative members into eunuchs. It has depreciated the value of the standing committees. It has permitted cabinet to arrogate all meaningful policy development. Worse, it has permitted the Prime Minister's Office to emasculate even cabinet.[36]

Politics is about power. Its appetite is never sated, the struggle for power never ends. In this perpetual battle for control the legislature loses each round, usually in the name of efficiency, and over time it is crippled.[37] Campbell Sharman, in a perceptive paper, points to yet another transfer of power to the cabinet. In 1973, B.C. amended the Constitution Act of 1871 to increase the size of the cabinet. A further amendment in 1980 removed all limits. The original 1871 limit meant members of the cabinet could not in number exceed 38 percent of the total government supporters in the legislature. This original provision Sharman interprets as a constitutional protection for the principle of responsible government. It constitutionally ensures the possibility that a caucus can out-vote cabinet.

> The removal of any limits at all on the size of the cabinet in a relatively small legislative assembly would seem to be a rather brutal expression of the cabinet dominance of the parliamentary process. It is certainly

a serious modification of the sort of government created in 1871. The changes of 1973 and 1980 might be
seen as amounting to a substantial alteration of the
mode of responsible government in the province
resulting not from changes to convention but from
amendments of a constitutional document.[38]

Hansard reveals that neither in 1973 nor in 1980 did anyone raise the
question of what impact these amendments might have on the principle of responsible government. Lorne Nicholson, NDP member for
Nelson/Creston came closest. Without elaborating he said, "We are
allowing the erosion of the legislature itself."[39] The amendment was
buried along with amendments to eighteen other statutes in the
Miscellaneous Statutes Amendment Act (No. 1) 1980. By convention
Miscellaneous Statutes Acts are not debated during second reading,
which is debate on principle. To bury such a significant change in a
basketful of housekeeping changes is itself shamefully autocratic.

During the last years of the Vander Zalm administration, the cabinet outnumbered the rest of caucus. Moreover, the ten parliamentary
secretaries and persons in other special positions all have a monetary
interest in supporting the cabinet. Maureen McTeer writes, "Cabinet
Ministers who go against the government on any matter must resign
their posts. The same applies to Parliamentary Secretaries and MPs
who hold other important parliamentary positions."[40]

"… IN A MANNER RESPONSIVE TO THEM"?

IN PITKIN'S VIEW, representation is action not only in the interest of the
represented, but also in a manner responsive to them. This requires
institutional arrangements through which the people can be heard. It is
also what the people expect, and what the courts mean by effective
representation. Clearly, the B.C. legislature, like all Canadian legislatures and Parliament, does not meet this test of representation. The
legislature lacks the power to deliver responsible government. Except
in the case of a minority government, it is virtually impossible for the
legislature to vote non-confidence in the cabinet.[41] Its ability to hold
the cabinet accountable is severely attenuated, and therefore the theory of responsible government, as outlined above, is not practised in our
system.[42] Lloyd George, British prime minister from 1916 to 1922, is
reported to have said, "Parliament has no control over the cabinet; it is
only a fiction."[43]

Representative and responsible government demands MLAs who
are independent. Prior to mass political parties, SMP could safeguard
that independence. Today the independence of government MLAs is
compromised at every point. As a link between the electorate and the

government, they are redundant,[44] and in their legislative function their vote is captive to the interests of the party. Although the situation in Great Britain is not nearly as severe, a similar concern exists there. "Party loyalty explains why government consistently wins votes in the House of Commons...Laws are described as Acts of Parliament, but it would be more accurate if they were stamped: Made in Whitehall."[45]

Should MLAs threaten a revolt the premier could retaliate by dissolving the legislature, and then they would face an election in which their fortunes depended entirely on the very same premier.[46] MLAs owe the premier almost everything; the premier owes MLAs almost nothing. It would help if the caucus could elect the parliamentary leader. Waltz believes that this British practice has led to a more responsible use of power, first, because it more effectively selects qualified persons with proven leadership abilities, and second, because it limits arbitrary use of power by leaders. In comparing the powers of a U.S. president and a British PM, Waltz notes, "The British mode of recruitment creates a condition that serves a a gross restraint on executive power."[47] I support going back to that system. It would correct, somewhat, the imbalance of power between the premier and caucus; it would help maintain an appropriate separation between the party and legislative leader; and it would probably allow more competent leaders to be elected. Allowing the membership of extralegislative parties to select a premier in the name of greater democracy is hopelessly misdirected. The increased democracy benefits a partisan group of activists who bought their membership, but weakens the legislative caucus, such that democracy for all citizens is frustrated in the legislature.

Finally, not only is the legislature weak, but increasingly it is completely bypassed. Examples include the following:

PUBLIC POLICY

Important public policy decisions are made and commitments entered into by the premier and cabinet long before they are submitted to the legislature. Examples include the present B.C. government's decision to recognize the inherent right to Aboriginal land title, and its policy to mortgage road construction. Both are firsts in our province's history and both will have profound, long-term effects.

ADMINISTRATIVE LAW[48]

This continues to grow at an alarming rate. We are moving in the direction from which the former Soviet Union is retreating. We do not have public ownership of the means of production, but a multiplicity of regulations imposed by faceless bureaucrats have the force of law, with the same end result. The public sphere unduly intrudes on the private. It is a form of largely unaccountable law-making outside of the legislature.

CROWN CORPORATIONS

These, too, are growing at a rate that should be cause for concern and similarly remove ever-larger chunks of government operations beyond the reach of the legislature. Vaughn Palmer, the respected political columnist, describes Crown corporations as follows: "They are less accountable to the legislature than any government ministry. They can borrow and spend large sums of money without it ever showing up as part of the provincial deficit. And they make an excellent repository for party hacks." Four more were created in early 1994 alone.[49]

"EMPTY SHELL" LAWS

These are bills that empower the cabinet to retain wide-ranging authority to draft regulations and other provisions, which often form the substance of the legislation.[50] Also, most legislation includes clauses by which cabinet retains the power to give effect to statutes or particular chapters of statutes at a time of its choosing – perhaps never. Again, the legislature is powerless. We have government by order-in-council, including special warrants – which allow cabinet to spend money we don't have on projects the legislature has not approved.

Bypassing the legislature in these ways renders the institution less and less relevant. Recall that in Pitkin's view representation requires institutional arrangements to facilitate the citizens' input, that citizens expect this, and that the courts see the legislature as the avenue by which citizens can exercise their slice of sovereignty. The notion of responsible government is usually described as fundamental to making the parliamentary system democratic; without it, the system is undemocratic.[51] The conclusion is unmistakable: we do not have a democracy. The legislature is either controlled by the cabinet, or it is bypassed. A comparative study of Canadian legislatures to determine how democratic they are concludes "In all provinces, institutional factors currently inhibit the ability of legislators to represent effectively the policy demands and needs of their constituents."[52] In view of this obvious truth, it is remarkable that the present system is still referred to as responsible government.[53] Perhaps, describing our present system as responsible government is one of Plato's "noble lies." But it is a lie, and needs to be debunked.

In 1985, the MacDonald Royal Commission identified two essential requirements for responsible government: the cabinet must be in *control* of government, and must be *accountable* to Parliament.[54] No Parliament or legislature can hold a majority government accountable when MPs and MLAs lack independence. In the present system responsible government means that the cabinet controls the operations of government and the legislature. Accountability is not to the legislature, but to the voters on election day, once every four or five years. If that is deemed acceptable, we should say so, drop the pretence that citizens participate in government through the legislature, and tell the courts, the people, and the theorists they have gotten it all wrong. Alternatively, we could try to bring practice in line with theory.

John Locke identified the legislative function as supreme. For him, representative government meant popular control of the legislative function over the executive and judicial, i.e., the supremacy of Parliament.[55] The nineteenth century saw the end of the long and arduous struggle to establish the authority of Parliament in the name of the people rather than that of the Crown. In Canada, this struggle for popular control culminated in "responsible government." This device to maintain the authority of the legislature over the cabinet is failing, and with it the Lockean concept of representative government. We have substituted cabinet for the Crown. The organization and effectiveness of large political parties have rendered the concept of responsible government void and empty. Our theories, intellectual justification, and institutional arrangements have been overtaken by political realities unforeseen when the parliamentary system began to evolve.[56] Edmund Burke could meaningfully debate whether to follow his own conscience and judgment or that of his constituents. Today's practitioners have no such choice. They take direction neither from their own beliefs nor from the wishes of those they purport to represent; they are partisans throughout. The struggle today is not against the Crown, but against the organizations and institutions that position themselves between the people and the exercise of governmental power. Large-scale organization tends to be anti-democratic; by design it entrusts power to the few. This is true of churches, labour unions, professional organizations, and business corporations, but especially political parties. Our tyranny is not that of the Crown; our oppressor is the tyranny of organization. The power of organizations such as political parties, and the peculiar results produced by our voting system, deprive representative and represented alike of independent judgment.

Without MLAs who have independence, responsible government cannot work, and the legislature's role is an empty formality. Chapters 2 and 3 have given two reasons why MLAs have lost their independence. First, SMP (single member plurality) generates majorities in the legislature where there are none among the voters. Second, these fake majorities permit political parties to have widespread power over the voters' representatives. These two factors combine to allow the cabinet to control the legislature. The proper relationship between cabinet and the legislature, which would allow responsible government to function, has been inverted, and cabinet is not accountable to the legislature, i.e., the people's representatives. Proportional representation (PR) voting systems stop faked, unearned majorities, and the single transferable vote (STV) variety of PR has the potential to lessen the power of political parties and give elected representatives the necessary independence.[57]

Parliament and the legislatures are marked by one dominant feature – power is concentrated totally, completely, at the top. To give one more example, during the 1996 B.C. election, premier Glen Clark placed a two-year moratorium on increases to tuition fees, hydro, and auto insurance rates. He did this unilaterally, without reference to the legislature, and for obvious partisan political purposes. The politically independent boards of directors mandated to administer the affected institutions in the public interest were bypassed. Should any premier enjoy such powers? This excessive concentration of power leaves much room for arbitrariness, for decisions based on political motives, and for subverting the rule of law. The rule of law, which undergirds the respect the British parliamentary tradition has rightly earned, is meant to guarantee the absence of arbitrary actions. Respect for Parliament and respect for law are not well served when the fundamental principle of the rule of law is not meticulously guarded. When all major decisions are made outside of the legislature, heavily influenced by non-elected political appointees, the process invites political interference, arbitrariness, and subversion of the rule of law. It happens all the time. Two recent B.C. premiers resigned under suspicion that due process had been tampered with for personal and political reasons.

But there is more than the danger of arbitrariness when power is so concentrated. Concentrating power violates every democratic instinct. We have government not by the many, but by the few. When the citizens' representatives have no power, the citizens have no power. Citizens' participation requires shared power, diffusion of power, and a consensual process. As it is, citizens are not drawn into assuming enlarged responsibilities. They are prevented from taking ownership of public issues. Their ability to exercise civic judgment is impoverished for want of use. Paternalism prevents maturity, and growth in citizenship remains stunted.

Three areas where citizenship is frustrated have been noted. Casting a ballot, the process of representation, and the operation of the legislature all block the possibility for the inclusion and participation of citizens. Some may think that, perhaps, it is different in the political parties – maybe *that* is an avenue to develop public-minded citizens, who will be able to influence public policies. It is not. The voting system that produces faked majorities, that concentrates power in cabinet, that excludes all minorities (except the largest) from active participation, also fails our political parties. Under SMP, parties are reduced to mere election machines, a vehicle for the leader but not for the people. It is helpful to understand why that must be so.

POLITICAL PARTIES

If we are going to keep representative gov-
ernment, the most important improvement
in participation is to find a way to force
parties to be more concerned with policy.
How do we do that? I can see only one
way of getting adequate change. This is to
change the electoral system.[1]

POLITICAL PARTIES ARE the gatekeepers to our system of government. No one can attain political office without entering
through the party gates. The reins of democracy are held in party
hands. Parties structure the ballot by selecting the candidates the public will vote on. That initial selection process eliminates from further
participation many diverse views, opinions, and interests. Such potential candidates, screened out by the party, never become accessible to
the voting public.

Anyone led into the party gate becomes party property. All members are bound by a duty of loyalty, candidates most of all, because of
the party's investment in them. Parties structure the parliamentary
groupings. As noted in the last chapter, party discipline for persons
elected to office is severe. The power and influence of parties is difficult to overestimate. But for all that, their power is hollow.

Parties have a formal function, but lack the enthusiastic support of
citizens. The rate of participation is abysmally low. The percentage of
citizens who carry a political party membership hovers between 1 and
2 percent, and only a fraction of those are active in making the important decisions. Between elections membership dwindles; parties are
dormant. Membership is fleeting and shifting. Increasingly, parties are
funded from the public purse by means of generous tax deductions for
political donations. Parties perform a function for the state, and may be
more accurately defined as agents of the state than as representatives

of society and citizens. Parties have not captured the imagination and loyalty of citizens. Citizens do not see parties as the road to self-rule, or as an influence on government. The power of parties is illegitimate. It is not an expression of the consent of the people.

The power of parties is used against the citizens. The day after the election the people's representatives become party property. In the mid-nineteenth century, when universal suffrage and democracy for the masses lay just over the horizon, J.S. Mill clearly perceived that mass political parties would quickly accompany universal suffrage, and that such parties would rob the people of their representatives. That is the paradox of universal suffrage – the offer of freedom contains the shackles of enslavement. Mill would not view our form of government as representative government. On the road to democracy for all, the agents of the people were captured by party interests. Mill ecstatically embraced the *single transferable ballot* (STV) as an effective remedy.

In theory, the main function of parties in a representative democracy is to involve citizens in the development of public policy, and to aggregate voters around alternative principles and platforms. Oddly, parties perform that function only partially at best. Again, theory and practice diverge widely. For policy formation elected persons, regional representatives, and the party network are redundant. In practice, their function is to legitimize, not to shape party policy; their role is to applaud, not to participate.

It is doubtful that under universal suffrage parties can be eliminated. This may not even be desirable. Politics deals with communal decision-making. But if citizens are to participate to attain democratic self-rule, parties must be restructured to fulfil their intended function. Before offering solutions, it is important to understand the failure of the current party system.

The Royal Commission on Electoral Reform and Party Financing, usually referred to as the Lortie Commission after its chairman, Pierre Lortie, was established in 1989, spent $19 million, reported in 1991, and has suffered the fate of most royal commissions – few of its many recommendations have been acted on. Its most useful contribution is a massive amount of research data. Among its many findings, Lortie asserted that "There is little doubt that Canadian political parties are held in low public esteem, and that their standing has declined steadily over the past decade."[2] Lortie attributes this loss of public confidence to the following factors.

SELECTION METHODS FOR CANDIDATES AND LEADERS.
As noted, the parties are gatekeepers for those seeking elected office. The process to select candidates is far from democratic. In a study prepared for Lortie, Carty and Erickson[3] found that in 1988 two-thirds of

all nominations were uncontested, that the majority of party members do not attend nomination meetings, that over half the constituency associations allowed non-residents to vote, that in two-thirds of the cases the timing of nomination meetings is determined by the local executive, that all parties engage in attracting quick, instant memberships when a few extra votes are needed, and that spending guidelines are in place in less than 15 percent of nomination contests.

Such evidence fuels the criticism that the nomination process is exclusive, secretive, and open to abuse. The abuse may be undue influence by local party elite, busing-in of instant members from outside the riding, excessive spending, or extending voting privileges to minors and those without Canadian citizenship. Increasingly, special interest groups attempt, sometimes successfully, to take over the nomination process. Intraparty competition seems weak. With the exception of the Reform Party of Canada, national party organizations exert little influence to prevent abuses in the nomination process and, in contrast to the U.S. and German federal system, electoral law does not regulate party nominations.

Public confidence in candidate selection is weak, and in leadership selection contests it is almost nonexistent. Lortie notes that leadership selection legitimacy is questionable when the delegate selection is readily open to abuse, and party membership is fluid, open to minors, non-voters, and instant partisans. Members often vote in ridings where they do not reside. Concentration of power attracts money, like filings to a magnet. Mulroney promised a full disclosure of who financed his bid for the leadership of the federal Progressive Conservatives in 1983, but the promise was never kept. Ten years later Kim Campbell secured that party's leadership, and with it the prime ministership. The same promise was made with the same empty result.

The Lortie Commission offers a number of worthwhile recommendations. Constituency associations of registered parties must register with the Canada Elections Commission to be allowed to issue tax receipts for donations to nomination campaigns. Candidates must be nominated by an open meeting of the constituency membership. Members entitled to vote at a nomination meeting must be voters, and can vote only once. Nominations are to be subject to spending limits, and there should be full disclosure of the source and application of all funds. Lortie contains many provisions that will lead to greater accountability. Very similar provisions are to govern the leadership selection process. Without mandatory spending limits, disclosure requirements, contribution limits, and restrictions on sources of funding, public confidence in leader selection contests will remain low. The Reform Party of Canada has done the most in voluntarily submitting to these suggestions. Their example and continued public pressure will bring the other parties in line eventually. Open and accountable processes for the selection of candidates and leaders are among the most easily remedied of the challenges facing political parties. Their solution is administrative and technical; the more difficult challenge is to find a satisfying role for the membership.

SIGNIFICANT PARTICIPATION

Lortie research notes that parties are in disfavour with the public partly because of the lack of meaningful participation offered to their membership. Since parties play a very weak role in public policy development, they have little to offer serious-minded citizens, apart from fundraising events. How many times can members be expected to look forward with anticipation to yet another fundraiser? The impact of modern technology allows the leader to bypass the party organization. Leaders communicate directly with the electorate. When New Democrat Glen Clark announced his candidacy for the B.C. premiership before a partisan, home-town crowd, conveniently arranged for an evening meeting so as to allow his predominantly labour union supporters the opportunity to attend, the long-awaited news was stale. Word had been out for two and a half hours. He had arranged an exclusive television interview for earlier in the day, provided it would be shown at a stipulated time during the 6:00 p.m. news hour. Making prime-time television is far more important than sharing this significant moment with one's own partisan supporters.

Parties have no meaningful function except at election time. But even then, the traditional role of members in shaping the party platform, devising strategy, and advising the leader about local needs has been eliminated; what remains is fundraising and helping to get the vote out. To ensure locals do not show too much originality, these last two functions must be conducted according to precise, detailed instructions head office has devised using the latest, state-of-the-art techniques. There is not much room for the creativity of talented members. It should come as no surprise that people are voting with their feet, and staying away from parties in droves. Based on a Carty study, Lortie notes, "Evidence indicates that on average a core of only 19 party members in each constituency association meets regularly."[4] Since this is an indication of the state of democracy in Canada today, it is imperative that corrective action be taken soon.

John Meisel gives a long list of reasons why political parties have weakened, and are unable to give their members any meaningful work to do. He mentions, among other things, the rise of the bureaucratic state, i.e., decisions made away from citizens and their elected representatives; increased consultation between institutions such as business, labour, and government; federal–provincial diplomacy; investigative journalism, the role of electronic media; pluralism, and the rise of special interest politics.[5] Increasingly, citizens turn from political parties to special interest groups and the media, or demand direct democracy through referenda and citizens' initiatives. Lawson and Merkl's study found that the U.S. bipolar party system cannot accommodate the growing diversity of interests, and as a result political action committees (PACs) have grown in number and increased in power: not only do they lobby extensively, they also help to elect or defeat candidates.[6] Similarly, in Canada so-called third parties play a significant role in elections. During the 1988 federal election, to ensure passage of the Canada/U.S. Free Trade Agreement, business interests advertised extensively in favour of the Progressive Conservatives.

The weakened role of parties and the declining influence of the membership on the party's head office is also present in Europe. In his study of European parties, Panebianco notes that the traditional ideological basis of party membership is in decline.[7] There, parties once run by large bureaucracies, which united people by class, religious, trade union, political, or ideological lines, have become electoral-professional parties. Parties run by professionals and geared to win elections focus less on their own membership and more on general issues that large segments of the voting public can agree on, such as economic development and public order. Their traditional membership is less loyal, and the electorate more volatile.

Canada's parties have never been based on class, religion, or even strong political or ideological differences. But as our parties have become more exclusively election machines, they too, are increasingly run by professionals. Communicating effectively to a broader audience by means of new technologies, particularly television, does not require the administrative skills of the bureaucrat or the mobilization of the local membership; it requires professionals – the communication consultants, and pollster/policy experts. Communication consultants are the image-makers and spin-doctors without whom no modern leader dare make an appearance or utter a word. They package whatever message the pollster/policy people propose. Their special expertise is marketing techniques that apply to any product.

The pollster/policy experts focus less on the traditional party principles and policies, and more on how the leader is perceived by the public. The policy concerns of citizens are increasingly diverse, specialized, and subject-specific. The subject matter requires experts. But in addition, public surveys and opinion polls need to be analysed and reinterpreted to discover people's fears, hopes, and personal preferences, within ever-increasing sub-groups. The communication experts then package the party and leader to maximum advantage. Even maintaining the membership and support base requires experts in telemarketing services, donor acquisition, acknowledgement, re-solicitation, list maintenance, and monthly sustainer programs. It is not a job for volunteers, amateurs, or the local constituency association. Thus the professional consultants, hired on contract, have displaced the traditional volunteer party workers and officials in gaining access to the leader, in providing advice, and in controlling the party. Television and special interest groups link party and electorate more than the party bureaucracy, organization, and members. Power and influence have shifted; members carry less weight, both as a source of finance and as links to the voters.

Party identification has declined. In Europe mass-bureaucratic parties were strong institutions with a loyal membership. Electoral-professional parties are hardly institutions. They are catch-all organizations with weak loyalty from a dwindling and ever-shifting membership. The trend for Canada's parties is unmistakably towards the professional-election model. Today, they are pragmatic organizations that consider image more important than platform, perception and personality more effective than principles and program. The NDP, like its high-minded predecessor the CCF, used to be the exception, but they could hardly be called that today. There is so little need for strong local party organizations with loyal, stable memberships that parties have almost become obsolete. This is true even during elections.

The process of professionalization, the undue focus on leaders, and hence the shift from the local membership, organization, and candidate to head office, consultants, and the leader, is particularly strong during modern election campaigns. The technology employed centres on television and computers. Television advertising and daily public opinion surveys have been perfected to make the campaign a closed feedback loop, self-fulfilling, self-correcting, and self-sustaining. The search for people's motives, attitudes, fears, and hopes is not only to discover what question or concerns are uppermost in people's minds, but also to unearth motives and emotions, because television advertising can powerfully affect the latter. This sophisticated use of technology has profoundly altered the nature of public policy discourse. Television reduces the full meaning of an event or proposition to a fleeting image or impression appealing to the emotions rather than the intellect. Television is not often used for rational debate or the vigorous exchange of substantial ideas. People expect to be spectators, not participants.

Modern campaign strategies are tailored to suit the television medium. The political operatives who mastermind the campaigns do not want people to think about the intrinsic merits of a public policy issue. Such thinking might produce decisions, and decisions lead to divisions. Success at the polls, particularly under single member plurality (SMP), requires uniting, not dividing people. Besides, most people are not interested in ideas, nor do they want to make decisions. Images and impressions bereft of content don't demand troublesome decisions.

Hence, public policy issues are advertised not on the basis of their intrinsic merit and objective meaning, but on some manufactured, secondary meaning. Robert Mason Lee, for example, shows how during the 1988 federal election campaign Liberal leader John Turner opposed the Canada–U.S. Free Trade Agreement on the basis that it represented the end of Canadian sovereignty; we would all become Americans. He turned a trade issue into one of nationalism.[8] The NDP, being more honest, dealt with it as an economic issue, which it was. Lee suggests they might have recast it as a question concerning the preservation of Canada's universal social programs. The Progressive Conservatives, noting public fears about an uncertain future, packaged the agreement as representing Mulroney's superior ability to control and manage world events. Lee suggests Mulroney lost the televised leaders' debate in part because, during the debate, he repeatedly characterized the agreement as a mere commercial contract cancellable on six months' notice. In telling the truth Mulroney lifted the symbolic or secondary meaning his entire advertising campaign had so carefully constructed around the trade agreement. During the Charlottetown Accord referendum, at least $120 million worth of advertising urged Canadians to approve the accord not on its merits, but on whether they truly loved Canada. Happily the people woke up in time, and eagerly pinned on buttons that turned the message around with the slogan "Friends of Canada Vote No." Modern election campaigns rely on strategies meant not to promote but to preclude rational debate.

Lee shows how ambiguity of meaning is the aim and purpose of political advertising and communications, and the appeal this has for a generation steeped in television. In politics, perception is everything. The naming of something is more important than the thing itself. For example, the Meech Lake *Accord* is preferable to the Meech Lake *Agreement*. "Accord" evokes balance, equanimity, and peace after interminable constitutional wrangling. Professional campaign experts, drawing on marketing techniques from the commercial world, develop slogans to which people from many groups, regions, and backgrounds can all attach their own meaning. In "Coke is it" the "it" is purposely left undefined. Young and old, rich and poor are all invited to subconsciously attach their own meanings. Such slogans lead to few mistakes, and can be universally broadcast on national television.

The extensive use of technology and the resulting professional election strategies lead to less democracy, not more, and renders parties hollow, empty shells. Party workers, members, and local organizations in elections are reduced to foot soldiers following instructions from head office complete with detailed manuals, and candidate seminars. Modern elections are contests between the leaders, the venue is the television, and the tools of the trade are craftily packaged messages and interpretations of survey results. Such tools are deftly manipulated by a few experts whose specialized knowledge and skills concentrate all power in the leader's office. The pollsters have replaced the poll captains. The significance of local candidates has diminished. The party no longer functions as the conduit carrying the people's concerns to the top. Policy positions and platforms that in former days might have been constructed from the ground up, and were rooted in a party's history, reputation, and a political ideology that had stood the test of time, are now an immediate creation concocted by a few political technocrats in response to the previous evening's polling results. Parties and local candidates are largely redundant, even at election time.

The Lortie Commission correctly identified the problem, but the solutions offered are entirely inadequate. It is mere tinkering when a root-and-branch change is what is needed. For example, to strengthen the policy development role of parties, Lortie suggests public funding for party foundations. Such foundations are to promote policy development, educate party members, and provide research support for their MPs.[9] Such publicly funded foundations for a party's private use will undoubtedly be gladly accepted, and promptly used to refine the party's communication strategy directed at its own membership. The money will be used not to undo the trend towards the professional-election machine, but to reinforce it. Party head offices will "educate" their membership about what dismal failures their opponents are. How will that assist greater democratic participation? Opposition parties will use the public money to help their MPs be more effective in their assigned role – oppose everything, support nothing, and bring the government down as often as possible. Just what Canada needs! It is laughable, but remember that the cost of producing this advice was $19 million. Lortie's recommendations are not sufficient to restore public confidence, nor do they empower Canadians as citizens.

Parties have no policy development role, because Parliament has no such role. Why should we expect parties to prepare their candidates and MPs for a function they will not perform? Citizens will show no sustained interest in joining parties unless party involvement offers them the prospect of actively and meaningfully contributing to public policy. What else are parties for? The goal of attaining power should not be an end in itself. Power must serve the citizens' interests. It must lead to social change and political goals. Parties are largely sidelined because in our present political regime parties are ineffectual. Citizens who want to work for specific social ends turn away from parties to interest groups of all kinds. This holds not only for citizens who are concerned about social justice – from the environment to arms reduction and the abortion battle – but also for business, commercial, and professional communities. Until Parliament, the legislatures, and politicians have a public policy role, parties have little to offer citizens who are interested in developing their skills for self-rule.

Franks's substantial study of Parliament found the following: 1)"No group is more systematically excluded from the process (policy making) than are MPs." 2)Parliamentary committees don't work. 3)In theory Parliament is a forum for discussing and debating policy, in practice it is not. 4)Budget and fiscal policy are virtually beyond the control of Parliament. 5)The greatest challenge to our parliamentary system is finding a role for Parliament in policy-making.[10]

In Canada, the structural obstacle to a policy role for Parliament and political parties is the voting system. SMP permits the concentration of power, thus eliminating MPs from participation. It fosters mass parties in an age of demassification. Since it aggregates votes in very restricted geographical territory, citizens with nonterritorial concerns, such as environmental protection, fiscal management, economic restructuring, unemployment, deindustrialization, immigration, consumer rights, AIDS, disarmament, occupational issues, cultural concerns, Aboriginal rights and women's issues, have all turned to special interest groups. Their concerns are sectorial, not territorial. There is a tension between the representation of sectorial interests through pressure groups and the territorial representation in Parliament, the legislatures, and parties. The formal political structure of parties, politicians, and Parliament provides inadequate channels to attain many political ends of the citizens. SMP permits the executive to arrogate policy decisions to itself. In addition, it induces the executive to forgo long-term, substantive policy considerations for immediate, short-term quick fixes.

Changing the voting system would remove the structural obstacle to a policy role for politicians, and political parties. However, some are of the view that change is quite unnecessary; that Canada's parties have never been motivated by philosophical or ideological perspectives; that election-machine parties suit our political culture; that Canada enjoys a broad consensus around liberal values, and sees government primarily as a dispenser of economic benefits. In this view, one party is really no different from another, because the basic liberal approach informs all of them, especially once they are in power. Therefore elections are not to determine shifts in policy, but simply to effect a change in personnel, to try to manage the system better, particularly the economy. Concerns that parties have a diminishing role are misguided, in this view, because they are based on a failure to appreciate that over time parties fulfil their roles differently, and that never in Canadian history was there a "golden age" when parties formulated policy. As so often, there are eminent political scientists on both sides of the debate.

Regardless of what might once have been, times are changing. The influence of post-modernism and post-materialism may well shatter the putative liberal consensus, especially when economic growth slows and governments are forced to reduce the flow of public benefits. Currently, our young people are the first generation of Canadians whose economic future will be less prosperous than that of their parents. Their reason for concern with public policy is very immediate. Also, the rise of the Reform Party of Canada suggests that citizens want greater honesty in politics, and accountability from their representatives. Reform's election platform in the 1993 federal election was a detailed and explicit statement constructed by its 130,000 members in extensive local constituency policy meetings and membership surveys. Their initiative forced the Liberals to produce the Red Book, which in turn demanded a belated, middle-of-the-writ-period response from the Progressive Conservatives with a published policy platform. Unlike the Reform Party, the mainline party documents were filled with platitudes designed to offend no one and appeal to everyone. The Reform approach represented a new direction, and at least a temporary break with contentless party politics.

Whether the trend of citizens' involvement in the preparation of detailed policy proposals holds remains to be seen. Already there are signs that Reform's promise to do politics differently is impossible to carry out in practice. Our system forces identical behaviour on all parties. To do politics differently will require changes more fundamental than Reform has yet proposed. Time may also prove that Canadians have only a limited interest in parties that involve their membership in providing direction to their representatives. However, that decision should be theirs to make; it should not be made for them. The voting system should be such as to remove all artificial, structural barriers. Then, if citizens choose bland, nondescript, one-size-fits-all parties of the centre, the debate can stop. Parties and citizens will be frustrated from assuming an enlarged, more participatory role in the attainment of democracy as self-rule until there is unrestricted choice. In selecting a new voting system, choice for citizens is of primary importance. Structural obstacles which prevent parties from functioning as the theories of democratic representative government suggest they should, must be removed.

Is there a need for political parties? To attain a fuller measure of citizenship for the voters, to make government more honest, responsible, and sensitive to the public good, to rescue public policy decisions from the corrupting influence of the immediate political ambitions of the party in power, to move from the peddling of perceptions and personalities to the presentation of platform and principles – all of these will require parties that are not mere election machines, but communities of like-minded citizens who share values and a vision of the common good. Parties exist to stimulate vigorous debate and serious reflection about the political good. Citizenship, like politics, is by its nature more than a solitary undertaking. Parties can assist in transforming individual persons into citizens. Canada needs a voting system that will permit parties to serve Canada's citizens, and to do so unhindered. The current structural incentives for parties to forgo developing public policy must be removed.

In summary, Canadian political parties are strong in demanding unquestioned loyalty from their parliamentary caucuses, but weak in mobilizing citizens in the development of public policy. Democracy would be served if this were reversed. The voting system Canada needs should emphasize a stronger policy role, not party discipline. A proportional system is needed, but not just any PR system will suffice. As noted above, Europeans with list and mixed-member PR systems have not prevented their parties from moving towards the professional-election, machine model, probably because those PR systems do not lessen party discipline. They concentrate power and influence at the top as much as SMP. Such PR systems ensure that power within Parliament is shared, but only among the leaders. If we are to have democracy as self-rule, if there is to be a policy role for parties, if parties are to be an instrument for empowering citizens, if parties are to compete effectively with the special interest groups, power cannot remain concentrated around the leaders, it must be shared with citizens. List and mixed-member PR systems are inadequate for weakening our parties where they are too strong, and strengthening them where they are now too weak.

CHAPTER FIVE

DEMOCRATIC REFORMS

The problem with reform lies not in the lack of recognition that change is necessary; rather the dilemma in Canada is change which will respect the tradition of representative responsible government in Canada with the current need for greater democratisation and accountability.[1]

THE SEARCH FOR more democratic participation, for effective representation and for institutional arrangements that will allow our country to be governed in a manner responsive to the people, has produced many and varied suggestions. This study looks to Europe for an answer, and suggests a form of proportional representation. Most proposals for reform look to the United States and suggest measures of direct democracy, such as referendum, initiative and recall. The U.S., from its inception, was a democracy – a polity ruled from the ground up. Not so Canada. Unlike the American and French, our history is void of any revolution establishing the rights of the people.[2] We have no blueprint of democracy to go back to. Hence, whenever we feel our governments and institutions are particularly autocratic, we look southward to see how a modern democracy works. In spite of many attempts to graft American solutions to the British parliamentary system, none have been successful.[3] The two systems are too different; there is no easy fit. However, neither a history of failure nor theoretical difficulties have prevented yet another round of popular demands for U.S.-style direct democracy.

In October 1991 the B.C. electorate accepted the principles of recall and initiative by a majority vote – 83 percent of those who voted in the referendum. As a result, the Recall and Initiative Act, Bill 36, was introduced on 16 June 1994, received royal assent on 8 July 1994, and was proclaimed on 24 February 1995. Federally, on 10 December 1992, the Reform Party of Canada's Deborah Grey introduced Bill C-392, the "Recall Act" in the House of Commons, following the adoption of recall as Reform Party policy (Blue Book 1991); she repeated this on 2 February 1994 as Bill C-210. The bills were defeated, but in the 1993 election Reform went from 1 seat to 52 seats, partly because it promised populist institutional safeguards that would make politicians listen to their constituents, rather than their party.

The ideas behind the campaign for referendum, initiative, and recall result from the search for greater citizen involvement and popular participation in government. They emanate from the belief that sovereignty rests not with Parliament, but with the people. In addition, the last decade has spawned a flood of proposals for parliamentary reform. These aim to make the parliamentary system more accountable and open to public participation, to lessen party discipline, and strengthen the role of private members. This chapter asks if direct democracy and parliamentary reforms are sufficient to rehabilitate responsible government.

DIRECT DEMOCRACY

REFERENDUM AND INITIATIVE, the first two measures of direct democracy, provide for direct law-making by the people. In 1919, B.C. followed the example of the other three most westerly provinces, and passed *An Act to Provide for the Initiation and Approval of Legislation by the Electors.* Since similar Manitoba legislation was found *ultra vires* by the British Judicial Committee of the Privy Council (which until 1949 was Canada's highest court of appeal), this first B.C. initiative legislation was never proclaimed. Current B.C. initiative legislation will not spawn a flood of activity; it is considered unworkable. The Canadian Taxpayers' Federation, among many others, suggests that the thresholds are too high and cumbersome, and is critical of the government's decision to make successful initiatives non-binding. Referenda have been part of the B.C. system of government from the beginning. Since 1871 there have been nine provincial referenda. The first, held in 1873, asked eligible voters to approve a pay increase for MLAs from five to seven dollars per day. It was defeated. Never again have B.C. MLAs asked the voters to approve a pay increase.[4]

Proponents of referendum legislation, such as Patrick Boyer, see direct democracy as a complement to, not a substitute for, Parliament.[5] On matters of significant interest, particularly on issues with a strong moral component, such as gaming legislation, capital punishment, euthanasia, and abortion, popular decision-making by referendum or initiative is entirely defensible as an important complement to

Parliament. Such measures can generate keen voter interest and vigorous public debate. For example, before Mulroney's August 1992 decision to allow popular approval of the Charlottetown Accord by referendum, popular interest in constitutional matters hardly registered, but during the six weeks preceding the vote citizen interest soared. After such an experience of citizen participation, further constitutional amendments of substance without popular approval are unthinkable. This is particularly so since British Columbia, Alberta, and Quebec now have constitutional amendment legislation which makes popular ratification a legal requirement. Workable referendum and initiative legislation will be essential to satisfy the Pitkin demand for institutional arrangements to govern "in a manner responsive to them." However, their application is limited. Effective referendum and initiative legislation does not preclude the need for fundamental reforms to make parties, politicians, and Parliament more effective instruments of democratic self-rule.

Recall, the third element of direct democracy, is the "power of a defined percentage of constituents to recall, or unseat, a representative,"[6] or "...a legal provision for the retirement of a public officer before his term of office expires, if he has forfeited the confidence of the voters."[7] Usually recall requires a petition signed by a percentage of eligible voters, which if successful triggers a by-election. It is a method for removing a representative in mid-term. Conceptually, recall is similar to impeachment, but it lacks the overtones of legal impropriety, and the person recalled may be a candidate in the by-election. Typically, one is recalled for failing to respond to the wishes or preferences of the electors. Recall is based on the delegate view of representation – representatives should do as they are told by their voters. Its purpose is to weaken the link between representative and party, and to strengthen the link between representative and electors.

Recall fits the congressional system, but can be misused in the British parliamentary system. Recall presupposes that representatives can be judged on individual performance. This is true under the American system, which separates the executive from the legislative. In the parliamentary system recall can be misapplied. For example, cabinet ministers fill two roles. In their role as representative of a constituency they are more like agents for their voters. Their second role is quite different. As ministers of the Crown they must be true to the oath of office and serve the wider national or provincial interest in a disinterested and nonpartisan way. Walter Lippmann, after defining the executive role, writes,

> When we move over to the representative assembly,
> the image is different. The representative is in some

> very considerable degree an agent, and the image of
> his virtue is rather more like that of a lawyer than of
> the judge. In the general run of the mundane business
> which comes before the assembly, he is entitled –
> indeed he is duty-bound – to keep close to the interests
> and sentiments of his constituents and, within reason-
> able limits, to do what he can to support them...But
> representation must not be confused with governing.[8]

In our parliamentary system, cabinet ministers fill both roles. They are
elected to the first role, and in that capacity they are responsible to the
electors in their own constituency. In the second role, to which they
are appointed, they are responsible to the Crown, through Parliament
or the legislature. Recall is designed to test performance in the first
role, but in practice can be used to pronounce judgment on performance in the second role. The presence of highly organized, well-
funded special interest groups makes it possible, even likely, that a perceived lack of responsiveness as minister of the Crown will trigger the
recall not in the legislature, or among all electors province-wide, but
within that minister's own constituency. The Lortie Commission found
that increased use of recall in the U.S. during the 1980s was partly due
to the strength and prominence of special interest groups.[9] Recall used
against a member of the executive is inappropriate; it constitutes a mis-
application of recall, and if done frequently would impair the possibility of responsible government. Such misuse of recall would be particularly tempting to an opposition bent on removing a prime minister or
premier. It is the possibility of such inappropriate use of recall that
lends some justification to Alberta Premier William Aberhart's retroac-
tive legislation withdrawing the recall when it was used against him by
a powerful oil industry lobby in 1937.[10] Hence, recall may be used not
to restore responsible government, but to deform it. The roles of the
various actors and their relationship become even more clouded.

Also, under a parliamentary system, recall of even one MLA may
bring down a government. Again, the repercussions go far beyond the
immediate relationship of one MLA and that member's electors.
Proponents dismiss such objections as unnecessary scaremongering,
because, it is claimed, the history of recall shows it is seldom used successfully.[11] However, such a defence is dishonest. Recall could be used
more frequently if the number of votes required to recall a member
were lowered.[12] But if recall is a meaningful solution to real problems,
the promise that it will be rigged so as to come into force rarely, say
once every eighty years, is a curious way of recommending it.
Proponents then shift ground and suggest that the value of recall is not
its use, but the possibility that it might be used. The possibility of recall

is said to be a deterrent; specifically, a deterrent to keep MLAs from submitting to excessive party discipline. But surely a deterrent with a near-zero probability of ever causing any inconvenience to a particular MLA is no deterrent at all, to that MLA or others. Recall can be fashioned to be either a deterrent and a cause of instability, or neither. The first is unacceptable, and the second not worth having.

Peter McCormick recommends recall as necessary to loosen the hold of party discipline, to strengthen the relationship between representative and voters, and weaken the relationship between representative and party. He pleads passionately for the need to lessen party discipline, and dismisses any concern that less party discipline would mortally wound the ability to govern.[13] The abiding interest in, and popularity of, direct democracy underscores the need to attain McCormick's goals, but is recall the best means to that end? Party discipline is so deeply entrenched that to assume recall will make a significant difference is wishful thinking. A recent, extensive U.S. study concludes:

> ... the recall device ... has not significantly improved direct communication between leaders and led ... Neither has it produced better qualified officeholders or noticeably enriched the quality of citizenship or democracy in those places permitting it. Whether it has strengthened representative government in any measurable way seems doubtful.[14]

Historically in Canada, populist parties that promised direct democracy have invariably retracted, weakened, or conveniently forgotten their bold promises upon attaining power.[15] U.S. experience shows that even where the congressional system lends itself to recall, it has been used very sparingly. Fifteen states have recall for state-wide elected positions, and thirty-six states for locally elected positions. Recall has successfully removed persons from office in the following instances: federally only once, in North Dakota in 1921; state legislators seven times, two in California in 1913, two in Idaho in 1971, two in Michigan in 1983, and one in Oregon in 1988. In Switzerland three cantons have recall but have never used it.[16]

Why does recall fail to live up to its promise? I submit that recall is misdirected because it treats the symptom and not the cause. Recall treats the relationship between electors and their representative. That relationship is distorted not because of some perversity on the part of elected representatives, but because of structural forces such as the single member plurality (SMP) voting system. Our electoral process gives parties and leaders power over representatives and causes voters on election day to discount the importance of the local candidate in favour of the party leader. Typically, the relationship between representative and elector does not sour at some time during a representative's term; that relationship is strained from its inception. In our system, political parties, their leaders, and the distortions of SMP stand between electors and the elected. Voters place an X beside a name while knowing little about the platform, principles, and competence of the person who carries that name. Voters are not particularly attentive to the person they vote for. Under our voting system an election selects a government; the local candidate is of little significance. For example, why vote for a brilliant, highly qualified person in a party that can't win? It is better to vote for a mediocre candidate of a winning party. Elections are first and foremost about party leaders, not local candidates. A letter to the editor of the Vancouver *Sun,* against recall, expressed the issue with a delicious touch of sarcasm: "Since we vote for people without any reason to think they have merit, what point is there in recalling them when they turn out to have no merit?"[17] If the vote, though cast for a local candidate, is actually for the leader, than those electors should not be offended at party discipline, which is loyalty to the leader. To complain about party discipline is to complain about the essence of the parliamentary system as practised under Canada's voting system. To remedy excessive party discipline and to strengthen the link between voters and their representatives requires far more than the recall.

Recall might be useful in a limited way, for instance, if a representative were elected with a hidden agenda, failed to show up for work, or switched parties in mid-term. But recall will not lessen party discipline, give representatives greater independence, or allow voters significant legislative input. Recall does not get to the root of what ails present parliamentary government.[18] A more fundamental overhaul is needed.

The Royal Commission on Electoral Reform and Party Financing turned down recall, but for reasons that are not impressive.[19] First, the commission suggested that in the parliamentary system representatives are elected to a national assembly not to be an agent for their constituents but to participate in deliberation on national interests: "...the House of Commons is a collective decision-making and representative institution that must weigh the competing interests of citizens against the national interest." On the contrary, it is precisely because the House is neither a decision-making body nor particularly representative that recall has such appeal. Would people clamour for recall if Parliament and the legislatures were actually deliberative bodies where competing interests are heard? Not every interest can have its way, but is it too much to expect that each significant interest should have a say? If we had such an institution, there would be less need for recall. Under proportional systems there is little demand for recall.[20]

Second, the royal commission pointed to the high turnover of MLAs and MPs as evidence of accountability, and concluded that recall is unnecessary: "The high turnover demonstrates Canadian voters are able to hold their MPs accountable for what they do ..." Suggesting Canadians should be content because they enjoy frequent opportunity to "throw the rascals out" is misplaced when the only choice available is more "rascals." Such alleged accountability has no substance if there is no significant difference among the available candidates, and in one pertinent respect all candidates are alike – they are all subject to party discipline.[21] As a result, none of the candidates are answerable to their voters to the degree recall proponents look for. Accountability results when voters have genuine choice. Structural factors such as SMP work against small parties, thus inhibiting choice. As long as the structural factors that prevent a representative from being accountable to the electors remain, no amount of turnover in personnel will make accountability flow downward. Under our voting system, the relationship of Parliament and the legislatures to cabinet, and hence the relationship between the elected and electors, remains unchanged regardless of who is in power. The problem is not people, but the system. As long as the voting system remains, changing MPs, no matter how frequently, will change nothing.

PARLIAMENTARY REFORM

FREQUENTLY, STUDENTS OF direct democracy suggest (as does the Reform Party of Canada) that measures of direct democracy might not be necessary if only Parliament were made to work as it is supposed to.[22] In particular, they urge a relaxing of party discipline and a greater role for private members. There have been numerous suggestions for parliamentary reform, from Trudeau's promise of participatory democracy to Kim Campbell's call for the politics of inclusion. Former B.C. premier Vander Zalm's first Speech from the Throne promised, "As a priority my government will expand the number and roles of the all-party committees of this assembly. I will ask members to become more involved in the business of our parliament."[23] His successor, Rita Johnston, also promised a greater role for private members including more free votes and a much stronger committee system.[24] Premier Harcourt must have inherited the same speech writer: "We will also take positive steps to more effectively include all members of the legislature in decision-making. We will seek to expand the role for committees of this House in areas such as the consideration of legislation, and the government spending estimates."[25] Federally, the 1993 Liberal Red Book promised less party discipline, and more free votes. However, to date (1996), every instance of breaking party ranks has been severely punished. The rhetoric, like party discipline, remains unchanged. Despite limited changes, such as an elected Speaker, and increased resources for members, power rests with the cabinet; in that area nothing has changed. Under Chrétien, party discipline is more severe than under any previous prime minister. Harcourt's promise to involve committees in legislation and estimates remains unfulfilled. In addition, about half the committees are not used. During the five years of B.C.'s 34th Parliament (1986-91) there were fifteen select standing and special committees; eight of those met twelve times or more, and the rest met once a year to reconstitute themselves. During the first two years of the 35th Parliament nine out of a total of eighteen committees met eleven times or more; the rest did not meet except to be constituted.[26] Committees cannot set their own agenda, but must be instructed by the legislature, i.e., the cabinet, and the majority of committee members are government members. As for the Speaker being elected, both in Ottawa and Victoria it has made no difference. Speakers are still drawn from the government ranks, which only serves to underscore the subservience of Parliament and the legislature to cabinet.

Federally, the very substantial report of the Special Committee on the Reform of the House of Commons was tabled in June 1985. Its goal was clearly stated:

> The purpose of reform of the House of Commons is to restore to private members an effective legislative function and give them a meaningful role in the formation of public policy.[17]

This report raised great expectations and many recommendations were implemented. Seven years later, some of the original committee members, parliamentarians, and academics studied and discussed its impact. Almost without exception, they expressed disappointment. For example, Question Period has not changed, ministers need not answer questions, image dominates over substance, private members' bills still face almost insurmountable obstacles, review of estimates and supply continues to be a farce, committees have not shown the independence hoped for, government ignores their recommendations,[28] and party discipline is as firm as ever. Ned Franks, in assessing the results against the goal of restoring the legislative function as noted above, commented, "I must say on this there has been no change."[29] He suggests that the problems are not procedural, "They are deep down in the way our system operates." He identifies structural arrangements as the leading causes for the disturbing fact that legislators do not have a legislative function, that is, the power to veto or amend legislation. Among such structural arrangements he includes party discipline, the rapid turnover of elected members, and an electorate voting primarily for party and leader, yet expecting to be listened to by the local member.[30]

The literature on parliamentary reform is vast, and the attempts at implementation many. In B.C., Gerry Kristianson and Paul Nicholson, two senior observers, have made nine specific recommendations, which they think would "...enhance the ability of the province's MLAs to play an effective legislative role."[31] They, like Preston Manning and others, suggest a redefinition of what constitutes an issue of confidence to achieve weaker party discipline. All such proposals fail miserably. Members are beholden to their leaders and party through a whole network of institutional arrangements. They don't even have to be whipped in line; instinctively they know their political survival depends on being a team member. It is not a legal or procedural problem. Contrary to what governments like us to believe, there is nothing in either law or convention that forces a government to treat every vote as a motion of confidence. Eugene Forsey said, in 1980: "Except in the case of a clear no-confidence motion, or a defeat of a measure the government has previously declared to be a matter of confidence, anything else is up to the government to decide."[32] Party discipline must be addressed, not by parliamentary procedural changes, but through fundamental change to the voting system. Since parliamentary reforms, like direct democracy, fail to touch the root of the problem, expectations will always be disappointed. Flanagan, in reviewing the many reforms that have been implemented, concludes: "All these measures were successful, and yet the basic situation has not changed."[33] Political parties offering simplistic solutions to complex problems do a disservice to our people and will deservingly reap the wrath of the electorate.

There are changes not mentioned by McGrath that would have real effect. Patrick Boyer, former MP, suggests that sitting members of the governing party select cabinet members, while the prime minister would retain the right to allocate the portfolios.[34] This splendid innovation, used by the Labour parties of Australia and New Zealand, would build partnership and participation at least among the members of the governing party. That, together with the earlier suggestion to have caucus select prime ministers and premiers, would diffuse somewhat the very substantial powers now concentrated at the top. Such sharing of power would do nothing towards a more positive role for the opposition, but at least the government side would participate. Under such conditions, most legislation and decisions of importance would be fully aired in caucus, and consequently caucus views would have considerable weight. Government decisions would be made by at least half of the people's representatives. Considering that today they are mostly made by non-elected consultants and appointees in the prime minis-

105

ter's office, it would be a leap forward toward democracy. As noted in the previous chapter, when caucuses have a policy role, parties are more likely to have such a role, giving citizens more opportunity for input.

Direct democracy and parliamentary reforms may, in certain limited circumstances, help attain a measure of citizen participation. But if it is expected that such measures will lessen party discipline, have elected members represent constituents instead of party, shift power from cabinet to Parliament and the legislatures, and thus restore responsible government, the expectations are misplaced.

SUMMARY AND TRANSITION

COMPREHENDING THE PROBLEM clearly is the first step to a solution. As has been noted, we think we are a democracy, and that this means more than periodic opportunities to vote, but we are not a democracy in that sense. We think the majority rules, but it doesn't. We think our voting system is fair, and we send international observers around the world to monitor others, but our own system is far from fair. The courts talk about Charter rights, votes of equal value, and effective representation, but in the most recent federal election it took 1,093,211 votes for each seat the Progressive Conservatives obtained, while adherents of the Liberal party platform needed only 31,730 votes per seat.[35] The vote of many Canadians was 34 times less valuable than the vote of many other Canadians. The PCs received 16 percent of the vote, and in fairness, they should have won 47 seats, but instead they won only two.[36] We say our system is responsible, but effective accountability started to disintegrate over a hundred years ago, and is gone today.

Political parties are powerful, but hollow. They lack their essential function of providing citizens a channel to influence policy. The citizens' role is dormant between elections. Power is concentrated at the top in parties and Parliament. From parties to Parliament, politics is a spectator sport; while the few rule, the many look on. The people vote primarily for party and leader, yet, ironically, they resent the local member taking orders from the party and leader. Our problems are structural. People yearn for answers, but enthusiastic support for the simplistic solutions offered by direct democracy proponents leaves them open to bitter disappointment.

The next chapters aim to provide viable, positive alternatives. Substantial change is needed to satisfy the popular conceptions of democracy held by an increasingly informed and educated populace. Politically significant blocs in our society must be represented. Change must satisfy Pitkin's demand for responsive institutions, and the court's notion of effective representation.[37] People deserve maximum choice and meaningful participation.[38] Change must lead to greater civility in

Parliament and the legislatures: to decisions by consensus in a place where everyone's talents are utilized, minority positions are respected, dissent is tolerated, and debate is genuine.

Moreover, the changes must respect both our vast geography and our unique history. It is a history shaped by, yet not wholly comfortable with, classical liberalism. Classical liberalism understood human rights as rights of individuals, and conceived the role of government as limited to the protection of private property. Our history reaches, via pre-revolutionary France and Britain, back into an older, European and classical tradition. That history precludes adopting the American congressional system in whole, while the congressional system's internal cohesiveness precludes adopting it in part. Our geography and history have combined to foster governments that are more communitarian and interventionist than those south of the border. The late George Grant, Canadian nationalist and political philosopher, expressed the difference between the Canadian and American political cultures with these words:

> Our hope lay in the belief that on the northern half of this continent we could built a community which had a stronger sense of the common good and of public order than was possible under the individualism of the American capitalist dream.[39]

Changes to strengthen democracy in the operation of the legislatures and Parliament must take account of these factors: the people, the country, and the influence of our history. Fortunately, proportional representation comes in many forms; a selection suitable to our peculiar needs is possible.

In particular, a new voting system must meet the following tests:

Accurate Reflection. The composition of Parliament and the legislatures is to be a micro picture, accurately mirroring, without distortion, the relative strengths of political diversity as it exists among the citizens.

Maximum Choice for Voters. Opportunity for voters to express at the ballot box an opinion on the optimum number of political issues.

Diffuse Power. In parties and Parliament, political power must be shared, not concentrated.

TOWARDS DEMOCRATIC
SELF-RULE

*Ultimately any form of democratic govern-
ment must stand or fall not so much by its
perfect subservience to majorities as by its
just treatment of minorities — a far more
difficult condition to fulfil. That minorities
must not rule is only the first canon of
good government; the second is that they
must not be ignored.*[1]

PROPORTIONAL REPRESENTATION

PROPORTIONAL REPRESENTATION (PR) is not, as is often
thought, a single, particular voting system. PR is the unifying
principle among a family of voting systems. The principle is that
representation in Parliament and the legislatures of groups of like-
minded voters is in proportion to that group's voting strength. For
example, if a party obtains 40 percent of the popular vote, that party
obtains 40 percent of the seats. Under proportional representation, votes
are translated into seats such that seat-share will equal vote-share. (To
see how far our present voting system deviates from the principle of
PR, consult Appendix B, Tables 2-5). The principle or ideal cannot be
attained perfectly, but there are many ways to approximate it. There
are many PR systems, and therefore any serious discussion must specify which system is talked about. After noting features common to most
PR systems, this chapter discusses one particular type of PR, the *single
transferable vote* (STV).

In North America and Great Britain, PR is often considered a deviation from the norm – an eccentricity; but in fact, many of the world's

stable democracies use PR, and others, such as Germany, use a mixed-member system to compensate for the inequities the *single member plurality* (SMP) system produces.[2] Among the most stable democratic regimes that use parliamentary systems, Great Britain and Canada may well be the exceptions in their use of SMP. New Zealand's 1992 referendum to change its SMP voting system carried by 84 percent; and in the 1993 referendum 53.8 percent favoured the *mixed-member proportional* (MMP) system, which is similar to what (West) Germany has used since 1949. It should be noted that in the US congressional system, because of its two-party system and separation of powers, SMP does not have the negative impact on fair results and the relation of the executive to the legislative that is the subject of this study. The first applications of PR took place in Denmark (1856), Belgium (1899), Switzerland (1901), and during the early decades of this century many other countries adopted PR.[3] Furthermore, very few have abandoned it once it was adopted.[4] PR cannot be dismissed as an anomaly, and should not be dismissed without being understood.

Why have so many democracies turned to PR? Why, for instance, would South Africa, in making a fresh start – in its first attempt at democracy, and while grappling with enormous racial, linguistic, and cultural diversity – opt for PR in both its national and state elections? Perhaps the answer is that the principle of PR, both in theory and in practice, most nearly embodies the essence of democracy. Vernon Bogdanor, who has studied PR extensively, writes:

> To meet the canons of democracy, an electoral system should perform two functions. It should ensure, first, that the majority rules and, secondly, that significant minorities are heard.[5]

SMP fails on both counts. It produces rule by minority, and all minorities except the largest are eliminated from participation in government. PR differs from SMP most strikingly in how it treats minority values, opinions, and interests. SMP aims to create a two-party system, which presupposes that all public policy issues, and the answers to those issues, allow no more than two possibilities. Such an assumption does not correspond to modern reality. Today, if ever, answers to significant public policy issues are not just black and white. Supposing otherwise imposes a straitjacket, suffocating the enormous diversity and creativity that drives a vibrant society. Out on the street, within society, there exists a rich diversity of principles, values, ideals, and ideas that people live by and pursue. PR provides a structure to capture that diversity, to bring it into the legislature, and to allow minority opinions to be heard. By including all significant minorities, PR promotes a consensual, cooperative form of social interaction and public policy decision-making, which is in sharp contrast with the adversarial politics SMP produces. PR changes the mechanics of translating votes into seats, and in so doing it fosters a profoundly different political culture – a culture of partnership and inclusion.

Why is it important to allow space for minority opinions and interests? First, it is a matter of fairness. SMP produces faked majorities in the legislature by preventing many of the votes from making it to the legislature. To manufacture a parliamentary majority from a minority of votes, the majority of votes are eliminated and wasted. This, to proponents of PR, is as wrong as dishonest weights and measurements, or winning an Olympic gold with the help of steroids. PR's concern with minority views need not arise from distrust of majorities, but to ensure that claims to majority status are justified and true. Proponents of PR do not question that someone voting with the majority should win, they protest winning without a majority. Majorities should be earned, not manufactured.[6] In brief, it is simply unfair to fix the rules so as to eliminate or deny a voice to significant minorities. Not everyone can have their way, but all should have a say. Why should only the largest minority have a voice in the deliberation and determination of public policy?

Beyond ensuring that majorities are arrived at fairly, the concern with minority rights has another dimension. If democracy is rule by the people, it cannot be exclusively rule by the majority, for then a minority is consigned to the status of non-people. In a democracy everyone counts. Voltaire said, "I disapprove of what you say, but I'll defend to the death your right to say it." Such respect for the differences among people lies at the heart of the democratic spirit. Majority rule must be limited majority rule; it has to be restrained by the rights of the minority. Without such restraint, majority rule is a form of tyranny. The essence of democracy is to respect different views, because people matter, persons are significant, every member of the human family has intrinsic worth. Democracy seeks unity in diversity; it is based on the worth of each person, and the importance of respecting diversity. The opposite is to seek unity in uniformity, which is totalitarian and the enemy of freedom. Sartori forcefully argues this position, and quotes Lord Acton, "The most certain test by which we judge whether a country is really free is the amount of security enjoyed by minorities."[7] Therefore, even when a voting system produces a legitimate majority, minorities deserve a limited degree of participation. PR systems institutionalize such protection by preventing the ruthless elimination of minority views at the various levels of the voting process as happens under SMP. For example, a voter under PR may still have some of his views represented even if just one of the candidates of his party's choice makes it to the legislature from that voter's district. In the event that the party of one's choice does not gain a majority in Parliament or the legislature, such a minority party is much more likely to still play a significant role in governing than would be the case under SMP.

The benefits of including minorities extend beyond the minority to the majority. Everyone benefits when no one is excluded. In a democracy, the collective wisdom steers the ship of state. All political elements and opinions have a hand on the tiller in proportion to their numerical strength. Unless all are present, the collective wisdom cannot emerge, and the public good will not be served. Our voting system excludes so many that the resulting ruling elite does not represent the collective wisdom of all citizens. Excluding even small minorities diminishes the quality of democracy. The minority must not rule, but neither must it be overruled.

A third reason for drafting the rules of a voting system so as to include minority views is that it helps to make election campaigns more honest, and to shift the focus from image to substance, from deceptive perceptions to principled policies.[8] Under SMP, parties tend to aggregate diversities of interests, bridge differences, and reach compromise before appealing for voter support. The result is a stronger tendency to pragmatic, "catch-all" parties, and election campaigns driven by personalities, images, and hollow promises. Parties are driven to seek such a large base of support that in the attempt to please all they satisfy none.[9] Voters not wholly comfortable with any of the parties are reduced to picking the best of a bad bunch. PR changes the dynamics, in that minority status does not prevent participation in governing. Under PR, parties have the option to state their principles and platform more openly without risking total elimination. The aggregation of interests and compromises necessary to the governing of any polity tends to occur after the election. In instances where two or three parties cannot honestly reflect all the plurality and diversity that exists in a given society, PR may lead to more parties. When this occurs the voter is given more choice, and the relationship between parties and their supporters is more authentic and positive, in that it is based more on substance. After Belgium switched to PR, one effect noted was that PR had "... introduced more sincerity into electoral platforms."[10] Parties can be honest about what they stand for, because their appeal is to fewer voters. As a result, PR, inasmuch as it allows for a greater range of political opinion to be represented, can lead to a Parliament and legislature whose make-up fulfils the requirements of descriptive representation as discussed in Chapter 2 above. It is more likely that every politically significant minority and majority interest will be represented.

OBJECTIONS CONSIDERED

OBJECTIONS TO PR are plentiful and arise for a variety of reasons. Unfortunately, PR seems to provoke strong feelings. Proponents sometimes present PR as a panacea for all inequities, while opponents may also overstate their case. Proponents might credit PR for all that is good and positive, while opponents may blame PR for all the ills that beset government and society. Such disputes usually draw on selective evidence, and therefore, are difficult to settle. For example, Hains supports his opposition to PR by observing that PR did not prevent the coming to power of Hitler in Germany and Mussolini in Italy. He forgets that historically most wars have been initiated by governments who attained power by means other than PR.[11] Voting systems are one component within a complex set of governmental institutions; institutions which themselves are deeply rooted in cultural, historical, social, and economic conditions, often unique to particular nation states.

This presents two problems: first, statements that claim PR as the cause of particular political behaviour, such as party formation, or the presence or lack of political extremism, should be considered suspect.[12] Second, even where inferences about the effects of PR in one country or culture are reasonably justified, such inferences may not hold in another time and place. These difficulties, which beset all the social sciences, should inform any consideration of the claims and counter claims, even when supported by empirical research. In addition, disagreements about PR are not always disagreements about the facts. Often opponents of PR readily admit that PR is fairer, and will produce a more descriptively representative Parliament than SMP, but to them other criteria and values are of equal or greater importance. A variety of objections will be noted in this chapter.[13] Some of these objections are based on claims that may or may not be true; others arise from a difference in priorities. Most consist of a mixture of the two.

PROLIFERATION OF PARTIES

There is a common perception that PR will naturally lead to an "Italian pizza parliament," a parliament fractured by a multiplicity of small, and perhaps extremist, parties.[14] Shortly after the Second World War, the French political theorist Maurice Duverger, troubled by the instability of French politics, looked enviously at Britain's two-party system and postulated that SMP produces a two-party system, while PR leads to a multiplicity of parties.[15] Duverger and others saw the voting system as determinative for the party system. However, the actual experience in many countries did not fit the model and defied the theory. Soon such theories came under attack. Turning Duverger's theory around, the critics postulated that voting systems derive from party configurations which themselves are the product of historical and cultural factors.[16] In response Duverger softened his position considerably, then suggested that SMP favours a two-party system, and while PR always produces more than two parties, it usually does not lead to a multiplicity of parties.[17] He also wrote:

> The relationship between electoral rules and party systems is not mechanical and automatic: a particular electoral regime does not necessarily produce a particular party system; it merely exerts pressure in the direction of this system, it is a force which acts among several other forces, some of which tend in the opposite direction.[18]

The theory that voting systems determine party systems was eclipsed. Under the leadership of Lipset and Rokkan, social cleavages in society were now considered as significant determinants of party systems. Where social cleavages such as religion and class are numerous, non-aligned, and pronounced, more parties will result.[19] Yet such theories did not prove entirely satisfactory either. For example, what then explains the strong correlation between electoral and party systems? Rae's research in the late 1960s concludes:

> In 75 legislatures elected under PR formulae, the mean minimal majority was 1.96 parties. Typically, the support of the two largest parties was required for the formation of the majority. In the 45 legislatures elected under majority and plurality formulae, the mean minimal majority was only 1.5 parties, suggesting that one-party majorities were more common.[20]

Rae's findings were substantiated by Lijphart in the early 1980s. To measure the association between voting systems and the number of parties, Lijphart studied twenty-two democratic regimes, and distinguished between three classifications of parties. The number of parties that contest elections is always greater than the number that gain parliamentary representation. The first he named electoral parties, and the second parliamentary parties. The latter requires a further subcategory, since some parties are much smaller in size, or carry less weight than others. Hence he devised a method to isolate "effective" parliamentary parties. Following Rae, he found that all voting systems tend to reduce the number of effective parliamentary parties compared to the number of electoral parties, but PR systems tend to eliminate fewer electoral parties from becoming effective parliamentary parties than SMP. Lijphart found the weaker version of

Duverger's sociological law to hold in all except two of the twenty-two democratic regimes studied. Because of the two exceptions, he concludes, "... proportional representation should not be said to *cause*, but only to *allow* multipartism."[21] Yet that seems excessively cautious. PR plays a more active role than the word *allow* indicates. PR, by design, eliminates fewer parties from attaining parliamentary status, and its correlation with the presence of a greater number of political parties is strong.

Why do some countries have many political parties, and others few? The answers are as complex as people and society itself. The mechanics of a voting system play a role, but factors such as the number and intensity of politically relevant interest groups and issues within a given society also play a role. Lijphart measured and found a strong correlation between the number of issue dimensions and the number of parties."[22] Taagepera and Grofman, inspired by Lijphart, suggest that the mechanics of a voting system, together with the number of issues in a given society, provide strong predictive power about the number of parties in that society. Recognizing the empirical presence of both voting system influences and the power of social diversity, they offer a synthesis of the two, and even provide a mathematical formula to express the relationship.[23] Though the formula does not hold in every instance, and the operational definitions require considerable qualification, it recognizes that at least two factors interact. It might explain why Austria, for example, has relatively few parties. That country's PR system's tendency for more parties is probably held in check by a society and political culture with few issues.

Empirical research shows that PR usually goes together with more than two parties, particularly in societies with a greater number of political issues. But does PR lead to a proliferation of parties? Blais and Carty found the number of "effective" parliamentary parties to be 20 percent lower in SMP systems than in PR systems.[24] That is not excessive. Rae's study confirms that PR does not lead to fractionalization due to multiplicity of parties. He had speculated that ballots which allow a voter to favour more than one party with a mandate (preferential voting) would lead to fractionalization, but concludes: "The reader will find that my theory is absolutely wrong."[25] Michael Cassidy lists extensive evidence that PR does not lead, in most cases, to unmanageable multiplication of parties and concludes: "... the differences between countries appear to be related more to the underlying political culture and cleavages than to the use of proportional representation."[26] Bogdanor, a proponent of PR, dismisses concerns about proliferation as fallacy.[27] Lakeman, also a proponent of PR, shows that European countries did not experience a marked increase in the number of parties after switching to PR.[28]

115

Proliferation of parties can be avoided. Most PR systems have minimum number-of-votes thresholds, ranging from 0.67 percent in the Netherlands to 5 percent in Germany; below such thresholds a party is denied parliamentary representation. Thresholds may be used to prevent excessive multi-partism. The Netherlands, with the lowest threshold of all, experienced an increase in parliamentary parties to 12, from 9 at dissolution, in the May 1994 election. That election was contested by 24 parties. Such numbers seem bewildering by Canadian standards. However, raising the Dutch threshold to 3.5 percent would eliminate all but 4 of the current 12 parliamentary parties. Under Lijphart's classification the Netherlands has only 4 effective parliamentary parties. It is not likely the Dutch will raise the threshold, since that would be considered an unacceptable suppression of minority views. Within Canadian political culture, which currently bars over 50 percent of its voters from participation, denying participation to 3.5 percent should be entirely acceptable.

In conclusion, comparative research shows, in most instances, a correlation between PR and an increased number of parties. But the increase is far from excessive and does not substantiate the claim, or fear, that PR leads to party proliferation. In addition, if desired, thresholds can effectively limit new party formation. The fear that PR must lead to an "Italian pizza parliament," is unfounded.

UNSTABLE GOVERNMENT

Opponents of PR do not always specify what they mean by the charge that PR leads to unstable government. For example, it might mean more turnover, in the sense of more elections and more frequent changes of both government and cabinet. PR is clearly associated with more frequent turnovers in governments and cabinets. Lijphart's study of twenty democracies between 1945 and 1980 shows that "...two-party systems are associated with stable cabinets, and as multi-partism increases, cabinet life tends to shorten."[29] Unstable government might also refer to the incidence of extremism or wild swings in law-making. The two are related; frequent turnover is assumed to lead to abrupt changes in public policies. PR has been blamed for the failure of the Weimar Republic and the rise of Hitler. Writing in 1941, Hermens asserted, "PR was an essential factor in the breakdown of German democracy."[30] This view is generally dismissed as exaggerated, yet it is feared PR may not exert the same moderating influence that the brokerage function of parties under SMP is credited with performing. By allowing a greater diversity into the legislature, PR gives status, recognition, and influence to minorities, some of whom will undoubtedly be extremist. Sartori described Italy's notorious instability – forty-eight governments between June 1945 and December 1988, an average of one every eleven months – as "polarized pluralism," with features that include extremism.[31] Sartori considered PR to contribute to instability and extremism by perpetuating social differences. He searched for a voting system that would bridge social and political differences.

In response: first, there are many PR countries, including Scandinavian countries, that have not given extremists undue influence. Therefore, the presence or absence of extremism in public policy cannot be attributed solely to the voting system.[32] Sartori's analysis may be valid for Italy, France, and Germany, for the period of those countries' history he studied, but it is invalid to generalize.

Second, the competition is not doing so well itself. Two-party regimes are supposed to produce moderation, since both parties are expected to converge on the centre for the swing vote in the middle. But this does not always happen according to script. B.C. is a counter example. Since the breakup of the wartime coalition, B.C. has enjoyed a virtual two-party system, yet provincial politics have been exceptionally polarized. A recent study concludes that: "...party competition in British Columbia has a sharper left/right focus than in any other part of English-speaking North America."[33] Similarly, in Quebec, SMP gave government power to an extreme faction determined to destroy Canada as we know it today. Under PR the national unity crises would probably not exist. Under SMP Quebec's nationalists either control government completely, or are entirely excluded. As Cairns has shown, and the 1994 Quebec election confirmed, SMP exacerbates social and regional differences.

On the matter of quick turnover, SMP does not guarantee unqualified stability. Far from it. The turnover in MPs and MLAs in Canada is among the highest world-wide. Franks considers this the most serious defect of the Canadian parliamentary system, and would for that reason consider PR, except that under list PR party discipline is too strong.[34] (There is no evidence Franks considered non-list PR systems, such as STV). The 1991 B.C. provincial election returned 25 incumbents and 50 rookies.[35] The 1993 federal election returned 90 incumbents, and 205 rookies. Defenders of such high levels of turnover should be cautious about presenting themselves as the guardians of stability. Cabinet might be stable, but is the governmental institution as a whole stable? Adding up the number of elections or cabinet changes under one voting system as opposed to another reveals little about the inherent stability of the regime as a whole.

Third, and perhaps most important, swings in public policy are more pronounced under two-party systems than under multi-party systems. It is easy to see why. Usually, successive governments and cabinets under PR are largely composed of the same parties and persons. Their relative influence may shift slightly, but the degree of continuity

117

is greater than under the complete swings of two-party systems. A change in government under the SMP, Westminster, winner-take-all model makes a dramatic shift in public policy possible, and more likely than under the PR, coalition, consensual type of governing. Peter Hains objects to PR, in part, because he sees it as providing government that is too moderate, middle-of-the-road, and supportive of the status quo. His political activism rebels against PR.[36] Similar sentiments might explain why in Canada the CCF/NDP has seldom spoken in favour of PR, even though they, as the third party, have suffered the unfairness of SMP more than any other party. It is doubtful Tommy Douglas, Dave Barrett, and Bob Rae could have implemented their entire agenda under PR. It would have had to be more incremental.

European experience shows that PR builds governing teams with staying power. Extremism, wild swings in policy, and abuses of political power are more likely when power is concentrated in the hands of the few. Critics of PR confuse cabinet instability with regime instability. One student of the effect of PR on Belgian political stability observed that "cabinets had weaker majorities and shorter lives, but there was much less danger of permanent and irreconcilable divisions within the country."[37] If the goal is to provide stability in public policy, PR, to the extent voting systems are responsible, is clearly the system of choice. Tom Kent, a longtime federal senior civil servant, supports PR for precisely this reason.[38] PR fosters continuity of public policy, and policy based not on short-term political gain but long-term public good.

PR should not be blamed for instability caused by cultural and social conditions that may precipitate unrest or extremism under any voting system, as seems to be the case in Italy.

Finally, one form of PR, the single transferable vote (STV), uses preferential voting. Such voting tends to prevent extremism more effectively than list PR and mixed-member systems. Under preferential voting, winning candidates enjoy a greater degree of support from the voters relative to any other candidates. This leads to remarkably different results, as shown in the following example. Suppose there are four parties – Left, Centre, Right, and Anarchist. The last has one objective – the overthrow of government. Due to its limited platform and extreme views, Anarchist enjoys the zealous support of 10 percent of voters; the remainder of voters have little sympathy for Anarchist. They would sooner support any party other than Anarchist. Suppose Centre and Anarchist each receive 10 percent of the vote. Under list PR, Centre and Anarchist will each receive 10 percent of the seats. In contrast, under preferential voting, Anarchist is not likely to obtain any seats, while Centre, as the probable second or third choice of some voters, is assured its share. If the majority of voters would sooner give their lower preferences to any candidate other than Anarchist, Anarchist may not win any seats, while Centre will. STV provides a greater safe-guard against extremism than any other form of PR.

To win under preferential voting requires, nearly always, second- and third-place support from voters whose first preference is for one's competitor. This feature moderates not only policy positions, but all political behaviour from election campaigns to decorum within Parliament. STV provides a powerful incentive to foster a less antago-nistic, adversarial political culture. The political actors need each other to win. No party or group can isolate itself and survive. There are those on both the right and the left who for this reason reject STV. Such views are shortsighted. In the real world, we all need each other. A voting sys-tem must not be designed to suit particular political or social agendas. Its sole purpose is to reveal the will of the citizens without distortion. The majority of citizens seldom harbour complete approval or com-plete rejection of candiates, parties and platforms. Preferential voting is sufficiently nuanced to capture the degree of public support various parties enjoy. Its results express the true intent of citizens more accu-rately than any other system. No one should object to that.

WEAK GOVERNMENT
Sartori labelled PR, in words that are quoted often, a "feeble" system. He described it as such because PR does not interpret or reassign vot-ing results. In his view, since PR faithfully reproduces in Parliament all the diversity, divisions, and contradictions that exist in society, govern-ment leadership is frustrated. Government should be able to lift itself above the petty partisanship and the fracturedness of society. Sartori does not hold PR responsible for generating "polarized pluralism," but thinks a more dynamic voting system would break Italy's chronic inability to take decisive action on creative, progressive ideas.[39] He con-sidered PR's capacity to govern weak; agreement can be found only on the most mundane, harmless, lowest-common-denominator issues. With the Italian example in mind, some defenders of SMP hold that the purpose of an election is to produce a government with a workable majority.[40] In that view, we must choose between two values. We can have a government with a strong capacity to govern, or we can have fairness of representation. Franks, for instance, argues against PR and a Parliament-dominated executive for Canada, because in his view our history and geography demand an activist, interventionist government capable of strong decisions.[41]

It need not be the case that PR leads to weak government. Rather than choose between fairness in representation and capable govern-ment, we should aim for both. There are many instances to prove both are possible. Were Franks to study western European PR democracies, could he still maintain that such governments are not "activist and welfare-oriented," and unable to promote "equality, justice, economic development, and other collective goals"? Franks credits "strong" government for Macdonald's national dream, the trans-Canada railway and road systems, and our valued universal social programs. Is he also grateful that "strong" government procured the Canada–U.S. Free Trade Agreement, the Goods and Services Tax, a $750 billion public debt, and an artificially aggravated national-unity crisis? Where Franks sees the fulfilment of national aspirations, others see relentless squandering of opportunity. Some applauded former B.C. Premier Vander Zalm's abortion funding policy as "strong" government, others saw dangerous extremism. Government cannot be strong unless it is responsible, and in a democracy that means being representative of and accountable to the people. Bogdanor holds that in the long haul, "strong" government is impossible without reflecting the majority view.[42] In a democracy, the strength of government is a function of its representativeness.

Decision-making by consensus is cumbersome, but is it necessarily weak? Is government stronger when the sole ambition of nearly half of the representatives is to be as destructive as possible? Is confrontation better than cooperation? Whether the consensus style of governing is considered weak depends on values and priorities, and often one's own political agenda. "Weak" is a relative term; weak in relation to what? As noted, J.S. Mill favoured PR because of its educative value. He believed that universal suffrage would destroy democracy unless the political institutions and culture included meaningful participation by the citizens. In that view, the contention that consensual, coalition-style government is cumbersome could be a recommendation. If the purpose of political leadership is to empower people, to enlist the creative energies of citizens for the benefit of the collectivity, if it is to lead people into self-rule for the purpose of lifting their horizons beyond immediate, narrow self-interest, then decision-making by consensus, partnership and conciliation is the epitome of strength, and the type of elected dictatorship our system produces is by contrast utterly feeble. PR issues from the premise that ruling should be by the many, not the few. Given those values, and judged from that perspective, PR produces the strongest form of government possible.

Perhaps not everyone shares those values. Today's society, unlike that of J.S. Mill's more reflective nineteenth century, places supreme value on efficiency. The materialism that characterizes our time measures efficiency primarily in economic terms. Hence, the administration of public justice (government) has become largely a function of economics. Most people today would measure a political system's strength by that system's ability to deliver economic benefits. Jankowski devised a study to measure economic results and efficiency under different voting systems.

If the yardstick is economic output, the conventional wisdom among political scientists – that the Westminster model of responsible government delivers strong government, while PR, coalition, consensual governments are weak – is turned on its head by Jankowski's findings. The study encompasses twelve democracies over a one-hundred-year time span reaching back into the last century, and measures per capita GDP (gross domestic product). Jankowski concludes:

> The statistical evidence rejects the responsible, or Westminster political parties argument. Strong, centralized two-party systems do not promote economic efficiency by making political parties more responsive to the electorate. Hence, this piece of conventional wisdom in political science requires either rejection, or substantial modification. ... Westminster parties actually reduce economic growth relative to weak, or multiparty systems.[43]

In addition, there is much circumstantial evidence that Japan, Germany, the Low Countries and the Scandinavian countries all have educational systems and economies that outperformed or did as well as Canada's over the past forty years.[44] Over the same time period, we have mortgaged our future to an unprecedented extent, just to keep up with these PR-run countries.

Finally, most governments cannot resist influencing the economy for purely political reasons. They inflate the economy before elections, and deflate the economy after elections. Edward Tufte studied the frequency of this self-serving practice, and found all but eight democratic governments world-wide are guilty. Each of the eight exceptions had a PR system.[45] The opportunity to manipulate the economy for short-term political gain is less likely when power is shared. Stubbornly insisting that decision-making by consensus is a form of weakness, in the face of so much contrary evidence, seems more dogmatic than reasonable. Whether we value widespread participation or crass economic output, PR forms of government are strong on both counts. The charge of weakness cannot be sustained. The facts are otherwise.

VOTERS DO NOT SELECT GOVERNMENT[46]

This objection maintains that under two-party, SMP regimes, voters have a choice between two alternative sets of policies, and elections clearly establish what people favour. However, the choice is more imaginary than real. As already noted, in the case of Canada, elections are seldom about policies, or won by majorities. Also, Lijphart observed that SMP frequently produces two parties, both of which seek to attract the swing vote in the middle. In this pursuit they often become so much alike as to offer the voter no genuine choice at all.[47]

Objectors in this category also suggest that under PR, government formation is subject to deal-making behind closed doors, and thereby removes government formation from the direct influence of the voters. To counter such criticism most European parties announce before the election which partners they deem acceptable for coalition-building. In addition, their compromises must be publicly defended. Bogdanor considers this objection at length and concludes the alleged secrecy is far from excessive and the objection itself a fallacy.[48] Finally, the criticism does not apply to all forms of PR. Some forms, such as STV, allow voters to determine what coalition they favour.

UNDUE INFLUENCE OF SMALL PARTIES
This objection suggests that PR gives each vote equal weight, but not each party, and that small parties may under certain circumstances have an undue influence. Lijphart reviews a number of studies that seek to measure the relative effectiveness of parties in a PR system, and how that effectiveness is achieved. His study confirms that usually the power of parties is commensurate to their numbers.[49]

The possibility for undue influence by minorities under PR must be evaluated against the alternative. Under SMP, minorities have an undue influence on public policy in two ways. First, SMP entrusts government power to minorities. Lakeman observes that seats won by narrow margins, which nonetheless decisively influence the outcome of an election, mean that the government is decided by a few voters acting in the secrecy of the ballot box. In contrast, small parties that participate in government formation do so under full public scrutiny, and are accountable for their actions to the voters in the next election.[50] If we must have a few decide the government, it is preferable to do so in public than in secret. The real difference is that under SMP a few voters decide on a government that arrogates all power to itself, eliminating other parties from participation, while under PR no government has absolute powers. Even in those few instances where SMP produces a party with more than 50 percent voter support, it must not be assumed that such voters identify wholly with that party. Particularly in two-party systems, many voters choose one party over another as the lesser of two evils, and not because they fully endorse that party's platform in every respect. SMP never produces government that truly reflects the mind of the voters.

Second, a two-party system is poorly equipped to represent the increasing diversity of a modern society. Therefore, people turn to special interest groups to more effectively influence public policy. Since SMP places the levers of power with the executive, such groups quickly learn to bypass political parties, MPs, MLAs, and the legislature to lobby directly those who can make quick and effective decisions behind closed doors in the prime minister's office, or cabinet. Some observers consider their influence so great as to speak of this as the "tyranny of minorities."[51]

If the concern is to minimize the occasions when power and influence fall into the hands of minorities, special interest groups, and small parties as opposed to the impossible goal of eliminating every such possibility, PR has the better record.

UNACCOUNTABLE GOVERNMENT

Critics of PR argue that in a two-party system responsibility is clearly placed with the governing party. If voters are dissatisfied with how their affairs are managed, they know who to blame. With a multi-party system and a government formed by coalition and consensus, responsibility is shared, making it more difficult for the voters to assign credit or blame to individual parties for government performance. Each party will point fingers, shift blame to others, and hope to leave voters confused. How seriously this will impair the electorate's judgment is a matter of speculation. A representative's vote on issues will be on the record. The congressional system shares power, and suffers potentially the same defect without much complaint. SMP is also capable of generating minority governments. Canadian experience with minority government is judged by some observers to have been very productive.[52]

More important, accountability has many dimensions. This entire study is about accountability. Between elections, our system is not accountable, cabinet is not responsible to the people's representatives, and the make-up of the government is not representative. At present, elections are more about personalities and perception than platform, principles, and programs. Therefore, while we may know clearly who is responsible, we hardly know what for. The question of accountability must be placed within the context of the larger enterprise, namely, to provide responsible government in fact as well as theory. Of all the different systems of PR, the most accountable is STV, because it gives voters the most choice, and it establishes the closest possible link between the represented and the representative. Under STV, the representative is held directly accountable by and to the represented; political parties need not come between the two.

The various objections usually raised against PR are often based on speculation rather than fact, or hold equally under SMP. There is a great need in Canada for informed, disinterested, and dispassionate discussion and deliberation about the values that undergird our voting system and those of other countries. Next, a consideration of one particular type of PR voting system.

SINGLE TRANSFERABLE VOTE (STV)

MOST PROPORTIONAL SYSTEMS are *list* systems. The parties select a list of candidates; this list is ranked in order of preference either by the party before the election, or by the voters during the election. The number of seats a party secures is relative to the number of votes a party receives, but who fills those seats is largely up to the party. Even where voters are asked to rank candidates, their vote must stay within the same party, and the ranking occurs within a particular party's list.[53] List PR voting systems favour a strong party system that allow parties a dominant role. In pure list PR systems such as practised in the Netherlands or Israel, the vote is much more for the party than for the individual candidate. As a result, representation is focused more on political program and interest than neighbourhood or geographical area. The link or sense of identity between the citizen and his or her representative is weak, while the link between representative and party has the potential to be strong. This results in strong party discipline.

By contrast, STV personalizes voting and representation. Because the British SMP system purports to establish a personal relationship between the represented and their representative (votes are for candidates, not parties), STV has been referred to as the Anglo-Saxon form of PR, and also as personal PR. This may explain that STV has been used only in countries with historical Commonwealth connections. It is used for the Irish and Tasmanian Lower Houses, the Irish and Australian Senate, Northern Ireland local and European elections, and the Maltese legislature.[54] Under STV parties have no formal role; as in SMP systems, votes are cast for candidates, not for parties. But in contrast to SMP, voters under STV have much more choice. STV functions with multi-member districts. Districts of five or more seats yield nearly proportional results. (Appendix A lists proposed electoral districts for British Columbia using STV. It suggests 15 multi-member districts to replace the existing 75 single-member districts). Voters are given a ballot paper listing all candidates for that district, but instead of selecting one candidate with an X, voters rank candidates in order of preference by placing 1, 2, 3 etc. beside one or more names. The preferences on the ballot papers are counted, assigned, and interpreted to elect candidates according to the expressed preferences of the electorate.[55] If a voter's higher preferences are not needed because those candidates have a surplus of votes, or those candidates are eliminated for having insufficient votes, that voter's ballot paper will be used to lend support to that voter's lower preference candidates. Hence, few votes are wasted, and most voters will assist in electing the winning candidates.

It should also be noted that lower preferences cannot hurt a voter's higher preferences, since the lower do not take effect until the higher preferences have either been elected or eliminated. There is no incentive to "plump" one's vote, although parties may attempt to persuade supporters not to rank candidates beyond those of its own party. The objective is to receive transfers from supporters of other parties without returning a similar benefit. Voters seldom follow such attempts at manipulation, and a party's rigid unwillingness to cooperate with others can be counterproductive at the ballot box.[56]

The system is somewhat similar to the run-off elections political parties use during leadership selection votes. In those instances, on each successive ballot the lowest candidates are dropped, and their supporters can transfer to the remaining candidates. STV earns its name because these successive votes are reduced to a single ballot. Also, the Reform Party of Canada uses STV at their candidate selection meetings.

STV is unique among PR systems in the amount of choice it gives to voters. Voters need not restrict their preferences to candidates of one party, and in addition, voters rank the candidates within the parties. STV provides a built-in primary election. Therefore, questions about whether elections should produce representations of geographical or personal interest or a mandate for a particular political program are left to the voters to decide. In contrast, under SMP all such questions, plus the wide diversity of policy positions on issues, are largely decided for the voter by the parties; and they must all be expressed in one single choice. A voter's ability to express a choice over a range of issues is severely restricted. Voters must support a party's entire package of policy proposals or reject them all – a most unsatisfying choice. Seldom do voters approve a party's entire package; the result is a dilemma for the voter. STV allows the voter to express degrees of preference for all candidates and parties based on their positions on a number of different issues, local as well as national or province-wide, and according to the perceived competence and past performance of both candidates and parties.

STV uses preference voting. Preference voting is to X-balloting as the dimmer switch is to the on/off light switch. Like the dimmer switch, preference voting allows for a range of options. Expressing a preference for a particular candidate, party, platform, or local issue does not compel the voter to reject outright all other options. Under X-balloting voters have only one option, and they cannot express whether their support for that one option is strong, weak, or in-between. Instead of outright approval or rejection, preference voting is like asking voters to register their likes and dislikes on a scale of one to ten. Preference voting registers the degree of support present among all voters for candidates, parties, and issues with exceptional precision. As a result, political convictions and opinions of citizens matter; most can be registered, not in a unrealistic, forced black-and-white fashion, but with great nuance. Citizens' participation becomes more meaningful and significant. Not only do most votes count, but their influence on public policy is immediate. Preference voting is a mechanism to more nearly attain government of the people by the people.

For example, because STV permits the voter to express a preference for a party's candidates, it allows the voter not only to help decide which party will govern, but also to influence the policies that party will follow. Parties are often coalitions aggregating a segment of the political spectrum under one umbrella. Voters decide under STV which part of that segment will be represented in the legislature. Under STV it is not uncommon for incumbents to be defeated by a candidate of their own party. In the 1977 Irish election 13 of the 32 defeated incumbents suffered defeat at the hands of their running mates. In effect, voters participate in a party's nomination and candidate selection process. Particularly well-liked candidates may escape their party's weak performance at the polls during a downswing.[57] Party machines need not come between voter and candidates. All voters, not just paid-up party members, get to select successful candidates. This feature encourages candidates to take positions of greater independence relative to their party, which in turn lessens the need for more parties; thus STV prevents party proliferation more successfully than list PR systems.[58] Like a dimmer switch, STV registers and expresses the true intentions of the citizens with great precision.

STV has the potential to offer more choice to the voters than any other voting system, including the German mixed system, which New Zealand has recently adopted, and which Michael Cassidy among others recommends for Canada. Taylor and Johnston conclude their study with these words: "If you want maximum choice for voters, then go for STV."[59] It is precisely this element of choice for voters that made J.S. Mill an early and enthusiastic supporter of STV. He clearly perceived and feared that the universal franchise would lead to mass political parties, and that such parties would radically change the relationship between the citizens and their representative. The single-member, riding-based voting system, designed to make independent representatives accountable to a particular, geographically distinct group of voters, would be distorted by the new-found influence and power of extra-parliamentary parties. The independence of MPs would give way to party discipline; as a result, representation of people within a territory would be replaced by representation of party. History has proven such fears amply justified. The vitally important direct link between citizen and representative has been eliminated.

To restore the link between voter and representative, Mill considered Hare's STV proposal brilliant, and uniquely suited to the need of the hour.[60] He wrote to Thomas Hare, the British inventor of STV:

> You appear to me to have exactly, and for the first time, solved the difficulty of popular representation; and by doing so, to have raised up the cloud of gloom and uncertainty which hung over the futurity of representative government and therefore, of civilization.[61]

Mill saw STV as the means to ensure that nearly every voter would have someone in government speaking for him, someone who shared his views and represented his interests. SMP is designed to represent a community or geographical territory, list PR represents party and platform, while STV represents citizens. Some citizens in expressing an opinion will opt for party and platform, others for their community and a local representative, and still others will select both, in a variety of combinations. The genius of STV is that such choices are left for the voter to make, and that such choices are registered accurately, without distortion. If Canadian politics is to promote vigorous citizenship, it must offer unrestricted choice to voters.

PROPORTIONALITY

STV has two essential features. It offers voters choice, and it prevents unearned, faked majorities in the legislature. Both features have the potential to significantly diminish the artificial, hollow power our political parties now enjoy. Parties receive their strength from attaining faked majorities in the legislature; majority government should result only when the voters are so minded, not as a byproduct of a divided vote against the winning party. As noted above, all voting systems over-reward the larger, stronger parties, but PR systems less than others. How effective is STV in preventing unearned majorities in the legislature? The answer requires a measure of its proportionality. Complete proportionality is attained when a party's seat share is equal to its vote share. Rae's 1967 study found PR systems, not surprisingly, to have a greater degree of proportionality than SMP systems.[62] Lijphart presents a more refined study. He classifies all PR systems into three subcategories and found STV to be within the intermediate range for proportionality among the three categories.[63] Katz adds a further refinement. He found STV to be less proportional than the average for all PR systems as determined by Rae, but notes that proportionality relates to district size. Since STV uses smaller district size than most PR systems, Katz compares STV to PR systems that use similar district size, and con-

127

cludes, "Surprisingly, for comparably small districts, pure PR systems appear to be less proportional than STV."[64] Bogdanor reports:"The single transferable vote has been found to yield a high degree of proportionality, not as great as list systems, but far higher than plurality or majority systems."[65]

The reason STV does not attain a higher degree of proportionality in Ireland relates to district size. Ireland uses mostly three-seat districts. In each district some votes do not help to elect anyone; in effect, they are wasted. Therefore, the more seats per district, the fewer the votes that are wasted. Districts beyond five seats attain only marginally greater proportionality. However, districts beyond five seats, except for densely populated areas, suffer a loss of local and community identification, thus cancelling the benefit of marginally improved proportionality. McLean concludes his comparative study of various electoral systems: "All are imperfect, but I think the least bad is STV... It compromises between proportionality and community representation."[66] Katz began his study to test whether STV could claim to be a PR system and found that its degree of proportionality warrants its inclusion among the PR family.

Measuring proportionality is not an exact science. Much depends on operational definitions. For example, what should count as a party? However, it seems safe to conclude that a relatively close approximation of proportionality can be attributed to STV, certainly much closer than is possible under SMP. The next chapter explores STV proportionality as it relates to the suggested STV electoral map for B.C. as found in Appendix A.

TRANSPARENCY

Finally, observers have noted that STV is particularly transparent. As noted above, public opinion and changing social trends find expression in governmental institutions relatively free of distortions. This is particularly evident in how STV responds to issues such as gender parity and representation of visible minorities. STV, like all PR systems, allows greater opportunity to historically disadvantaged groups. It does so naturally without the need for affirmative-action gerrymandering. However, the countries that use STV – the Irish Republic, Tasmania, and Malta – have not removed barriers to elected office for disadvantaged groups as effectively as some of the countries using list PR. Under list PR, political correctness can be enforced from a party's central head office, while under STV change comes only when society is so minded, and expresses itself through a free, unrestrained exercise of its collective will.[67]

Scholars note how a society's political culture, history, and traditional way of doing things are more determinative than the formal structure of its voting system.[68] For example, in a largely rural, tradition-bound society, such as Ireland, where politics has always been local, personal, and based on parish-pump patronage, STV changes little. It merely reflects and perpetuates society's expectations. In such societies, STV's potential for minority representation, cross-party voting, or a coalitionist, rather than a largely bipolar government, has not been used much.[69] Consequently, Carty, among others, considers PR and STV weak voting systems.[70] Such systems faithfully reproduce in government the expectations, prejudices, and cleavages that exist in society. This may be considered a weakness where a society is more tradition-bound, or particularly fractured, as is the case in Northern Ireland, but the same transparency will provide dynamic government in a more progressive society.

Complaints that STV in Ireland has not significantly reduced the negative role of parties, or improved access to elected office for traditionally disadvantaged groups, may be less a complaint about STV and more about the lack of dynamism in Irish society. Both the British Labour party's Plant Report and New Zealand's Royal Commission on Electoral Reform dismiss STV on the basis of its practical effect in Ireland. This is shortsighted, since in a different society STV's results would be different. Similarly, Sartori's characterization of PR as feeble is really directed at Italian political culture. STV allows society to influence government, and has the potential to make government responsive in the manner prescribed by Pitkin and classical democracy. Whether it is so used is up to the citizens. Such responsiveness or transparency, in my view, is hardly a weakness. Government exists to serve society; society is prior to government. In a democracy the correct criterion on which to judge a voting system is its ability to capture and express, without distortion, a society's collective wisdom.

PROPORTIONAL REPRESENTATION, LIKE ice cream, comes in many colours and flavours. It need not be the Italian variety. It need not be unsuitable to Canada's geography and history. PR meets the test of accurate representation. More closely than most systems, it gives votes equal value, thus leading to descriptive representation. Society can reproduce itself in miniature in the legislature. All politically significant sectors of society will be represented in proportion to their vote share. As a result, the court's demands for fairness and effective representation are best met by PR. In addition, PR, particularly STV, is transparent. Social concerns, changing values, and people's expectations will quickly find representation in the legislature. The demand that government listen to the people can be met more effectively with PR, particularly the STV variety. To meet the needs of our history, PR's transparency will make government more – or less – interventionist, as and when the people are so minded. Finally, STV's compromise between representation of territory and other interests uniquely suits our vast and unevenly populated country and provinces. Of all the PR systems, STV suits both our geography and history best.

It remains to be seen how STV will affect the operation of the legislature. In particular, it must be established that STV can diffuse power, give elected representatives independence from their parties, and thus restore responsible government. And if it holds promise for responsible government, will it also provide institutional safeguards, such that representing people's interests will be conducted in a manner responsive to them, as Pitkin stipulated?

CHAPTER SEVEN

IMPLEMENTATION

There is nothing more difficult to plan, more dubious of success nor more dangerous to manage than the creation of a new system. For the initiator has the enmity of all who would profit by the preservation of the old institutions and merely lukewarm defenders in those who would gain by the new ones.[1]

ALMOST ANY COMMENT and prediction about what might or might not happen should the single transferable vote (STV) replace single member plurality (SMP) must consist largely of speculation. There is only one assertion that cannot be denied: STV would allow voters to shape politics as they wish. How Canadian or British Columbian voters would use it remains open to speculation.

The interrelatedness and complexities of society, political culture, and the voting system are manifold. STV has not been applied except in small, rural, traditional, agriculturally based, homogeneous societies. There are no current examples that readily apply to B.C. or Canada. It is also known, from comparative studies, that structural arrangements such as voting systems are less able to influence political behaviour than social and historical factors.[2] For example, Mill and other nineteenth-century proponents of STV thought it would encourage legislators of exceptional talent; what has happened in fact, at least in Ireland, is almost the opposite. Irish politics is so localized that elected representatives are not well qualified for law-making, and parties are prevented from articulating a meaningful national political agenda.[3] In theory, STV has no need of political parties; in practice, where STV exists, political parties operate much as they do anywhere else. Perhaps STV is a necessary, but not a sufficient, condition for change. Even that is too strong; change could come even under SMP, particularly under conditions of minority government. Party discipline need not be enforced; not every vote needs to be treated as a vote of confidence; a cabinet need not treat Parliament and the legislature with contempt; parties, if listened to, would develop policies. Power might be shared. Change is possible, even under SMP. But how likely is it? It would take men and women whose motivation was radically different from the kind that has been around for most of recorded history.

This study suggests that change in the relationship between cabinet and the legislature is likely under STV. Incorporating the findings of previous chapters, this final chapter suggests why this might be so, considers the impact of that on the legislature and political parties, and briefly assesses the probability of actually changing our voting system, given political and historical realities both here and elsewhere.

THE LEGISLATURE REVISITED

CABINETS AND GOVERNING political parties derive their power from unearned majorities, compliments of SMP. Would STV end all unearned majorities? There can be no guarantee. The possibility would be greatest under a province-wide, one-district, list PR system. In addition, list PR systems have a propensity for consensual, coalition-based government after the European model. Such government would attain the goal of involving more meaningfully all political parties represented in the legislature for the development and implementation of public policy. Power would be shared between parties, and cabinets would have shorter lives but greater continuity. All political parties would have a more constructive role, all would have a say, and only in the end would the majority have its way.

There is one substantial drawback to a list PR system – choice for voters is limited, and power resides with parties, not people. Under list PR the power of Parliament is carved up and parcelled out to the parties; it need not reach down to the citizens. Private members of Parliament and the legislatures (those not in cabinet) need independence from parties to make responsible government work, and to be agents for citizens. List PR is able to give more power to legislators, but cannot guarantee that such power will be used in the interest of the people or in a manner responsive to them. For democracy to work within the British parliamentary system requires both an end to unearned majorities, and a weaker party system. The appeal of STV is its potential to limit both unearned majorities and party power. In contrast to list PR, STV gives the voter choice, and through choice, power – the power parties now hold. Unlike list PR, STV allows voters to express a preference among candidates from more than one party. Such voter choice will realign the loyalties of elected representatives.

Attaining a party's nomination means little when the voter has the last word and unrestricted choice. In addition, when voters have real choice, leaders at the top cannot attain majorities unless the voters are so minded. Demands for loyalty from such leaders are more easily resisted, and a representative's first loyalty will more easily stay with the voter. At the bottom end, voter choice ensures that demands for representation of voters' wishes can be registered more effectively. The bond between citizen and representative is strengthened. Putting an end to artificial majorities, and enlarging choice for voters, would allows such a redistribution of power.

To sum up, Canada's governing institutions suffer two defects. The first is the undemocratic distribution of seats – a majority of seats are awarded to a minority of the voters. The second is the unequal distribution of power within Parliament and the legislatures. This inequality has two aspects: first, the ruling party excludes all other parties from participation in governing, and, second, party discipline rules supreme. List PR systems and mixed-member systems address the first, and therefore part of the second defect. But list PR systems fail in the second aspect – party discipline is not eliminated. In fact, because entry to elected office is absolutely controlled by parties, party discipline under list PR and mixed-member systems tends to be ironclad. As a result, the distribution of power within Parliament is not between members, but between parties. List PR's inability to weaken party discipline and restore the link between citizens and their representatives is sufficient reason to reject the mixed-member system that New Zealand recently adopted and some advocate for Canada.

The argument against STV is that it might not absolutely end all unearned majorities. However, STV would certainly diminish their frequency, ending the worst abuses; and it *could* end them altogether, if that was what the voters wanted. Appendix B, Table 2 projects the 1991 B.C. election results over fifteen STV districts. In 1991, SMP translated the NDP's 40.7 percent popular vote into 51 seats, or 68 percent of seats, for a comfortable majority government. Assuming that STV does not alter voting behaviour as it relates to party support, then under STV that same 40.7 percent popular vote would translate into 36 seats, or 48 percent, for a minority government. As Table 2 indicates, both SMP and STV over-reward the largest party, and under-reward the smallest party, but STV less so than SMP. The middle party is slightly over-rewarded by STV, and slightly under-rewarded by SMP. The index of disproportionality for SMP is 8.7 percent, and for STV it is 2.5 percent.[4] While STV comes much closer to true proportionality than SMP, and therefore would have prevented an unearned majority in 1991, it would still have placed the largest party within two seats of a majority government, with only 40.7 percent of the popular vote. The B.C. general elections between 1903 and 1996 inclusive produced eighteen unearned majority governments, and eight of these had a popular vote share of less than 41 percent. Therefore, it seems reasonable to assume STV would have prevented eight unearned majorities since 1903.

Preventing eight unearned majorities out of eighteen is helpful, but far from satisfactory. However, these projections assume political behaviour by voters will not change or in any way be affected by the voting system itself. What if that assumption is wrong? Bogdanor found that voting system and social forces both influence political behaviour.[5] For example, the voting system itself affects voter turnout; it is 8 percent to 11.4 percent greater under PR than under SMP. The reason appears to be that people under PR know their vote counts, and will not be wasted.[6]

Does the voting system affect voting behaviour other than in voter turnout? The political history of B.C. offers strong evidence that institutional structures affect voting behaviour. In B.C., provincial politics is more polarized than federal politics. The study of Cairns and Wong attributes the more pronounced two-party provincial system to voter fears that splitting the right-of-centre vote would allow a CCF/NDP victory. For nearly forty years, Social Credit warned their potential voters that on the provincial level a Liberal or Conservative vote was a vote for the socialists. The voting system justified that warning, and because of the voting system many B.C. voters continue to vote strategically in provincial elections. During the 1996 election, Liberal leader Gordon Campbell issued the same warning, with considerable success. For fear of wasting their vote, or inadvertently electing some undesired party, many voters were herded into supporting the main parties against their wishes. Their choice was constrained.

On the provincial level, the two structural components – the SMP voting system, and a cabinet-dominated legislature – often force voters to forgo their true wishes and vote strategically. For B.C. voters, it is different in federal elections. B.C. voters know from experience that, federally, their vote will not determine the government. Every election night, when the polls close, and before one B.C. vote has been counted, British Columbians turn on their TV to be told who has won. Provincially, the fear of wasting one's vote drives voters into the direction of a two-party system; federally, in every election, except for rare instances of minority government, all B.C. votes are wasted, inasmuch as they do not help form government. Hence, federally, the structural systems do not induce citizens to vote strategically.[7] The lesson is clear: for B.C., changing the voting system would change voting behaviour.

The extent to which people will vote their true wishes, and stop voting strategically, depends on how easy it is for any group of like-minded citizens to elect a representative without the risk of wasting their vote. As noted in Chapter 6, new party formation is related to two factors: district size and the number of politically relevant issues. District size beyond ten is unmanageable for STV, because the ballot paper would have too many names. Also, where district size is too large, STV's advantage of maintaining a local connection between representatives and voters is lost. STV, as proposed in Appendix A, would reduce B.C.'s present seventy-five districts to fifteen, thus significantly enlarging district size. To measure the opportunity this creates for new party formation, we need to know the threshold, that is, the minimum number of votes needed to elect a candidate. The threshold varies with district size. In a 5-seat STV district, one-sixth plus 1 of valid ballot papers cast will elect a candidate. The formula is: votes cast divided by N, add 1, where N equals number of seats for that district plus 1. In Vancouver every 36,030 votes will elect a candidate; or less, if voter turnout is lower than 83 percent. For Victoria, Okanagan, and Peace River respectively, the numbers are: 32,750; 31,606; 19,390.[8] These numbers expressed as a percentage of valid votes are as follows: Vancouver 9 percent; Victoria 14 percent; Okanagan 17 percent; Peace River 25 percent. The rising threshold is a function of the increasingly smaller district size. The average threshold for all STV districts in B.C. is 16.2 percent plus 1 of valid votes cast. In contrast, under SMP, few candidates win with less than 30 percent of valid votes cast. Hence, the number of like-minded voters able to win a seat is considerably smaller under STV than SMP.[9] That alone is an incentive to exercise choice far beyond what is possible under SMP. But the real benefit of STV is evident when one considers the probability of wasting one's vote under either system. As Table 2 indicates, the wasted vote drops from 55.35 percent under SMP to 16.2 percent, or less, under STV. Both the lower threshold and the reduced probability of wasting one's vote will alter voting behaviour.

In addition, the second factor in new party formation relates to the number of non-aligned, politically relevant issues. Would a change in the voting system allow issues that are now suppressed to come to the surface? STV is uniquely designed to represent interests, opinions, and political beliefs; in contrast, SMP represents territory. As noted above, in this respect SMP is out of step with the times. Increasingly, people's interests are not bound to any particular geographical place. The main provincial political issues are unrelated to where one lives within the province. SMP suppresses policy choices that cross district boundaries, and restricts choice for voters even on issues peculiar to a district, because voters must express preferences on any number of issues through one vote for one person. It seems highly probable that SMP frustrates the full diversity of issues present in our society from finding expression in our political choices on election day. When structural conditions ensure that votes for smaller parties and less popular issues are not wasted, such parties and issues will attract more votes. Again, the Cairns/Wong study shows that the B.C. electorate will choose a more diverse range of issues, and hence render B.C. politics less polarized, provided the threat of manufactured government majorities is removed.[10]

There are two reasons why STV is likely not just to diminish the frequency of unearned majorities but perhaps to prevent them completely. First, as noted, the threshold is much lower, and fewer votes are wasted. Second, if given an opportunity, issues will assume a greater salience, and their diversity will be of greater relevance when citizens cast their vote. The issues are present in our society; we need a structure, such as STV, that will allow them to surface within the legislative process. If any group in Vancouver numbering 9 percent of the voters can secure a seat, the special interest groups will successfully capitalize on that opportunity. When people have more than one vote, they'll reserve lower ballot preferences for what could be deemed fringe candidates. A longtime Vancouver councillor, Harry Rankin, left-wing and extreme in most of his views, virtually always topped the polls when running for one of ten council seats, but was twice unsuccessful as mayoralty candidate. If voters are given a chance to register a preference over a range of issues, candidates like Rankin, environmentalists, and other special-interest groups will get elected under STV.

Comparative studies show that PR systems respond quickly to social changes. In Europe, the Greens have been inside the doors of the legislature for over twenty years. In B.C., they crash the doors of the legislature, clog the courts at legal-aid expense, and eventually are trundled off to jail. SMP excludes environmentalists, PR includes them. This vividly illustrates SMP's structural incapacity to deliver government in a manner responsive to the people. STV is transparent; it reflects accurately the current concerns of the people, and responds quickly to changing social trends. People get what they want. If, as is the case in Ireland, voters expect their MP to primarily deliver local and personal benefits, then the system will respond to that need. If the focus shifts to law-making and public policy issues, STV will force the system to respond. New issues will be addressed through political channels, including the legislature; and the response will be quick.

A combination of low threshold and diversity of interests can break the strength of political parties; and the special interest groups are likely to initiate the process. This is to be welcomed, not because every special interest group should have their way, but because they should have a say – not outside on the steps of the legislature, but inside. It may appear that STV is designed to give special status and undue prominence to minorities and special interest groups. In fact, the opposite is true. STV will give them clout, but only in proportion to their numbers. The current system allows special interests access to the levers of power out of proportion to their numbers. STV will make it easier for minorities, such as Aboriginal citizens, to gain legislative representation, but not more than their percentage of the population warrants. Minorities would have less access to backroom deal-making than they do now. During the ten years of constitutional debates following the patriation of 1982, both Aboriginals and representatives of women's issues sat at the constitutional table along with premiers and the prime minister. Recently, the B.C. government has come under severe criticism for negotiating land-claims settlements behind closed doors. Minorities, special interests and fringe parties, such as Christian Heritage, Natural Law, and Libertarians, should be given their rightful, proportionate place. If not, they are either suppressed or given favoured treatment. Both are unhealthy. Women's groups lobby for PR, but from a tactical point of view it is a mistake, as some have recognized.[11]

Suppose the combined force of a lower threshold and the diversity of issues has resulted in the necessary structural changes and their intended effect. STV is in. Unearned legislative majorities are no more. The power of parties is diminished. Voters can use their ballot paper to express an opinion across a greater range of issues by means of preference voting. MLA careers depend more on voters than parties. What effect will this have on the composition and functioning of the legislature? The details depend on particular circumstances, but comparative studies, based on long experience with PR in countries not much different from ours, suggest some general changes can be predicted with considerable confidence.

First, the composition of the legislature will be more descriptively representative. It will be a microcosmic picture, far more exact than what SMP can produce. Aboriginals, women, ethnics, racial minorities, and small political parties will be represented to the extent voters want them to be represented. It will happen without the coercion which taints affirmative-action gerrymandering when imposed on society by politicians, the courts, or boundary commissions.

Second, a wider range of ideas, interests, and policy proposals will make it to the floor of the legislature. Voter choice will largely prevent legislative majorities that can dictate the agenda, and voter choice will engender greater responsiveness from the politicians, making government more transparent to changing social conditions and concerns.

Third, as in most European democracies, power will be shared, lasting coalitions will be formed. SMP invites coalitions of short duration, because a small shift in popular support translates into large shifts in the legislature. STV, like all voting systems of high proportionality, does not provide an incentive to force quick elections for political gain. STV removes the electoral advantage of bringing a government down. The premier will consult, and not every bill, budget, or ministerial estimate will enjoy automatic approval. The legislature would have the power to meaningfully hold government responsible; responsible government could be practised. The legislature would help shape public policy; legislators would have a legislative function.[12] Cabinets would change frequently, but the continuity of their membership, and MLAs who stay beyond their training period, would render public policy less open to short-term, politically driven goals, and more receptive to the long-term public interest. Our adversarial, confrontational political process would be replaced by a more cooperative, consultative, consensual style.[13] Good manners would start as early as the campaign trail. The need to attract second-place support from voters whose first preference is for an opponent is a powerful incentive to show considerable civility to that opponent. It might even become accepted that persons can differ on public policy issues without being deemed guilty of bad faith, lying, deceit, or high treason. Good manners – the hallmark of a civilized society – might grace the legislature, and teachers would take their students into the public galleries without shame.[14]

Changing the voting system cannot guarantee such results, but it does provide opportunity for new patterns of behaviour. Unbending party discipline will always be a temptation. It is an instrument of control that leads to power. Governing demands groupings of some kind in the legislature. Not all party discipline and coalition-building is subversive. Party discipline is destructive when it robs representatives of their independence. Loose, shifting, freely entered coalitions are possible only if legislators have independence. To achieve such independence, choice for voters is essential. That alone is capable of delivering the independence needed for responsible government based on the British parliamentary model. Legislators who are free from control by party or cabinet are also the prerequisite to satisfy Pitkin's demand for government "in a manner responsive" to the voters. The oligopolistic patterns of power must give way to the self-correcting mechanism of an open market, free of constraints. Society must assert its preeminence over government. The structure must allow voters' wishes to be heard. STV's low threshold and high transparency, in a dynamic society with a diversity of issues, will either make existing parties more responsive and diverse, or lead to more parties. In either case, the legislature will be fundamentally changed in composition, operation, and distribution of power. Government will connect to people, citizens will become participants, because their representatives speak for them, and Pitkin, J.S. Mill, and Aristotle will smile their approval. The need for direct democracy measures and parliamentary reforms will be diminished.

WOULD TURKEYS VOTE FOR AN EARLY THANKSGIVING?[15]

WHAT ARE THE possibilities of actually changing our voting system? UBC professor Alan Cairns starts his influential critique of SMP with the warning that in Canada any suggestion of alternatives is "a fruitless exercise."[16] Cairns did not feel obliged to heed his own advice; therefore, he won't take it ill if others do likewise. William Irvine, a proponent of electoral reform, wrote in 1985 that "Election results in Canada are usually accepted, if only because few Canadians bother to think that the results could have been other than what they were."[17] Realistically, voting reform will not happen for some time, but pointing the way to a better social order is never fruitless.

Technically, changing the system is entirely within the legislature's jurisdiction. As noted above, the Constitution Act is regularly amended by the legislature. The difficulty is not jurisdictional but political. Under majority governments, the legislature is impotent to act except on instruction of the government. No majority government is likely to destroy the mechanism by which they obtained their majority. Until we have meaningful initiative legislation, the only persons who can change the electoral system are those who benefit from not changing it. SMP, universal suffrage, and the resulting strength of mass political parties have eroded the independence of political representatives, weakening Parliament and the legislatures. These developments have served the interests of political parties. Within our present system there is no incentive for parties to serve the public interest in electoral and parliamentary reform, particularly when serving the public interest entails political suicide. Even the smaller and opposition parties do not want the system changed. While in opposition, political leaders sometimes express a fondness for electoral reform, but as Kristianson has observed, their enthusiasm is quickly dampened when they are in power.[18] An example of such political opportunism is W.A.C. Bennett's abandonment of the alternative vote after it won him government in the 1952 and 1953 B.C. elections.[19] Most smaller parties believe that the unfairness that works against them while out of power is a guarantee that someday they will have power.[20]

Minority governments open the possibility of change; but as noted above, SMP provides an incentive to end coalitions quickly for political gain; thus the idea of change is seldom seriously explored. Under a minority government the political actors expect the system to return to normal soon, and to the benefit of their own party. Neither does a minority situation weaken a party's desire for self-preservation. SMP favours parties, not people. Under SMP parties can win big. Just as turkeys will not express fondness for an early Thanksgiving, so parties will not voluntarily withdraw from a system that offers them potentially

139

unlimited power. STV has the potential to undermine the unlimited power of parties,[21] and therefore our history shows resistance to STV from political organizations. Minority governments, which enforce compromise between parties, might have a positive effect if it were illustrated that cooperation and decision-making by consensus work as well in peacetime as they do in wartime. Successful and sustained minorities would have a salutary psychological effect, but fundamental change must come from the people; it will not come from parties and party activists.

For example, the report of the New Zealand Royal Commission on the Electoral System recommends against STV, in part because it might weaken the cohesiveness of parties by promoting intra-party competition. The report does not sufficiently consider the positive results that flow from greater independence for elected representatives, particularly on the operation of the legislature. Mill's enthusiasm for STV was primarily based on its promise of independence for MPs, which alone can preserve the essence of representative government. Had the New Zealand Commission given greater weight to this aspect of the matter, its recommendation might have been different. One explanation for this omission is that New Zealand's political culture has not developed a history of party discipline as severe as Canada's.[22]

If hope for electoral reform rests with the people, where is the popular demand for electoral reform? Unfortunately, most people are not interested, and are appallingly ignorant. Every boundaries commission receives strong emotional appeals about the absolute importance of maintaining and not diluting the present local representation, and that access to one's own local member is of the greatest importance and among the highest of all political goods. It is difficult to take such requests seriously when in fact votes are much more often cast for the party than for the local candidate. I agree with Henry Angus, who, when confronted with such appeals while travelling the province of B.C. as a commissioner, concluded that in an impersonal, unresponsive system, where all the questions of real importance are decided once every four years on election night by a minority of the population, the only way it remains possible for the individual voter to have an effect is to ensure that the local representative is around to help people, on a personal level. Angus concluded the people know their local member has no power to affect public policy; therefore, the only remaining useful function for MLAs, relative to their voters, is the ombudsman's role, fighting bureaucratic red tape.[23] The role of MLAs outside cabinet is largely restricted to personal and constituency-based service, and since the people know that, it is not surprising that everyone wants to have their own MLA close by. Boundary commissions that pander to such attitudes, concentrating on what happens on the way to the legislature but stopping short at its door, prevent the legislature coming into its own. If they were to study what happens inside the legislature, their comments about the essence of representation would be less influenced by the predictable pleadings heard on the road. It is a vicious cycle: legislators have no legislative role, so people plead for a glorified ombudsman, and compliance with such requests reinforces the restriction on the legislators' role. To break the cycle, people must be given choice. STV allows people to decide how important locally based interests are. Then we will know if voters really prefer a politician who shares their neighbourhood to one who shares their political views. Resistance to electoral reform is based on misunderstanding, even ignorance.

The ignorance is perpetuated by our educational system. An important text, widely used from its publication in 1949 to this day, instructs young Canadians about our form of government as follows:

> The first and most important characteristic of Canadian government is that it is a democracy, a government controlled directly or indirectly by the greater part of the people. The second characteristic of Canadian government is that it is founded on the representation of the great bulk of the people.[24]

Canadian government is neither controlled by nor representative of the majority, let alone the great bulk of the people. Lest we think such comfortable myths are the product of the more complacent, deferential, postwar era, a recent book for children by the wife of a former prime minister explains how Canada's democracy works:

> Democracy is one way for a group of people to make decisions on what is best for the largest number of them – called the majority ... If the people do not agree with the decision made by their elected representatives, they can tell them so. The majority (50 percent of the voters plus one) can vote any elected representative out of his or her job at any election.[25]

We believe this, because we have been taught to believe it. McTeer describes democracy, but not the kind Canada practises. The words of McTeer ring true until we force ourselves to consider their real meaning, and understand the actual workings of our governmental system. Even the academic community is guilty of placing careless inaccuracies before our school children. Goddard's study of the B.C. government notes W.A.C. Bennett's near-dictatorial control of the legislature, and then justifies it because "Their [the people's] will for the past two decades has supported the Social Credit Party and the leadership of Premier Bennett."[26] Bennett's majorities were manufactured by SMP; they were not an expression of the will of the people. But for writing this, Goddard was awarded his Ph.D. Change must start with awareness-raising, from the streets to the universities. Until there is greater awareness, the people will not instigate electoral reform.

There are some glimmers of hope. For example, demands for employment equity are based on the principle that a typical workplace should reflect the demographic diversity of society. If, by force of law, the workplace is made more representative, how long can the legislature be left unrepresentative? Society is increasingly multicultural. The Charter of Rights and Freedoms has induced Canadians to think of themselves as citizens who possess rights; the Meech Lake process convinced Canadians that political leaders and parties do not represent them; and the 1992 Charlottetown Accord referendum gave the people a taste for exercising the sovereignty they possess. The referendum was an attempt to avoid the Meech Lake process. Peter Russell notes that the excessive secrecy of the Meech Lake round engendered a loss of faith in the representative capacity of the Canadian legislatures. He writes, "...the Meech Lake experience may well have made reform of executive/government party domination of the legislature the most popular constitutional cause of the future."[27] One can only hope Russell is correct.

Others see hope in post-modernism's rejection of the politics of confrontation.[28] Perhaps these social trends, together with the desire for gender equity, the campaign for inclusion of Aboriginals, and the greater diversity of interests in evidence among all citizens, are harbingers of public attitudes more open to electoral reform. The Lortie Commission found:

> Our attitudinal survey showed that many Canadians want the electoral process to be made more accessible to the non-traditional parties, so that voters have a broader choice in the selection of their elected representatives.[29]

Sociologist Reginald Bibby remarks in the conclusion of his influential book on current social trends in Canada:

> The confrontational politics that have characterized our federal and provincial governments are increasingly out of touch with where the world is going. Tired by wars and tension that yield few winners, more and

more people in this country and elsewhere are recognizing the need to choose peace and cooperation, then work to bring them about ...[30]

Such positive trends would receive enormous stimulus from some form of PR. If we wish to be a country that regards diversity as an asset, respects differences, and encourages the mosaic of cultures, our governmental structures must be more flexible and responsive.

STV, NATIONAL UNITY, AND LEADERSHIP
CANADA HAS TWO pressing public policy issues – national unity and massive government debt. At the time of writing, 30 percent of Canadians think Canada will break apart, while in fact the probability of this happening is even greater. As to the national debt, it currently consumes 38 cents of every dollar the federal government takes in as revenue. STV might have prevented both issues from reaching a point of crisis.

It is inconceivable that Canada, which by any measure is one of the most favoured countries on earth, should be unable to accommodate its linguistic and regional diversity. Countries such as Belgium, Switzerland, and South Africa have successfully incorporated differences more numerous and more pronounced than Canada's. These countries have PR. How would PR affect our national unity issue? First, under STV, or any PR system, the separatist premier, Parizeau, would not have received a majority government from a minority of the votes. Lucien Bouchard would not have been leader of Her Majesty's Loyal Opposition. Both men used the considerable power, influence, and prestige of their office to promote separatism. In addition, under SMP Quebec's nationalists are either in complete control of government or entirely excluded. No system that can effectively exclude 40 percent of the population is satisfactory. Significant minorities should neither be excluded nor given total control.

Second, SMP exacerbates Canada's traditional linguistic, cultural, and regional divides. For example, during the Trudeau years, the federal Liberals did not elect anyone west of Winnipeg, even though the Liberal vote share there was frequently not less than 20 percent. Such votes are wasted. The Progressive Conservatives suffered similar results in Quebec. In 1993 the Reform Party of Canada received only slightly more votes in Ontario than in B.C. and Alberta combined. The nearly one million Ontario votes obtained one seat, while B.C. and Alberta yielded 51 seats. Such skewed results prevent national parties from performing the bridging and brokerage function that would help heal differences, engender understanding, and build national unity. The Reform Party of Canada is seen as a regional party, unable to articulate national interests or attract national support. Worse, the party

143

thinks of itself that way. Parties invest resources and build where their strengths are. Thus our political structure reinforces the isolation of the two solitudes. Canada's problems are partly of our own making. SMP works reasonably well in a homogeneous society with a two-party system and few cleavages or issues. Where all these are lacking, PR works best. Canada has precisely the wrong voting system.

Third, under SMP those who have get more, and those who do not have lose the little they have. That is to say, in a cabinet-dominated Parliament, and a confederation consisting of provinces with widely divergent populations, the most densely populated provinces are king, master, and tyrant. Those provinces will control cabinet, and hence, the House of Commons. Provinces with smaller numbers are prevented, under the rules of the game, from playing. Their participation is window-dressing to preserve the appearance of democracy. All decisions of importance are made by those who can deliver the numbers. Minorities don't count. During the Trudeau years the West voted Progressive Conservative. The West's representatives watched from the opposition benches, powerless, as Trudeau pillaged $60 billion worth of resources from Western Canada under the National Energy Program. Finally, in 1984 the West's wilderness experience ended when Mulroney's Progressive Conservative sweep rivalled John Diefenbaker's landslide victory of 1958. Expectations ran high. At last the West would be heard, historical wrongs righted, and regional animosities healed. Little changed. When the Progressive Conservatives from the West took their seats on the government side at last, they were lost among the Central Canada crowd. Warming a government back bench yields no more power than haranguing the government from an opposition front bench. In 1984, after years of frustration, the West had merely traded ineffectual opposition seats for equally ineffectual government backbench seats. In a cabinet-dominated Parliament, sharing seats in the government benches brings no more power than being in opposition. It may even reduce power, because party discipline ensures quiet acquiesence. After the next federal election B.C. will have an additional two seats. But what difference will it make? Thirty-four times zero is still zero. The decisions of importance will always gravitate towards the most populous regions. It is an inevitable function of our system.

To correct the imbalances that our voting system visits on the House of Commons, and to strengthen the federation through regional participation, Western Canada has put forward numerous proposals for Senate reform, a project to create a House of Provinces, and other suggestions for constitutional innovations, only to meet outright rejection by Central Canada. The West should consider accepting the abolition of the Senate in return for House of Commons elections by STV. It would guarantee that the minority populations of the Western provinces will have power in proportion to their numbers.

It must not be just any form of PR. STV alone provides the independence necessary for MPs to place their voters above party interests. Within the Canadian federation, the list PR and mixed-member systems would provide representation only marginally more responsive to regional and minority needs than SMP. Parties would continue to be instruments for the most populous regions.

STV has the potential to yield maximum accountability, and to ensure that regional voices can be heard. For that reason it holds promise not only for national unity but also for other significant public policy issues. Canada's debt has been allowed to grow, largely for short-term political gain. A similar, structurally induced lack of public responsibility has depleted fish stocks and other natural resources. Our governments are out of control, literally. No one looks after the public interest. STV holds the promise that through choice for voters, shared power, and accountability, citizenship will be an enlarged experience for Canadians. Unless our citizens are enlisted, mobilized, and equipped, policies that are intended to deal with our problems of national unity, debt, environmental protection, and much else, will not be informed by the criteria of good stewardship. Organizations, groups, and collectivities have a propensity to become self-serving, to blunt the sense of responsibility that is evident at the personal level. Organized collectivities shield the human conscience, and negate personal responsibility. Think of what an army organization does to people. Army training starts by destroying whatever is individual, because individuality undermines the unthinking, unquestioning herd instinct necessary to get one person to kill another. To be human is to be social; organizations are inevitable and necessary. But they can be shaped to help people keep their ideals and their sense of responsibility. In politics, organizations can foster what is highest and best in a people's concept of citizenship, and help them develop toward that goal.

It is said that Canada today lacks strong leadership. If this expresses a fond wish for a person who will bestride the political stage like a colossus and single-handedly impose solutions, it is a dangerously misguided sentiment. We need a different model of leadership. Switzerland's president is appointed by the cantons in turn, to a one-year term. Such presidents function like chairmen of boards of directors. For one year they are the first among equals. They lack both the time and the power to develop a personality cult. Money's corrupting influence is not felt, since business does not invest in temporary team-coaches. Money flows wherever power concentrates. U.S. Congressmen now spend 50 percent of their time in fundraising. The Lortie

Commission spent $19 million to produce numerous recommendations to effect financial accountability in politics. The simplest, most direct means of keeping money from tainting the political process is to diffuse power. Swiss presidents do not engage in expensive leadership contests or extensive election campaigns masterminded by consultants and experts in manipulating information and moulding public opinion through multimillion dollar advertising blitzes. Our style of leadership is weak because it invests too much in the few, and not enough in the many.

Increasingly, Canadian leadership contests take on the dimensions and features of American presidential elections. Our prime ministers, enjoying direct access to the people through television, assume presidential roles without the restraining influence of Congress. It is a recipe to subvert the rule of law. The human desire to elevate one strong leader to the pinnacle of power is a form of hero-worship. It belongs in a former time of paternalism, when the unwashed masses were deemed incapable of self-rule. Hero-worship is a primitive instinct, absolving people of personal responsibility for their fate. *Citizens* do not harbour impossible expectations from a single, superhuman, Führer figure. They expect that the wellspring of a civilized social order lies deep within every human breast. Hope lies not in one person, but in the inclusion of all persons.

In the current debate about national unity, proponents of the status quo often assert that Canada is among the most decentralized of all federal systems. That is a myth that must be debunked. Most tax dollars flow through Ottawa. Our voting system concentrates power at the top. Canadian prime ministers appoint cabinets, parliamentary secretaries, the Supreme Court, the Senate, boards of directors of Crown corporations, the Bank of Canada, and numerous regulatory agencies and public institutions. Canada is run out of the prime minister's office, away from the scrutiny of Parliament. Not only Parliament, but all positions of importance are under the full control of the prime minister. As the Swiss experience shows, it need not be thus. The suggestion that the Canadian federation is among the most decentralized of all is simply not true.

Our voting system concentrates power. STV diffuses power. The hidden assumptions, values, and goals of the one are diametrically opposed to the openly expressed aims of the other. SMP does not lead to democracy as self-rule; it does not equip citizens with the tools of self-government. It is out of touch with the times. STV fulfils better than any other voting system the three requirements of democracy: accurate representation, maximum choice for voters, and diffused power.

NEW ZEALAND'S MMP

ANY ATTEMPTS TO change Canada's voting system will be influenced by the New Zealand experience. Both are Commonwealth countries that inherited the British voting system. In both countries respect for politicians reached an all-time low during the 1980s. In both countries voters express revulsion at the adversarial nature of their politics, and yearn for a politics of cooperation, negotiation, and compromise. However, whereas during the last decade Canada focused its energy on constitutional reforms, particularly to maintain national unity in the face of Quebec separatism, New Zealand was forced to deal with economic restructuring. The economic upheaval of the 1980s precipitated social and political changes, including a change in the voting system. As always, crisis breeds opportunities for new beginnings.

New Zealand's switch from SMP to a German-style mixed-member proportional (MMP) system was popularly endorsed in two referenda. The first, held in 1992, established that 85 percent of participants favoured changing the voting system, and the second, held in 1993, selected MMP with 54 percent of support.

In the general election held on 12 October 1996, New Zealand inaugurated its new system. Each voter has two ballots. The first is to select their favourite local-riding candidate, the second to indicate support for the party the voter deems most capable of governing the country. To ensure proportionality, half the parliamentary seats are filled with local-riding MPs, and half with list MPs. The allocation of list MPs between parties is such that a party's total parliamentary seat share will be equal to that party's vote share. For example, if a party obtains a 25 percent vote share on the second ballot, but only 20 percent seat share from the first ballot, that party will receive an additional 5 percent seat share from the list MPs. These MPs will be drawn from that party's list in the order in which they are listed. Unlike many list PR systems, New Zealand's MMP does not allow voters to express a preference among the candidates on a party's list. This seems an unfortunate and unnecessary restriction on choice for voters. The politicians inserted this provision to protect their party's interests prior to the 1993 referendum.

Under New Zealand's MMP, voters need not cast both votes, and disqualifying one vote does not disqualify the other. Voters may select a local candidate from one party and their choice for government from another. The two votes are for different purposes, and are counted differently. Votes for local candidates are counted using SMP, hence the majority of those votes will be wasted. But the second, the government vote, is counted on a proportional basis, and the number of votes in this category that are wasted depends on how many votes are cast for parties that do not meet the threshold.

To prevent splinter parties, a political party must win at least 5 percent of the party vote (the second vote), or win at least one local riding seat (the first vote) to receive any allocation of the proportional seats in Parliament. Votes for parties that do not meet the threshold are discarded, therefore parties that cross the threshold may receive a slightly higher percentage of all seats in Parliament than they would be entitled to under strict proportionality.

In recognition of their special interests, New Zealand's aboriginal community, the Maori, are designated their own seats, as they have been since 1867. Maori citizens choose to be enrolled on the Maori voters' list or on the general voters' list at each five-year census. Following each census the number of Maori seats and their riding boundaries are established in proportion to the number of voters on the Maori voters' list. Voters on the Maori list cast their first ballot for the Maori candidates in the riding in which they live, and their second ballot along with all voters on the general voters' list.

This important provision means the Maori need not become politically ghettoized, for the two-vote feature gives mainstream parties an incentive to compete for the Maori's second, or party votes. Also, if the Maori choose to join the general voters' list, they can eliminate the special Maori seats. Their destiny is largely in their own hands, as it should be. Maori support for MMP in the 1993 referendum was 2–1, considerably stronger than in the population overall. In the 1994 preparations for the new system, Maori registered in record numbers, nearly doubling their seat share from 4 percent to 7.7 percent. Perhaps, in a paradoxical fashion, these group rights may lead to a fuller integration of the Maori into New Zealand politics since proportional representation provides for equal and effective participation of all minorities.

The Electoral Act of 1993 requires a parliamentary select committee to begin reviewing the MMP system in the year 2000 and to report to parliament by mid-2002. The committee must also consider whether there should be a further referendum on changes to the electoral system.

What made New Zealand citizens change their voting system? Prior to 1978 New Zealand enjoyed a stable two-party system, with the two major parties, Labour and National, alternating government between them. The country's poor economic performance in the following years challenged this stability. Neither Labour nor National seemed able to find the necessary economic solutions. The two-party system suffered breakdown. In the elections of 1978, 1981 and 1984 third parties won 20 percent of the total vote. Under SMP that 20 percent was virtually without representation. In addition, in both 1978 and 1981 the Labour opposition gained the most votes overall, but fewer seats than the governing National. On such occasions, when the party with the most votes loses the election, the unfairness of SMP is cast in stark relief. For a minority to rule a majority is intrinsically undemocratic.

The movement for electoral reform gained sympathy, particularly within Labour party ranks. Labour won government in 1984 on the promise of wide-ranging institutional reform including a royal commission on electoral reform. The royal commission was appointed in 1985, and unlike its Canadian equivalent appointed by Prime Minister Mulroney a few years later, it was given sweeping terms of reference. The following year it produced a thorough report recommending MMP, but also a referendum allowing citizens to express a preference between voting systems.

Their report, *Towards a Better Democracy*, precipitated public debate on electoral reform, focusing on three concerns. First, the failure of parties in power to deliver on pre-election promises. For instance, economic necessity forced Labour to abandon its manifesto once in power. Reforms seemed to be pushed through without public debate and consultation. Secondly, people questioned the legitimacy of governments elected by a minority. How can government be representative and responsive when 60 percent of the people have voted against its leader, party, and platform? The economic crises precipitated a crisis of confidence in the governing institutions. A public opinion poll measuring confidence and trust in politicians showed 32 percent support in 1975. By 1992, a similar poll registered merely 4 percent support. Third, public discontent focused on the adversarial nature of the Westminster model of parliamentary democracy. Reform of the voting system was seen as essential to introducing a different political culture. A culture of cooperation, consensus, and coalition, instead of unproductive confrontation in a cabinet-dominated parliament. The Hon. Justice John Wallace, chairman of the 1985 royal commission that recommended MMP, in urging acceptance for changing the voting system, wrote in the NZ Herald on the eve of the 1992 referendum:

> There is a strong argument that New Zealand would benefit from increased consultation and negotiation in government under a system where at least half of the voters' representatives in Parliament have to be convinced of the desirability of any given policy. A change to MMP should help reduce our confrontational approach to politics.

A majority of both Labour and National MPs opposed electoral reform. However, public support was growing, and the Royal Commission report had generated expectations. Labour postponed a decision by referring the matter for further study to a select committee. The select committee reported in 1988, and, reflecting the views of most politicians in both caucuses, dutifully rejected MMP, proposing a more limited adjustment.

While the politicians dithered, public opinion for electoral reform grew consistently. In response, the 1990 election platform of both Labour and National contained the promise of a referendum on electoral reform. Following the election, National honoured its commitment. The 1992 referendum was preceded by an effective and extensive public information program conducted by an independent electoral referendum panel. The information program was strictly neutral, but highly educative. The debate was joined by academics, journalists, and politicians. The Electoral Reform Coalition, an umbrella organization of citizens' groups formed after the 1986 royal commission report, backed change and supported MMP. The Electoral Reform Coalition produced an impressive amount of research showing the advantages of a political culture based on consensus. Included in this research was documentation showing improve credit ratings, per capita gross national product, and average annual economic growth rates for parliamentary democracies using PR, as opposed to those using SMP. In spite of considerable public participation, just one month before the referendum date 64 percent of those polled acknowledged not knowing enough about the various voting systems to express a preference.

Opposition to change and arguments for maintaining SMP came primarily from politicians and party activists from within the two major parties. Organized under the name "Campaign for First-Past-the-Post," they warned against the weaknesses of coalition governments, the possibility that minor parties might have undue influence, the evils of backroom deal-making, and the confusion that can arise from not knowing which party is responsible for broken promises or shifts in policy. But public opinion could not be reversed. In eight polls between October 1991 and August 1992, support for change ranged from 51 to 62 percent. That spokespersons for the major parties opposed change may well have solidified support for change. These were the same persons that could be blamed for the country's economic and political troubles, and to a cynical electorate their efforts seemed self-serving.

After the referendum, the government struck a select committee, which decided the threshold, the total number of seats, how many would be elected from lists, and whether voters would be allowed to rank the candidates on such lists (they are not). Most important, it decided to hold a binding referendum at the next general election in which citizens could make a final decision. That referendum confirmed support for MMP with a 54–46 margin. Thus, 100 years after New Zealand was the first nation to enfranchise women, it again made electoral history.

150

The New Zealand experience shows how parties tend to resist a change to proportional representation. Since 1911, eight private member's bills sponsoring PR had been introduced unsuccessfully. Three times, in 1912, 1924, and 1928, parties elected on the promise of electoral change had conveniently forgotten their promise after winning government. This time a very thorough royal commission report, profound economic and social restructuring, an extensive public information campaign, persuasive analysis, determined grassroots advocacy, and above all the tradition of fair play triumphed over vested political party interests. New Zealand demonstrates that the iron law of political self-preservation, whereby parties are unlikely to undo the mechanism by which they attained the pinnacle of success, can be broken. It provides comfort to those whose idealism is often shattered in the world of real politics.

THE BRITISH EXPERIENCE

NOTHING WOULD ASSIST electoral change in Canada so much as a similar change in England. Canadians still regard Westminster as the mother of parliaments. There is no Canadian institution more British than our Parliament and provincial legislatures. Within these institutions, reliance on the British model is as strong today as it was at Confederation in 1867. The change in New Zealand is significant, but a change in England would be decisive.

What are the possibilities for electoral reform in Britain? PR is not foreign to Great Britain. Northern Ireland uses STV for its local and European elections, and a list PR system for the Forum elections. The Republic of Ireland has used STV continuously since 1921. In Britain the Liberal-Democrats, as the third party, would lose the most under SMP, and therefore have the most to gain from reform. In 1992 they received 20 seats, but under STV would have received 102. They zealously support STV.

After nearly two decades of Conservative rule made possible by a centre and centre-left split between Labour and the Liberal-Democrats, Labour's leader Tony Blair seems open to establishing a working relationship with the Liberal-Democrats, if not a formal coalition. The price is the Liberal-Democrats' demand for proportional representation. Although the polls suggest Labour is poised to win government from John Major's Conservatives without the aid of the Liberal-Democrats, compelling reasons for seeking an alliance remain. Mid-term polls are no reliable indication of the next election's results. Also, Labour's commitment to far-ranging constitutional proposals will require strong parliamentary support. The Labour government of 1964–70 made two unsuccessful attempts at reforming the House of Lords, and the two attempts by Labour between 1974 and 1979 to set up assemblies for

Scotland and Wales also failed. If Blair is to succeed where others failed, he may need the Liberal-Democrats. And finally, Tony Blair's ambitions reach beyond a one-term Labour government. A united opposition against the Conservatives is the only hope for continued electoral success of the left.

Today, in mid-1996, there are indications that Blair, though personally unconvinced of the merits of PR, is willing to endorse the alternative vote. Proponents of PR interpret this as a promising first step towards full PR. Officially, Labour is still committed to SMP for the House of Commons, but it has adopted PR for elections to the European Parliament, any new Scottish Parliament, and possibly for Wales. In addition, Blair has consistently supported a promise first made by his predecessor, John Smith, that Labour will allow a referendum on electoral reform. Much will depend on the results of the next election, but for the first time the major opposition party is committed to some change.

Additional pressure for electoral change comes from Britain's membership in the European Union, by which it is bound to the terms of the Treaty of Rome. The Treaty of Rome requires uniform electoral procedures. The unfairness of Britain's voting system, compared to those of its European partners, was particularly evident in the 1989 European elections, when the two million British citizens who voted Green were effectively disenfranchised. While receiving 15 percent of the vote – the largest Green vote in all of Europe – the British Greens won no seats in the Strasbourg parliament. Just as SMP fails to represent the full diversity of British political opinion, so it also fails to reflect the plurality of modern society. The 1992 election elected only sixty women and six black persons out of a total of 651 MPs. This is in stark contrast to most parliamentary democracies on the European continent, where PR ensures fair representation of women and visible minorities.

In Britain, unlike Canada, the movement for reform of the voting system enjoys popular support, even public agitation. For example, Charter 88, a non-partisan lobby and political activist group has the support of 60,000 signatories. Its objective is to attain far-ranging constitutional reforms, including PR. Its methods are public education, youth mobilization, and staged public events to highlight democratic abuses. In 1991 the Joseph Rowntree Reform Trust–commissioned MORI survey found 50 percent of respondents in favour of PR, and 20 percent against. A similar survey four years later found a slight drop, with 46 percent in favour, and 21 percent against. In 1991 support for PR among Labour voters was 53 percent, with only 18 percent opposed. In November 1990, the Labour party formed its working group on electoral reform. With Prof. Raymond Plant as chair, eighteen academics, politicians, and party members produced an extensive report, which leaned toward recommending the mixed-member, German system. That report prompted Labour's promise to hold a referendum on electoral reform.

In addition to citizens' activist groups, such as the Voting Reform Group – launched in 1995 with the promise to present the next parliament with a petition of six million names demanding fair voting – more venerable organizations such as the Electoral Reform Society of Great Britain continue to promote PR through education and research. The Electoral Reform Society has been in existence for over one hundred years, is well funded, supports STV, and has produced a wealth of research documentation. Yet in spite of these efforts, the country of Thomas Hare, the inventor of STV, and J.S. Mill, its ardent supporter, remains locked in its old traditional ways. Why?

Peter Mair observes that for most parliamentary democracies the switch to PR accompanied the introduction of universal male suffrage in countries that contained significant minorities – ethnic, linguistic, or religious.[31] Their inclusion in political decision-making and allegiance was necessary for long-term political and social stability. Among these are Belgium, Holland, Switzerland, and, very recently, South Africa. When the franchise was extended in the United Kingdom in the late nineteenth century, no significant groups were excluded in virtue of SMP. The Irish Catholics were sufficiently concentrated geographically to ensure their participation under SMP.

However, Mair notes some significant changes to traditional British social homogeneity. SMP functions best in a society with few divisions and a two-party system of government. During the last two decades a three-party system has emerged in British politics. In the 1950s, and 1960s the combined Conservative and Labour vote ranged from 94 to 89 percent, thus dwarfing the combined minor parties' vote. But the combined Conservative and Labour vote dropped to 80 percent in the 1970s, and 71 percent in the 1980s. Such results show the unfairness of SMP in starker relief. For example, in the 1992 election it took 42,357 votes for each Conservative seat, 42,876 votes for each Labour seat, and 304,183 votes for each Liberal-Democrat seat. The chronic exclusion of the Liberal-Democrat vote may well offend the traditional British regard for fair play. Charter 88's slogan, "One person, one vote, one value" expresses a basic democratic ideal shared by most citizens. How long will voters tolerate the discordance between a three-party electoral system and a two-party parliamentary system?

Electoral reform in Britain is not only motivated by revulsion at the unfairness inherent in SMP; there are also demands for a more participatory form of government. The objective is to change the mechanics of translating votes into seats, but additionally to foster a different political culture. A political culture based on consensus, participation, accountability, a less executive-dominated parliament, and political parties that are instruments of the popular will, not of the state. The goal is a power-sharing democracy and a culture of genuine citizenship.

Electoral reform in Britain depends in the short term on the Labour party's fortunes at the ballot box, and the imperative of an alliance with the Liberal-Democrats. But in the long run, Britain's increasing social fragmentation and pluralism, the need to achieve gender parity, the almost universal distrust of governmental institutions, the growing divide between politicians and their constituents and the accompanying desire for participatory, consultative forms of governing, the pressure from the European Union, and Britain's long list of demands for constitutional reforms all mean that the country is inexorably gravitating towards the kind of citizenship and democracy that can be attained only under proportional representation.

LESSONS FROM CANADIAN HISTORY

IN THE SEARCH for a more responsible order of governing, it is instructive to briefly consider the history of PR in our country. In the present day, occasional appeals to consider PR may be found in the scholarly journals that collect dust in university libraries, but there is little public awareness of the idea. It was not always so. During the early decades of this century, PR enjoyed substantial popular appeal. For example, the substance of the arguments made in this study can be found in a pamphlet that the Proportional Representation Society of Canada published in 1916 in Vancouver.

> ...a popularly elected Representative Assembly ... is the necessary organ for carrying into effect the Will of the People. If any "House" be, for any reason, not truly representative, legislation and the control of government ceases to be in harmony with the Will of the People. Self-government is replaced by an undemocratic and unrepresentative form of "cabinet control", and the "House" becomes merely an assembly for the registration of decisions, arrived at without its deliberative assistance.[32]

Alberta passed enabling legislation permitting cities and municipalities to adopt PR in 1916. B.C. followed in 1917, Saskatchewan and Manitoba in 1920. The thirteen B.C. local councils that switched to STV included: Vancouver, Victoria, West Vancouver, New Westminster, South Vancouver, Port Coquitlam, Mission, and Nelson. Most of these lasted no more than two or three elections. The reasons for abandoning STV included: the alleged complexity of the system, fears that extremists might be elected, and interference from political machines that jealously guarded their interests from the encroachment of too much democracy.

154

> In Victoria...the abolition of the system after a single
> election in 1921 was due to a campaign against it by a
> local paper, which spread the false statement that bal-
> lots were transferred under PR to persons for whom
> those who cast them had not voted.[33]

Complaints about STV's complexity and long delays before results were
known are understandable: this was before the advent of computers.

Winnipeg, Calgary, and Edmonton changed to STV for both city and
provincial elections. Winnipeg changed in 1920 to dispel, successfully,
the bitterness left by the general strike of 1919. For the provincial elections, STV lasted in Edmonton and Calgary until 1956, and in Winnipeg
until 1957, where the Liberals abandoned it for political reasons (which
backfired badly).[34] In most places, enthusiasm for PR weakened after
the early '20s. In 1923, a resolution was passed by the House of
Commons favouring the alternative vote; and a Bill to effect this was
given first reading on 26 May 1925; however, the constitutional crisis
between MacKenzie King and Byng pushed electoral reform into the
background.[35] Resistance from vested interests and fear of extremism
seem to have been the main reasons for PR's fading popular support.

More recently, a faint but renewed interest in PR can be detected.
The motivation comes from two sources. In the late '70s and early '80s
politicians and scholars turned to PR out of concern for national unity.
PR, particularly some form of the mixed system, was seen to be a remedy necessary to preserve national unity.[36] By 1984, the debate about
electoral reform had slowed and the election put a virtual stop to it. The
massive Conservative sweep assured government representation in caucus, cabinet, and Parliament from all regions and in particular, from
both major language groups. In 1984 and 1988, the electoral system
bridged the English/French division, and could no longer be blamed for
contributing to the national unity crisis. This respite proved temporary.

A second source of concern with electoral reform is motivated, not
by the goal of attaining national unity, but by the wish for a fairer representation of groups such as women, Aboriginal communities, and ethnic
minorities.[37] The Charlottetown Accord of 1992 provided for an elected
Senate. Such Senate elections would have allowed provincial and territorial flexibility to provide for gender equity in the composition of the
Senate. Initially, at least three premiers expressed a commitment to
make such provisions, by means of PR. The Accord also called for additional, Aboriginal Senate seats.[38] The Accord did not enjoy approval by
referendum, but it did generate public discussion about electoral
reform. Concern about national unity and group rights will undoubtedly
continue to provoke the debate about a fair and just electoral system,

particularly in view of recent election results, federally in 1993 and in Quebec in 1994, and the court rulings discussed in Chapter 2.

In Canada, enthusiasm for PR could not be sustained beyond the early decades of this century. Twice this century, war of global dimensions broke out in continental Europe. Abroad, Canadian blood drenched the soil that had spawned PR, and at home support for PR understandably vanished. In contrast to the destructive forces unleashed in continental Europe, Britain and the United States seemed to offer a political order of security, stability, and hope to a world gripped by fear of political extremism. To this day, both in the scholarly literature and among the public, PR evokes images of excessive factionalism and dangerous extremism. That image is an undeserved but enduring reality. As Canadians we fear extremism and, therefore, if we give it a thought at all, we fear PR. In contrast, our relationship to the U.S. system of government is not one of fear, but ambivalence. Today, as during so much of our history, we are strangely fascinated by and yet unsure about the dynamic, overwhelming presence of the United States. If our irrational fears of PR do not subside, and the southern continental pull maintains its strength, we will continue to invest energy in direct democracy measures, and keep attempting to graft bits of the congressional onto the parliamentary system, and PR will not grip the popular imagination.

It need not be so. Through the United Empire Loyalists, and through links before them to pre-revolutionary France, our cultural taproots reach back into an older European tradition, inspired by the classical cultures that first conceived of citizenship and democracy. Here in British Columbia, nearing the end of the twentieth century, these impulses may seem particularly faint. But it is precisely here, far out on the edge of the Pacific, in a culture open to new beginnings, that the classical view of democracy might receive new impetus from the infusion of an even older, Oriental tradition. This is a tradition of social order based not on the pursuit of individual happiness through competitive, adversarial relationships, but a social order anchored in tradition and aimed at preserving respect for family and community through relationships founded on co-operation and consensual decision-making. As we open ourselves to the Pacific, the mixture of these ancient cultures may give birth to a politics as different from our present political practices as the Japanese corporate and industrial relations are different from their North American counterparts. Should the ancient Far East and a West formed by the classical and biblical Near East meet on these Pacific shores to shape our political future, governing will be more fully everyone's business, and citizenship will approximate Aristotle's vision, when he wrote:

> The full and complete definition of a citizen is confined
> to those who participate in the governing power.[39]

NOTES

NOTES FOR INTRODUCTION

1   J. Davis, *Popular Politics* (Vancouver: Jack Davis, 1984), 221.

2   Royal Commission on Electoral Reform and Party Financing, *Report,* vol. 1 (Ottawa, Minister of Supply and Services, 1991) 223-24.

3   Our voting system is commonly referred to as the "first-past-the-post" system. Here preference is for the technical term *single member plurality,* because there is no post, or fixed number of votes a candidate must attain to be elected, nor is there a spatial or time sense in which a winning candidate must be first.

4   *Vancouver Sun,* 5 March 1988, polls by Angus Reid and Marktrend.

5   B.C. Civil Liberties Association vs BC (AG) (1988), 24 BCLR (2d) 189 (BCSC).

6   *Vancouver Sun,* 13 September 1994, 1.

7   The issue in Item 1, for the purpose of this paper, concerns the process of decision-making, not the merits of funding abortions. The author's view on abortion is largely pro-life, and on public record as far back as 19 October 1983; see *Richmond Review* of that date.

8   A term used to denote the British parliamentary system, which selects as prime minister or premier the leader of the political party with the largest number of seats, who in turn selects a cabinet from the popularly elected members of the House. Cabinet is said to be responsible to the House in as much it cannot remain in power unless it enjoys the support of a majority of the Members of the House.

9   Peter W. Hogg, *Constitutional Law of Canada*, 2nd ed. (Toronto, Carswell, 1985), 197.

10   Douglas Rae, *Political Consequences of Electoral Laws* (New Haven: Yale University Press, 1967), 74-75; Michael Cassidy, "Fairness and Stability in Canadian Elections: The Case for an Alternative Electoral System" (1992, Ottawa: Parliamentary Centre for Foreign Affairs and Foreign Trade), 3.

11   This is confirmed by many studies. See P.J. Taylor and R.J. Johnston, *Geography of Elections* (New York: Holmes and Meier, 1979). They conclude their study by noting, "If you want maximum choice for voters, then go for STV," 486; Iain McLean, "Forms of Representation and Systems of Voting" in David Held, ed., *Political Theory Today* (Cambridge: Polity Press, 1991), 172-196.

12   Confirmed by many studies. Andre Blais writes on this point, "This assertion is plainly indisputable." A. Blais, "The Debate over Electoral Systems," in *International Political Science Review* (1991), vol.12, no.3 (Butterworth-Heineman) 239-260; R. Taagepera and M.S. Shugart, *Seats and Votes,* (New Haven: Yale University Press, 1989).

13   Not to be confused with the alternative vote system used in B.C. for the 1952 and 1953 elections. The alternative vote ensures each representative has

majority support, but it is riding based, and therefore, it does not yield proportional results. It is marginally better than SMP. Instead of wasting over 50 percent of the votes, it wastes just under 50 percent.

14 Alan C. Cairns, "The Electoral System and the Party System in Canada, 1921-1965," *Canadian Journal of Political Science*, vol. 1 (March 1968), 59.

15 See: Paul Hirst, *Representative Democracy and Its Limits* (Cambridge, U.K.: Polity Press, 1990).

16 A. de Tocqueville, *Democracy in America*, trans. by H. Reeve (Boston: John Allyn Publisher, 1882), vol. II, 395.

17 Ibid., 392.

18 J.S. Mill, *Utilitarianism, Liberty, Representative Government* (London: J.M. Dent, 1910), 206 and 268.

19 P.J. Taylor and R. J. Johnston, *Geography of Elections* (New York: Holmes and Meier, 1979), 414-15.

NOTES FOR CHAPTER 1

1 Aristotle, *Politics*, bk. IV, 4.

2 Quoted in *Representative Democracy in the Canadian Provinces*, by Alan Kornberg et al. (Scarborough, Prentice-Hall Canada, 1982), 2.

3 B. Russell, *Power* (London: Unwin Books, 1960), 186.

4 Quoted in *Democracy, Eh?* by J. Deverell and G. Vezina (Montreal, Robert Davies, 1993), 101.

5 For a full elucidation of Manning's position see *Waiting for the Wave; The Reform Party and Preston Manning*, by T. Flanagan (Toronto: Stoddart, 1995).

6 During the 1993 election, Reform produced an extensive policy position on agriculture, but nothing on women's issues. Addressing women's issues was seen as catering to special interest groups, something old-line parties were castigated for doing. As though farmers were not a special interest group! At Assembly/96, Reform passed a resolution expressing equal treatment for persons and denying rights to groups. Later, with hardly a note of inconsistency, the Assembly passed a resolution defining the family. If the family is not a group, what is? As Reform commits itself with increasing firmness to a particular, and rather narrow, political agenda, the populism with which it started must decrease. Reform's inability to overcome the inner contradictions of populism suggests that parties with a definite, if not ideologically based agenda will remain part of politics. The remedy is for such parties not to abandon their agenda, but to devise a voting system permitting them participation commensurate with their level of public support.

7 P. Drucker, *Post Capitalist Society* (New York, HarperCollins, 1993), 130-33

8 *Two Treatises of Government*, bk. II, chap. V, 25. ed. P. Laslett (Cambridge University Press, 1963), 327.

9 In political theory this organic view of social structures is associated with the red, or radical Tory strain of conservatism. Within the Dutch Reformed tradition it is known as sphere-sovereignty, and in British writings as the theory of subsidiarity. For a detailed statement of sphere-sovereignty see *The Society of the Future*, by H. Van Riessen, trans. by D.H. Freeman (Philadelphia, Presbyterian and Reformed Publishing Co., 1952), Chap. 3.

10 A. Solzhenitsyn, "A World Split Apart," speech delivered at Harvard University, Cambridge, Massachusetts, 8 June 1978.

11 B. Barber, *Strong Democracy* (Berkeley, Los Angeles: University of California Press, 1984), 158.

12 De Tocqueville, *Democracy*, vol. 1, 252

13 C. Pateman, *Participation and Democratic Theory* (Cambridge University Press, 1970).

14 Annual Reports, Ministry of Labour, Victoria, B.C., Queen's Printer.

15 P. Stothart, "How We Can Own Our Own Industry," *Policy Options Politiques*, July/August, Ottawa 1989, 19-22.

16 Cited in Barber, *Strong Democracy*, Berkeley, Los Angeles: University of California Press, 1984, 1.

17 C. Taylor, 82.

18 R. Gwyn, *Nationalism without Walls: The Unbearable Lightness of Being Canadian* (Toronto: McClelland and Stewart, 1995).

NOTES FOR CHAPTER 2

1   Carl Cohen, *Democracy* (Athens: University of Georgia Press. 1971), 86-7.

2   A. Toffler, *The Third Wave* (New York: William Morrow, 1980), 438.

3   Cf. Raymond Plant, "Criteria for Electoral Systems: The Labour Party and Electoral Reform," *Parliamentary Affairs*, vol. 44, no. 4, October 1991, Oxford University Press.

4   F. Hanna Pitkin, *The Concept of Representation* (Berkeley, University of California Press, 1967).

5   Ibid., 81; 111; 139; 165.

6   Quoted in *Elections British Columbia*, by T. Patrick Boyle (Vancouver: Lions Gate Press, 1982), 4.

7   Simon Sterne, "Proportional Representation," in *Representation*, ed. H.F. Pitkin (New York, Atherton Press, 1969), 37.

8   Quoted by Iain McLean in "Forms of Representation and Systems of Voting," in *Political Theory Today*, ed. David Held (Cambridge: Polity Press, 1991), 173.

9   J.S. Mill, *Utilitarianism, Liberty, Representative Government* (London, J.M.Dent and Sons, 1957) 239;257.

10 Royal Commission on Electoral Reform and Party Financing, *Report*, vol. 1, 1991 (Ottawa: Minister of Supply and Services), 93.

11 Pitkin, *Concept of Representation*, 87.

12 Descriptive representation need not imply affirmative gerrymandering, nor that members of a particular sociological group will vote for no candidates except those of their group.

13 Pitkin, *Concept of Representation*, 182.

14 Ibid., 175; and *Edmund Burke and the Critique of Political Radicalism*, by Michael Freeman (Chicago: University of Chicago Press, 1980), 118.

15 Vernon Bogdanor, *What Is Proportional Representation?* (Oxford: Oxford University Press, 1984), 121.

16 "Parliamentary constituencies as natural communities are a sociological myth and the British MP's electoral dependence on constituents rather than party is, of course, a political myth." So concludes a British study of the relationship of ridings, communities, and the MP–constituent link, by I. Crewe. ("MPs and their Constituents in Britain: How Strong Are the Links?" in V. Bogdanor, *Representatives of the People?* [Hants.: Gower Publishing 1985], 62.)

17 F.L. Morton and R. Knopff, "Does the Charter Mandate 'One Person, One Vote'?" (Calgary: University of Calgary, Occasional Papers Series, Research Study 7.1 1991), 23.

18 STV makes the task of boundary commissions easier. Most shifts in population are accommodated by adding seats to existing districts. It saves money, and people will more readily know their district.

19 H.F. Pitkin, ed., *Representation* (New York: Atherton Press, 1969), 19.

20 Pitkin, *Concept of Representation*, 209.

21 For example, see "The Puzzle of Representation: Specifying Components of Responsiveness," by H. Eulau and D.P. Karps (in *Representation and Electoral Systems,* by P.J. Johnston and H.E. Pasis [Scarborough: Prentice-Hall,1990], 44-60). The authors note that Pitkin's formulation of responsiveness does not "specify the content or target of responsiveness" (49). They then proceed to fill the void and suggest that responsiveness may be measured by output in areas such as policy, service to constituents, etc. But Pitkin's stipulation "in a manner responsive to them" is directed at process, not output. Pitkin dismisses those whose sole concern is with output. She writes," A representative government must ... not merely promote the public interest, but must also be responsive to the people," and "Representative government is not defined by particular actions at a particular moment, but by long-term systematic arrangements — by institutions and the way in which they function." (Pitkin, *Concept of Representation*, 232, 234). Also, the authors criticize Pitkin for failing to observe Wahlke's findings that citizens are not significant sources of input for representatives, since citizens lack either the ability or the willingness to develop and express meaningful opinions on policy questions (47). Again, this misses the mark. Pitkin's concern is with process, not content, a means for allowing people to express an opinion, whether that means is used or not.

22 Pitkin, *Concept of Representation*, 231.

23 Ibid., 181-2.

24 Self-rule is important to Canadians. "Our political values ascribe a high priority to the right — even obligation — of its citizens to be self-governing." Canada, Royal Commission on Electoral Reform and Party Financing, *Report,* vol. 1, 1991 (Ottawa: Minister of Supply and Services).

25 For example, "Constituency Influence in Congress," by W.E. Miller and D. Stokes, *American Political Science Review* 57 (March 1963), 45-56. And A.H. Birch writes, "The responsiveness of elected representatives ... has been the subject of a great deal of research" (Birch, *Representation* [London, Pall Mall Press, 1971] 127).

26 Elkins's study defines strategic voting as voting for one's "second choice'" and suggests this happens infrequently. (D.J. Elkins, *Manipulation and Consent* [Vancouver: UBC Press, 1993], chapter 7.) Yet, it is common wisdom that in our system govenments do not get voted *in*, but *out* of office, and that for many their choice at elections is to choose the "the least of all evils." Also, what is the motivation of the 25 to 30 percent of eligible voters who abstain? Perhaps each ballot should have a box for "None of the above."

27 H.D. Clarke et al., *Absent Mandate* (Toronto: Gage Educational Publishing, 1991), 114-15. I don't know of a similar study covering B.C. politics.

28 C.E.S. Franks, *The Parliament of Canada* (Toronto: University of Toronto Press 1987), 222; 249; 260; 268; A.H.Birch, *Representation* (New York: Praeger, 1971), 115.

29 *British Columbia, Electoral History of British Columbia 1871–1986* (Victoria: Elections B.C., and Legislative Library), 1988. Creating legislative majorities artificially is intrinsic to SM. See D. Rae, *Political Consequences of Electoral Laws* (New Haven: Yale University Press, 1967), 27.

30 Tom Kent, *Getting Ready For 1999* (Ottawa: Institute for Research on Public Policy, 1989), 10. On negative advertising and campaign strategies that attack incumbents without offering alternatives, see R.M. Lee, *One Hundred Monkeys* (Toronto: Macfarlane Walter and Ross, 1989); J.Laschinger, *Leaders and Lesser Mortals: Backroom Politics in Canada* (Toronto: Key Porter, 1992); G. Gagnon and D. Rath, *Not Without Cause* (Toronto: Harper Row, 1991).

31 In July 1991 the B.C. Social Credit Party drew two thousand delegates to its convention. Reluctantly, and only at the eleventh hour, after the minister of finance, M. Couvelier, had publicly denounced the backroom organizers, did they allow one and a half hours, out of two and a half days, for policy discussion under conditions of strict control. For example, they allowed written questions only, subject to screening.

32 K. Carty et al., *Leaders and Parties in Canadian Politics* (Toronto: Harcourt Brace Jovanovich Canada, 1992). They note that delegates of the Social Credit party choose a leader for "ability to win," not for policy, and "...as in other Canadian party systems, electoral competition in BC focusses much on personalities and character of the party leader."

33 Findings indicate feelings of political powerlessness and dissatisfaction with politicians and political processes. Canada, Royal Commission on Electoral Reform and Party Financing, *Report*, vol. 1 (Ottawa: Minister of Supply and Services, 1991) 25-43.

34 J. Laschinger, *Leaders and Lesser Mortals: Backroom Politics in Canada* (Toronto: Key Porter Books, 1992), 217-18.

35 Royal Commission on Electoral Reform, *Report*, 208.

36 Ibid., 226; Franks reports a Gallup poll in which only 7.9 percent of Canadians felt MPs should vote as their party requires (Franks, *Parliament of Canada*, 29). See also Richard Johnston, *Public Opinion and Public Policy in Canada: Questions of Confidence* (Toronto, University of Toronto Press, 1986); and Peter Dobell and Byron Berry, "Anger at the System: Political Discontent in Canada," *Parliamentary Government*, no. 39, January 1992 (Ottawa: Parliamentary Centre for Foreign Affairs and Foreign Trade) 3-11.

37 A. Blais, and E. Gidengil, *Making Representative Democracy Work* (Canada: Minister of Supply and Services Canada, 1991) 59-61.

38 H. C. Clarke et al., eds., *Parliament, Policy and Representation* (Toronto: Methuen, 1980), xv.

39 Reform Party of Canada, *Blue Book 1994* (Calgary: Reform Party of Canada, 1994), 3.

40 Blais and Gidengil, *Making Representative Democracy Work*, 55.

41 There is some recognition of that. See, for example, C. Maille, "Primed for Power: Women in Canadian Politics" (Ottawa: Canadian Advisory Council on the Status of Women, 1990), 31.

42 I think such concerns may be overstated. A recent study designed to detect differences in political behavior between men and women found: "On the major questions of policy and government priority, women and men in aggregate tend to concur with each other. The areas in which there tends to be disharmony are usually less relevant to the electorate as a whole." P. Wearing, "Does Gender Make a Difference in Voting Behavior?" in J. Wearing, ed., *The*

Ballot and its Message: Voting in Canada (Toronto: Copp Clark Pitman, 1991), 348.

43 Pitkin, *Concept of Representation*, 51.

44 C. Boyle, "Home Rule for Women: Power-Sharing Between Men and Women," *The Dalhousie Law Journal* (October 1983) vol. 7, no. 3 (Halifax: Dalhousie Press), 796.

45 Royal Commission on Electoral Reform, *Report,* 269.

46 Canadian Advisory Council on the Status of Women, "Women in Politics," *Issue Summary* (November 1993) (Ottawa: CACSW), 1.

47 D. Blake et al., *Grassroots Politicians: Party Activists in British Columbia* (Vancouver: UBC Press, 1991), 28.

48 L. Young, "Electoral Systems and Representative Legislatures: Consideration of Alternative Electoral Systems" (Ottawa: Canadian Advisory Council on the Status of Women, 1994); S. Day, "The Key Isn't Quotas, It's Proportional Representation," *Vancouver Sun,* 22 September 1992; L. Smith, and E. Wachtel, "A Feminist Guide to the Canadian Constitution" (Ottawa: CACSW 1992), 56; C. Maille, "Primed for Power: Women in Canadian Politics" (Ottawa: CACSW 1990), 33; see also CACSW's *Brief to the Royal Commission on Electoral Reform and Party Financing* (Ottawa: CACSW, June 1990), 10-11.

49 A study of factors, such as electoral structures, political parties, and socio-economic conditions that contribute to the election of women in twenty-three countries found that the type of electoral system is the most important predictor of the number of women elected. W. Rule, "Electoral Systems, Contextual Factors and Women's Opportunity for Election to Parliament in Twenty-Three Democracies," *Western Political Quarterly.* vol. 40, no. 3 (1987). See also P. Norris, "Women's Legislative Participation in Western Europe," *Western European Politics* (1985) no. 4: 90-101.

50 B.C. electors strongly supported both recall and initiative legislation by referendum in 1991.

51 D. Thomas, "Turning a Blind Eye: Constitutional Abeyances and the Canadian Experience" (Calgary: Mount Royal College, 1992), 25, note 7.

52 A. Cairns, "The Limited Constitutional Vision of Meech Lake," in *Competing Constitutional Visions: The Meech Lake Accord,* J.K.E. Swinton and C. Rogerson, eds. (Toronto: Carswell, 1988), 256; A. Cairns, in *Disruptions: Constitutional Struggles: From Charter to Meech Lake,* D.E. Williams, ed. (Toronto: McClelland and Stewart, 1991).

53 Dixon v. B.C. (A.G.), (1989) 4 W.W.R.

54 Ibid., 404.

55 Ibid., 406.

56 The Vander Zalm administration responded with the Fisher Commission, whose recommendations shifted power from rural to urban B.C. They were implemented in time for the 1991 general election.

57 Dixon v. B.C., 413-14.

58 Reference Re: Provincial Electoral Boundaries (1991) 3 W.W.R. (Saskatchewan Court of Appeal).

59 Ibid., 609.

60 Reference Re Provincial Electoral Boundaries (1991) 5 W.W.R, 1 (Supreme Court of Canada). McLachlin was elevated to the Supreme Court of Canada shortly after the Dixon case, and wrote the majority opinion, which Norman

Ruff has dubbed McLachlin II. See J.C. Courtney et al., eds. *Drawing Boundaries* (Saskatoon: Fifth House, 1992), 128.

61 Ibid., 12.

62 Ibid., 20.

63 Ibid., 12-13. Emphasis added.

64 Reference Re Electoral Boundaries Commission Act (1992) 1 W.W.R., 481 (Alberta Court of Appeal).

65 Canada West Foundation, *Conference Report: Renewal of Canada — Institutional Reform*, Calgary, 1992.

66 Courtney, *Drawing Boundaries*, 152-55.

NOTES FOR CHAPTER 3

1 A. Westell, *The New Society* (Toronto: McClelland and Stewart, 1977), 39.

2 Veteran parliamentarian Stanley Knowles, in defining the tradition of parliamentary government in the Commons on 2 June 1975, said, "The government makes the decisions and all we can say is yes or no." Quoted in Westell, *New Society* (28).

3 See R.R. March, *The Myth of Parliament* (Scarborough: Prentice-Hall, 1974); A. Hill and A. Whichelow, *What's Wrong with Parliament* (London: Penguin Books, 1964).

4 See, for example, J. Wahlke et al., *The Legislative System: Explorations in Legislative Behavior* (New York: John Wiley and Sons, 1962); A.M.Goddard, *Legislative Behavior in the British Columbia Legislative Assembly* (Ann Arbor: Ann Arbor University Press, Microfilms, 1973); A. Kornberg, *Canadian Legislative Behavior* (New York: Holt, Rinehart, and Winston, 1967); A. Kornberg and W. Mishler, *Influence in Parliament* (Durham: Duke University Press, 1976); A. Kornberg and L.D. Musolf, *Legislatures in Developmental Perspective* (Durham: Duke University Press, 1970).

5 For a complete constitutional description of responsible government see P.W. Hogg, *Constitutional Law of Canada,* 2nd ed. (Toronto: The Carswell Co., 1985), 189-213.

6 R.W. Langstone, *Responsible Government in Canada* (London: J.M. Dent and Sons, 1931), 87. See also R. MacGregor Dawson, *Democratic Government in Canada* (Toronto: University of Toronto Press, revised ed., 1963), 8.

7 Quoted in Langstone, *Responsible Government*, 158-59. Up to then cabinets were selected largely by representatives of the Crown. See also Hogg, *Constitutional Law*, 189.

8 "The 14th Article of the Terms of Union had pledged the Dominion to consent to representative government when desired by the people of British Columbia, and Governor Musgrave had intimated, at the opening of the Session of 1871, his intention to introduce such a measure. This resulted in the Constitution Act, 1871." F. W. Howay and E.O.S Scholefield, *British Columbia* (Vancouver: S.J. Clark Company, 1914), vol. ii, 327.

9 P. Weller and D. Jaensch, eds., *Responsible Government in Australia* (Victoria: Drummond Publishing, 1980), 2.

10 H.F. Angus, *Citizenship in BC* (Victoria: King's Printer, 1926), 33-4.

11 Only three times has a B.C. premier resigned as a result of a vote of non-confidence. The last time was 29 January 1883, well before the formation of political parties in 1903. Source: *Electoral History of BC 1871–1986*, 545.

12 C. Saunders, "Rethinking the Parliamentary System: Contributions from the Australian Debate," 29 *Alberta Law Review* 336 (1991), 336-50, Edmonton.

13 N. Ruff argues that the legislature influences policy, not directly, but by giving voice to public opinion. See T.J. Morley, *The Reins of Power* (Vancouver: Douglas and McIntyre, 1983), 12. Occasionally, cabinet is embarrassed into withdrawing legislation, e.g. Finance Minister Glen Clark's super surtax on property. In other instances it ignores public opinion, e.g. dropping the secret ballot for union certification votes.

14 Recent works that give an insider's view include: G. Gagnon and D. Rath, *Not Without Cause* (Toronto: Harper Collins,1991); R. M. Lee, *One Hundred Monkeys* (Toronto: Macfarlane Walter and Ross, 1989); K. Laschinger, *Leaders and Lesser Mortals: Backroom Politics in Canada* (Toronto: Key Porter Books, 1992).

15 Matters referred to committees preclude debate in the legislature until after the committee reports. G.E. MacMinn, *Parliamentary Practice in British Columbia*, 2nd ed. (Victoria: BC Government, 1987), 118.

16 F.I. Greenstein and N.W. Polsby, eds., *Handbook of Political Science* (Reading, Massachusetts: Addison Wesley), vol. 5, 235.

17 J. S. Mill, *Utilitarianism, Liberty, Representative Government* (London: J. M. Dent and Sons, 1910, reprinted 1957), 231.

18 C. Schmitt, *The Crises of Parliamentary Democracy* (trans. by Ellen Kennedy, Cambridge, Massachusetts: MIT Press, 1985), 33-50.

19 "Parliament" derives from the French *parler,* to speak.

20 Quoted in *The Myth of Parliament,* by R.R. March (Scarborough: Prentice-Hall of Canada, 1974), 65; 121-22.

21 Vancouver *Sun,* 10 November 1995 (D2c). An edited excerpt from D. Barrett and W. Miller, *A Passionate Political Life* (Vancouver, Douglas and McIntyre), 1995.

22 P. Boyer, *Hands On Democracy,* 74.

23 Occasionally, the opposition MLAs would have knowledge of pending legislation prior to the government backbench. The government House leader in consultation with the opposition House leader works out a legislative agenda. This requires deal-making, and disclosure of cabinet's intentions. Government backbenchers often complained, not without some justification, that to know what cabinet was up to it was best to consult the opposition. Under Bill Bennett, Vander Zalm's predecessor, it was no different. One day his caucus pinned mushrooms on their lapels, indicating they were always in the dark.

24 Goddard's extensive study of B.C. MLAs notes that 71.4 percent of Social Credit respondents selected "consensus building" as the most important function of caucus. A.M. Goddard, *Legislative Behavior in the British Columbia Legislative Assembly* (Ann Arbor: University Microfilms 1973), 170.

25 P. Boyer, in Canadian Study of Parliament Group, *Proceedings,* Year 7: *A Review of the McGrath Committee Report of the House of Commons,* 2 December 1992, 37-8.

26 B. Russell, *Power* (London: Unwin Books 1938, fifth printing 1967), 132.

27 Boyer, *Hands On Democracy,* 196.

28 Ibid., 77-83; see also N. Ward, "Confederation and Responsible Government," *Canadian Journal of Economics and Politics,* 24:1 (February 1958), 49.

29 Robert Marleau, Clerk of the House of Commons, describes the review of estimates and supply in the parliamentary system as a "dismal, farcical, absolute-

ly silly exercise." He also notes that the 1985 McGrath committee ran out of time to address this issue. Goddard, *Legislative Behaviour,* 18.

30   E. Forsey, *How Canadians Govern Themselves* (Ottawa: Publication Canada, 1980), 28.

31   March, *Myth of Parliament,* 56; and N. Ward, "Confederation and Responsible Government," in *Canadian Journal of Economics and Politics,* xxiv (February 1958), no. 1, 49-56.

32   D.Kilgour, and J. Kirsner, "Party Discipline and Canadian Democracy," *Canadian Parliamentary Review,* 1988, 11:10.

33   In M. Cassidy, *Democratic Rights and Electoral Reform in Canada* (Toronto: Dundurn Press, 1991) 287.

34   G. Aiken, *The Backbencher* (Toronto: McClelland and Stewart, 1974), 7-8.

35   James Mowat was the last independent to be elected in B.C., for Alberni in 1949. He was first elected for Alberni in 1941 as a Liberal, and re-elected in 1945 under the Coalition. Without that record it is doubtful he would have won as an independent in 1949 (*Electoral History of BC*).

36   D. Johnston, *Up the Hill* (Montreal: Optimum Publishing International, 1986), 263.

37   For an account of recent transfers of power to the cabinet see G. Leslie, *Breach of Promise* (Madeira Park: Harbour Publishing, 1991), part 3.

38   C. Sharman, "The Strange Case of a Provincial Constitution: The British Columbia Constitution Act," *Canadian Journal of Political Science* (March 1984), 102-03.

39   Hansard, 25 June 1980, 3039.

40   Maureen McTeer, *Parliament: Canada's Democracy and How It Works* (Mississauga: Random House, 1987), 75.

41   In 1980 Prime Minister Joe Clark had a minority government but decided to act as though he had a majority, and lost on a motion of non-confidence.

42   Many studies conclude that provincial legislatures do not hold the cabinet accountable in an effective manner. A. Kornberg et al., *Representative Democracy in the Canadian Provinces* (Scarborough, Prentice-Hall Canada, 1982); H.D. Clarke et al., eds., *Parliament, Policy and Representation* (Toronto: Methuen, 1980), chaps. 8, 9, and 11.

43   J. McLeod, ed., *Agenda 1970: Proposals for a Creative Politics* (Toronto: University of Toronto Press), 217.

44   Lee, *One Hundred Monkeys,* especially 46-48.

45   R. Rose, *Politics in England* (London: The McMillan Press, fifth ed., 1989) 112. For a study of decreasing party discipline in Britain see P. Norton, "Behavioural Changes: Backbench Independence in the 1980s," in *Parliament in the 1980s,* J. Norton ed. (Oxford: Blackwell, 1985).

46   Two studies have shown independently that in Britain at least, individual MPs can add or subtract no more than 5 percent of the votes a party would get regardless who won the nomination. (See March, *The Myth of Parliament,* 12). This suggests people vote for the leader or party, not for the candidate. In the 1986 B.C. provincial election, candidates of the same party in each of the twelve dual-member ridings had less than 4 percent spread in popular vote, including Richmond where the premier received only 3.9 percent more votes than his relatively unknown running mate.

47   K. Waltz, *The Theory of International Politics* (Reading, Mass.: Addison-Wesley, 1979) 83-84. Neither Vander Zalm nor Johnston would have been premier.

Also, see: J.C. Courtney, "Leadership, Conventions and the Development of the National Political Community in Canada," in *National Politics and Community in Canada,* by R.K. Carty and W.P. Ward (Vancouver: University of B.C. Press, 1986), 92-111.

48 This refers to powers of bodies such as the Workers' Compensation Board, the B.C. Utilities Commission, the Labour Relations Board, the Motor Carrier Commission, etc. For a full discussion see J.M. Keyes, *Cabinet Legislation* (Toronto: Butterworth, 1992); J.R. Bowers, *Regulating the Regulators* (New York: Praeger, 1990); K. Puttick, *Challenging Delegated Legislation* (London: Waterlow Publishers, 1988).

49 Vancouver *Sun,* 13 May 1994.

50 Examples include: The Environmental Assessment Act, 1994; it gives the minister and cabinet powers to enforce environmental protection at their discretion. The Build BC Act, 1993, gives cabinet unlimited spending power for any type of capital construction without approval of the legislature, except that a financial report must be tabled once a year. It also gives unlimited power to tax the sale of gasoline and car rentals, and to place tolls on highways. The Residential Tenancy Act, 1994, allows cabinet to set limits to rents. See also: G.L. Seens, "Awesome, Sweeping Powers: The Land Commission Act, 1973; The Mineral Royalties Act 1974, and other 'Blank Cheque' Legislation: the NDP Years, 1972-75," Victoria: Political Science, BC Project, University of Victoria, 1983.

51 For example, the MacDonald Commission. (Canada, Royal Commission on the Economic Union and Development Prospects for Canada, *Report,* Ottawa, Supply and Services Canada, 1985, vol. 3, part 4, 36.)

52 Kornberg, *Representative Democracy,* 267.

53 For a brief overview of the history of the idea of responsible government, see C. Dunn, "The Meaning of Responsible Government," in *Canadian Parliamentary Review* (Ottawa: vol. 11, no. 3, 1988) 12-3.

54 MacDonald Commission, *Report,* 36.

55 J. Uhr, "Cabinet–Legislative Relations: Learning from Locke," *Canadian Parliamentary Review,* 10:1 (Spring 1987), Ottawa, 9-11.

56 For a discussion on how political parties replaced independent notables, and the effect of this on responsible government, see March, *The Myth of Parliament.*

57 Westell, *New Society,* 30: "If a major change were made in the electoral system to introduce some form of proportional representation, the powers of the prime minister and the cabinet would probably be reduced ..."

NOTES FOR CHAPTER 4

1 Tom Kent in *Sovereign People or Sovereign Governments,* H.V. Kroeker, ed. (Montreal, Institute for Research on Public Policy, 1979), 34-5.

2 Canada, Royal Commission on Electoral Reform and Party Financing, *Report,* vol. 1, 1991, Ottawa, Minister of Supply and Services, 223.

3 H. Bakvis, ed., *Canadian Political Parties: Leaders, Candidates and Organization* (Toronto, Dundurn Press, 1991).

4 Royal Commission on Electoral Reform, *Report,* 228.

5 J. Meisel, "The Decline of Party in Canada," in *Party Politics in Canada,* H. Thorburn, ed., 1979, 111.

6 K. Lawson, P. Merkl, *When Parties Fail,* 1988, 566.

7   A. Panebianco, *Political Parties: Organization and Power,* 1988.

8   Lee, *One Hundred Monkeys.*

9   Royal Commission on Electoral Reform, *Report,* 298.

10 C.E.S. Franks, *The Parliament of Canada* (Toronto: University of Toronto Press, 1987), 97; 162; 204; 214; 219.

NOTES FOR CHAPTER 5

1   J.H.A. Dyck, "Representative Recall and Initiative Legislation: Two Forms of Direct Democracy," University College of Cariboo, paper prepared for Select Standing Committee on Parliamentary Reform, 29 September 1992, 3.

2   For one among many discussions of this theme see: P. Resnick, *Parliament vs. People* (Vancouver: New Star Books, 1984), Chap. 1.

3   For a detailed history of direct democracy in Canada see P.J. Boyer, *Lawmaking by the People* (Toronto: Butterworth, 1982); and for B.C. see N.J. Ruff, "Institutionalizing Populism in British Columbia," *Canadian Parliamentary Review* (Ottawa: Winter 1993/94), 24-32.

4   Source: *Electoral History of BC,* 409. Thomas Jefferson had a better idea. He thought Congress could vote themselves a pay raise provided that it would not take effect until after a subsequent election.

5   P. Boyer, *The People's Mandate* (Toronto: Dundurn Press, 1992).

6   W.L. Morton, *The Progressive Party in Canada* (Toronto: University of Toronto Press, 1950), 16.

7   E.M. Phelps, *Selected Articles on The Recall* (New York: The H. W. Wilson Co., 1915), 1.

8   W. Lippmann, *The Public Philosophy* (New York: Mentor Books, 1955), 47-8.

9   Canada, *Reforming Electoral Democracy,* vol. 2, Ottawa: Canada Communication Group-Publishing (1991), 243.

10 Canada's only experiment with recall, so far.

11 P. McCormick, "Provision for the Recall of Elected Officials," in *Democratic Rights and Electoral Reform in Canada,* by M. Cassidy (Toronto: Dundurn Press, 1991), 270; 288.

12 For example, critics charge that the B.C. legislation has a threshold so high as to make it virtually impossible to be used. It requires that within 60 days 40 percent of voters eligible in the previous election must sign the petition. This compares to 25 percent in most U.S. jurisdictions, and even that level is seldom attained. Considering that average voter turnout in general elections is about 70 percent, it would require almost 60 percent of those who voted in the previous election for recall to even get off the ground. However, it is equally true that the vagaries of SMP will sometimes elect members with 30 percent or less of the popular vote, in which case a large majority of voters have a bias against the member from the start. Also, in the only historical example in Canada, the threshold was much higher, and was attained. "By the fall of 1937 they had the necessary 66.66 percent of the voters supporting the recall petition. In order to save Aberhart's seat, the government revoked the Recall Act retroactively to the date of its passage." (D.R. Elliot and I. Miller, *Bible Bill* (Edmonton: Reidmore Books, 1987) 273.

13 McCormick, 288-92 (see note 11 above).

14 T.E. Cronin, *Direct Democracy: The Politics of Initiative, Referendum and Recall* (Cambridge: Harvard University Press, 1989), 155.

15 Canada, *Reforming Electoral Democracy*, 230-233; and McCormick, 274.

16 Canada, *Reforming Electoral Democracy*, 242-43.

17 Gail Bell, Letters to the Editor, *Vancouver Sun*, November 30, 1993.

18 Graeme Bowbrick rejects recall and suggests the concerns of proponents are more effectively met by replacing SMP with PR. G. Bowbrick, "Revisiting the Implications of Recall and Initiative and their Potential Implementation in British Columbia," unpublished paper, UBC Faculty of Law, 24 April, 1992) 38.

19 Canada, *Reforming Electoral Democracy*, 244-47.

20 T. Flanagan, "Reform of Canada's Parliamentary Institutions," unpublished paper for Reform Party of Canada, June 1991, 45. Flanagan also writes, "In my opinion, the recall would not really come into its own unless we restructure the Canadian parliamentary system more radically than the Reform Party has yet proposed" (47).

21 In spite of the rhetoric, it is doubtful the Reform Party will be different. Their interim policy states, "Until parliamentary reform is enacted,... Reform MPs shall vote with the Reform Party majority in the House unless a Member is instructed to abstain or vote otherwise by his/her constituents." (Reform Party of Canada, *Principles and Policies*, 1991, 10.) Thomas Flanagan comments that while this is advanced as an interim policy, no relaxation of party discipline within the Reform Party is likely as long as the Westminster model remains. See Flanagan (note 20 above), 23. In addition, Manning's concept of representation can accommodate many positions. It suggests party discipline, following constituent instructions, and following one's own best judgment are all appropriate, depending on the circumstances. See P. Manning, *The New Canada* (Toronto: Macmillan, 1992), 321-22. For an additional voice skeptical about relaxing party discipline in the Reform Party of Canada, see D. Laycock, "Reforming Canadian Democracy? Institutions and Ideology in the Reform Party Project," *Canadian Journal of Political Science* 27:2 (June 1994) 213-48.

22 For example, see Dyck (see note 1 above), 6. Also, Lortie (Royal Commission on Electoral Reform) makes this point repeatedly.

23 Hansard, 9 March 1987, 3.

24 *The Province*, 19 June1991; *Times Colonist*, 16 August 1991.

25 Speech from the Throne, Hansard, 17 March 1992.

26 Source: Clerk of Committees.

27 Canadian Study of Parliament Group, *Proceedings*, 6.

28 For a particularly chilling account of how standing committees can be used by an cabinet to "manufacture consent" for decisions already made elsewhere see Lee, *One Hundred Monkeys*, 49-50.

29 Canadian Study of Parliament Group, *Proceedings*, 11.

30 Ibid., 10.

31 G. Kristianson and P. Nicholson, "Improving the Image and Operation of the British Columbia legislature," Brief to the Standing Committee on Standing Orders and Private Bills of the Legislative Assembly of British Columbia, 1984.

32 Quoted in Flanagan, 12 (see note 20 above).

33 Ibid. 16.

34   Boyer, *Hands On Democracy*, 75-77.

35   Chief Electoral Officer of Canada, *Official Voting Results for 35th General Election*, Ottawa, 1993

36   Sometimes such unfairness is dismissed with the suggestion that parties, once in office, are all the same anyway. Not true, empirical studies show otherwise. See Kornberg, *Representative Democracy in the Canadian Provinces*, 266. Also, consider the impact of the election of the Bloc Québécois on national unity. They obtained 18 percent of the seats with 14 percent of the popular vote, making them the official opposition.

37   A comparative study of the conditions that help a legislature contribute to national integration found that all groups must be represented, they must be heard, and the structures must facilitate compromise. See A.F. Eldridge, ed., *Legislatures in Plural Societies* (Durham: Duke University Press, 1977), 267.

38   Participation in political decision-making contributes to human self-actualization. See J.L. Walker, *American Political Science Review*, 60:2 (1966), 285-95; L. Lipsitz, "If, As Verba Says, the State Functions as a Religion, What Are We to Do Then to Save Our Souls?" *American Political Science Review*, 62:2 (1968) 527-35.

39   G. Grant, *Lament for a Nation* (Ottawa, Carlton University Press, 1970), x.

NOTES FOR CHAPTER 6

1   C.D. Sharp, "The Case against the Referendum," Fabian Tract No.155 (London: The Fabian Society, 1911), 10.

2   For a crude classification see Appendix A.

3   M. Balinski and H.P. Young, *Fair Representation* (New Haven: Yale University Press, 1982), 87.

4   E. Lakeman, *How Democracies Vote* (London: Faber and Faber, 1974), 168. Canadian experience at the municipal level is one of the exceptions; see chapter 7 of this study.

5   V. Bogdanor, *What Is Proportional Representation?* (Oxford: Martin Robertson, 1984), 157.

6   All electoral systems, including PR, are capable of manufacturing majorities, but this effect is far less likely under PR than SMP. See A.Lijphart, *Democracies* (New Haven: Yale University Press, 1984), 167.

7   G. Sartori, *The Theory of Democracy Revisited* (Chatham, New Jersey: Chatham House, 1987), 31-4.

8   D.J. Amy, *Real Choices/New Voices* (New York: Columbia University Press, 1993), chap. 3, 55-75.

9   As noted above, many observers have made this point. Former MP and cabinet minister Don Johnston writes about his experience as a leadership candidate: "The so-called policy sessions were well-chaired... but policy content was minimal... The dominant strategy seemed to be to play it safe and avoid broaching controversial subjects. In the hope of winning supporters over the long haul, each tried to be the candidate to offend the fewest people" (D. Johnston, *On The Hill* (Montreal: Optimum Publishing International, 1986), 122-26.

10   "The Crises in Party Politics," in *Westminster Review* (Vancouver: Westminster Review Publishing Office, September 1916), 11.

11   P. Hain, *Proportional Mis-Representation* (Hants.,England: Wildwood House, 1986), 38. For a discussion about differences between Imperial and Weimar

169

Germany that are more significant than the change in electoral system, see V. Bogdanor and D. Butler, eds., *Democracy and Elections* (Cambridge University Press, 1983), 252-53.

12   Ibid., 254. Bogdanor and Butler conclude their study with this, "It should be clear then, that any theory making the electoral system a fundamental causative factor in the development of party systems cannot be sustained."

13   The important link between voter and representative, and the merits of coalitions, will not be treated in this chapter, but in other contexts below.

14   This and the following objections can be found, among many others, in P. Barker, "Voting for Trouble," in *Contemporary Political Issues*, M. Charlton and P. Barker, eds., 2nd. ed.(Scarborough: Nelson Canada, 1994), 292-303.

15   M. Duverger, *Political Parties*, 2nd. ed. (Toronto: Methuen 1959).

16   Bogdanor, *Democracy and Elections*, 254-55. Bogdanor lists the following theorists: J.H. Grumm, "Theories of Electoral Systems," *Mid-West Journal of Political Science* (1958); L. Lipson, "Party Systems in the United Kingdom and the Older Commonwealth: Causes, Resemblances and Variations," *Political Studies* (1959); L. Lipson, *The Democratic Civilization* (New York: 1964).

17   Duverger, *Political Parties*, 273-45.

18   Quoted in *Electoral Laws and Their Political Consequences*, B. Grofman, and A. Lijphart, eds. (New York: Agathon, 1986).

19   S.M. Lipset, and S. Rokkan, eds., *Party Systems and Voter Alignments: Cross-National Perspectives* (New York: Free Press, 1967), chap. 1.

20   D. Rae, *The Political Consequences of Electoral Laws* (New Haven: Yale University Press, 1969) 99.

21   A. Lijphart, *Democracies*, (New Haven: Yale University Press, 1984), 158-59. Canada being one of the two. This confirms what Cairns showed in 1968, namely, that SMP does not always deliver a two-party system as promised.

22   Ibid., 149.

23   R. Taagepera and B. Grofman, "Rethinking Duverger's Law: Predicting the Effective Number of Parties in Plurality and PR Systems — Parties Minus Issues Equals One," *European Journal of Political Research*, 13 (1985), 341-52.

24   A. Blais, and K. Carty, "The Psychological Impact of Electoral Law: Measuring Duverger's Elusive Factor," *British Journal of Political Science*, 1991.

25   Rae, *The Political Consequences of Electoral Laws*, 127.

26   M. Cassidy, *Fairness and Stability in Canadian Elections: The Case for an Alternative Electoral System* (Ottawa: Parliamentary Centre for Foreign Affairs and Foreign Trade, 1992), 35.

27   Bogdanor, *What Is Proportional Representation?* 167.

28   Lakeman, *How Democracies Vote*, 173.

29   Lijphart, *Democracies*, 110. Lijphart says this confirms analysis of others, even though everyone uses slightly different operational definitions. For a list of studies see A. Blais, "The Debate over Electoral Systems," *International Political Science Review* (1991), vol. 12, no. 3, 239-60.

30   F.A. Hermens, *Democracy or Anarchy? A Study of Proportional Representation* (New York: Johnston Reprint Corporation, 1972), 293.

31   Quoted in "Government Stability and Electoral Systems: The Italian Example," by P. Furlong, *Parliamentary Affairs*, vol. 44, no.1 (January, 1991), Oxford University Press, 50-60.

32   See Bogdanor, *Democracy and Elections*, 253.

33 D. Blake et al., *Grassroots Politicians* (Vancouver: University of British Columbia Press, 1991), 124.

34 Canadian Study of Parliament Group, Proceedings, Year 7: A Review of the McGrath Committee Report on the Reform of the House of Commons, 2 December 1992, 13.

35 Six seats were newly created, but this is still unacceptably high.

36 Hains, *Proportional Mis-Representation,* 45.

37 Quoted in Blais, 'The Debate over Electoral Systems,' 245. (See note 24 above)

38 T. Kent, *Getting Ready for 1999* (Ottawa: Institute for Research on Public Policy, 1989), 45.

39 See Furlong, *Parliamentary Affairs,* 56.

40 P.J. Taylor and R.J. Johnston, *Geography of Elections* (New York: Holmes and Meier, 1979), 469: Guy Lardeyret, quoted in Amy, *Real Choices/New Voices,* 162.

41 C.E.S. Franks, *The Parliament of Canada* (Toronto: University of Toronto Press, 1987), 268.

42 Lijphart, *Democracies,* 157.

43 R. Jankowski, "Responsible/Irresponsible Westminster Parties," *British Journal of Political Science*, vol. 23 (January 1993), 107-29.

44 To document fully this assertion is beyond the scope of this study. Some evidence comes from the World Bank which ranks annual per capita income in most of these countries above that of Canada, even apart from considering Canada's per capita debt which is among the highest in the world. Source: *Vancouver Sun*, 29 December 1994, 1.

45 E. Tufte, *Political Control of the Economy* (Princeton, N.J.: Princeton University Press, 1978).

46 Blais lists a considerable number of scholars who have raised this objection. ("The Debate over Electoral Systems," 242.)

47 Lijphart, *Democracies,* 113.

48 Bogdanor, *What Is Proportional Representation?* 62-7, and 148-51.

49 Lijphart, *Democracies,* 116-23.

50 E. Lakeman, *Power To Elect* (London: William Heineman,1982), 161-2.

51 T. Flanagan, "Reform of Canada's Parliamentary Institutions," Calgary: Reform Party of Canada, unpublished paper, June 1991, 6.

52 See for example R. Thompson, *The House of Minorities* (Burlington, Ontario: Welch, 1990), and G. Woodcock, *Power to Us All* (Madeira Park, B.C. Harbour Publishing), 1992.

53 M. Marsh, "The Voters Decide?: Preferential voting in European List Systems," *European Journal of Political Research*,13 (1964), Amsterdam: Elsevier Science Publishers, 365-78.

54 Bogdanor and Butler, *Democracy and Elections,* 2 and 8.

55 For a detailed description of the procedure see Appendix C.

56 V. Bogdanor, *The People and the Party System* (Cambridge: Cambridge University Press, 1981), 243.

57 Ibid., 140.

58 Ibid., 244; Bogdanor, *What Is Proportional Representation?,* 161 and 173-74. Also see J.F.H. Wright, "An Electoral Basis for Responsible Government: The Australian Experience," in *Choosing An Electoral System,* by A. Lijphart and B. Grofman (New York: Praeger, 1984), 133.

59 P.J. Taylor and R.J. Johnston, *Geography of Elections* (New York: Holmes and Meier, 1979), 486.

60 Hare's original proposal was slightly different; it suggested one nation-wide district, instead of multi-member districts.

61 Bogdanor, *Democracy and Elections,* 9.

62 Rae, *Political Consequences of Electoral Laws,* 89.

63 A. Lijphart, *Electoral Systems and Party Systems* (New York: Oxford University Press, 1994), 159

64 R.S. Katz, "The Single Transferable Vote and Proportional Representation," in A. Lijphart and B. Grofman, *Choosing an Electoral System* (New York: Praeger, 1984), 136

65 Bogdanor, *Democracy and Elections,* 10.

66 I. McLean, "Forms of Representation and Systems of Voting," in *Political Theory Today,* D. Held, ed. (Cambridge: Polity Press, 1991), 187.

67 F.G. Castles, "Female Legislative Representation and the Electoral System," *Polity* (November, 1981).

68 Among others see R.K. Carty, *Party and Parish Pump* (Waterloo: Wilfrid Laurier University Press, 1981); and the contributions in *Representatives of the People?* V. Bogdanor, ed. (Hants.: Gower Publishing, 1985).

69 Carty, *Party and Parish Pump,* 27; 64.

70 Ibid., 100; 124; 150.

NOTES FOR CHAPTER 7

1 N. Machiavelli, *The Prince* (New York: Oxford University Press,1952), 49-50.

2 V. Bogdanor and D. Butler, eds., *Democracies and Elections* (Cambridge: Cambridge University, 1983) 251.

3 Ibid., 10. Confirmed by K. Carty, *Party and Parish Pump* (Waterloo, Ontario: Wilfrid Laurier University Press, 1981), 140-43; 146.

4 These results use Lijphart's Index. On that Index Ireland's disproportionality is 2.4 percent, and Canada's 8.1 percent. A. Lijphart, *Democracies* (New Haven: Yale University Press, 1984), 160-65.

5 "There is reciprocal interaction between social and electoral change." Bogdanor, vii (see note 2 above)..

6 A. Blais, and K. Carty, "Does Proportional Representation Foster Voter Turnout?" *European Journal Of Political Research* (Dordrecht: Kluwer Academic Publisher, vol. 18, no. 2, 1990), 167-82; Royal Commission on Electoral Reform and Party Financing, *Report,* vol. 1, 19.

7 A. Cairns and D. Wong, "Socialism, Federalism and the BC Party Systems 1933-1983," in *Party Politics in Canada,* H.G. Thornburn, 6th. ed. (Scarborough: Prentice-Hall Canada, 1991), 468-506.

8 See Appendix B, Tables 2 and 3.

9 Threshold is the most important aspect of an electoral system's ability to influence political behaviour. See chap. 7, "Electoral Engineering: Limits and Possibilities," in A. Lijphart, *Electoral Systems and Party Systems* (New York: Oxford University Press, 1994), 139-52.

10 Cairns and Wong, in *Party Politics in Canada.*

11 For example, C. Maille, "Primed for Power: Women in Canadian Politics" (Ottawa: Canadian Advisory Council on the Status of Women, 1990), 31.

12 German and Scandinavian legislatures have a more effective role in the scrutiny of legislation than the British House of Commons. See V. Bogdanor,

ed., *Coalition Government in Western Europe* (London: Heineman Educational Books,1983), 271.

13 For a full comparison between the Westminster, adversarial and the consensual models of governing see, among others: A. Lijphart, *Democracy in Plural Societies: A Comparative Exploration* (New Haven: Yale University Press, 1977); and also, Lijphart, *Democracies,* chaps. 1 and 2.

14 STV's civilizing effect on legislators is well documented. Among others see D.J. Amy, *Real Choices/New Voices* (New York: Columbia University Press 1993), 74.

15 Not to be read as a slur against politicians, but a metaphor for political parties acting in their self-interest.

16 A. Cairns, "The Electoral System and the Party System in Canada, 1921-1965," *Canadian Journal of Political Science,* 1 (March 1968), 56.

17 W. Irvine, "A Review and Evaluation of Electoral Reform Proposals," in *Institutional Reforms for Representative Government,* P. Aucoin, ed. (Toronto: University of Toronto Press, 1986), 102.

18 G.L. Kristianson, "The Non-partisan Approach to BC Politics: The Search for a Unity Party–1972-1975," *BC Studies* (Vancouver: UBC Press, no. 33, Spring 1977), 13-29.

19 Bennett had supported the alternative vote as early as 1947, and by his own admission, the Coalition government adopted it at his urging. D.J. Mitchell, *WAC Bennett* (Vancouver: Douglas and McIntyre 1983), 88 and 127. Also D.G. Steeves, *The Compassionate Rebel, E. Winch and His Times* (Vancouver: Evergreen Press, 1960), 181; and D.J. Elkins, "Politics Makes Strange Bedfellows: The BC Party System in the 1952 and 1953 Provincial Elections," *BC Studies,* No. 30 (Summer 1976), 3-26. The alternative vote is not PR; it ensures candidates are elected by the majority of the votes cast in each riding, but it does not give government to candidates supported by the majority of provincial voters.

20 J.S. Woodsworth supported PR in 1930, but some within the CCF opposed PR on the grounds that a system which now worked against them would help them eventually, as was confirmed in the 1944 Saskatchewan election. H. Philips, *Challenges to the Voting System in Canada, 1874-1974* (London, Ontario: University of Western Ontario, 1976), 198 and 260-63.

21 A. Blais, "The Debate over Electoral Systems," *International Political Science Review* (1991), vol. 12, no. 3, 248.

22 G. Palmer, *Unbridled Power,* second edition (Auckland: Oxford University Press), 70-77.

23 H. Angus, "Report of the Commission of Inquiry into Redefinition of Electoral Districts" (1966), 16-21.

24 R. MacGregor Dawson and W.F. Dawson, revised by N. Ward, *Democratic Government in Canada* (Toronto: University of Toronto Press), fifth ed., 3 and 5 (first published 1949).

25 Maureen McTeer, *Parliament: Canada's Democracy and How it Works* (Toronto: Random House, 1987), 18-19.

26 A.M. Goddard, *Legislative Behavior in the British Columbia Legislative Assembly* (Ann Arbor: University Microfilms, 1973), 185.

27 P. Russell, "Can the Canadians Be a Sovereign People?" *Canadian Journal of Political Science,* XXIV 4 (December 1991).

28 Among others, R. Sigurdson, "Preston Manning and the Politics of Postmodernism in Canada," *Canadian Journal of Political Science*, XXVII:2 (June 1994), 249.

29 Royal Commission on Electoral Reform and Party Financing, *Report*, vol. 1, 228.

30 R. Bibby, *Mosaic Madness* (Toronto: Stoddart, 1990), 200-1.

31 P. Mair, "The Question of Electoral Reform," *New Left Review* (July/August 1992), no. 194, London, England, New Left Publishing.

32 PR Society of Canada, "The Crisis in Party Politics," (Vancouver: Westminster Review Publishing Office, September 1916), 3. Note that PR is seen as necessary for self-government.

33 C.G. Hoag and H. Hallett, *Proportional Representation* (New York: MacMillan, 1926), 223-234, quoted in private correspondence from Enid Lakeman, Editorial Consultant for Electoral Reform Society of Great Britain, 9 February 1994. The author has tried and failed to locate a copy of this book.

34 Contemporary newspapers in both Edmonton and Calgary also accused Social Credit of political motivation, but Social Credit, unlike the Liberals in Manitoba, largely escaped the voters' wrath.

35 Much of this historical information is drawn from P.J. Harris, "The Practical Workings of Proportional Representation in the United States and Canada," in *Supplement to the National Municipal Review* (New York: National Municipal League, May, 1930), vol. XIX, no. 5, 365-67; Enid Lakeman's correspondence to the author; and E. Lakeman, *Power to Elect* (London: Heineman, 1982), 116-22; and H. Philips *Challenges to the Voting System in Canada, 1874-1974*. The first two of these works are by authors supportive of PR, the last author less so.

36 Proponents include: E. Broadbent, House of Commons Debates (Ottawa: Queen's Printer of Canada, 1978), vol. VI, 6974; D. Smiley, "Federalism and the Legislative Process in Canada," in *The Legislative Process in Canada: The Need for Reform*, W. Neilson and J. MacPherson, eds., Proceedings of Conference, March 31-April 1, 1978 (Victoria: University of Victoria) 73-87; The Task Force on Canadian Unity (Pepin-Robarts), *A Future Together* (Ottawa: Minister of Supply and Services Canada, 1979), 105; W. Irvine, *Does Canada Need a New Electoral System?* (Kingston: Queen's University,1979), 53-54; D. Elton and R. Gibbens, "Electoral Reform: The Need Is Pressing, the Time Is Now" (Calgary: Canada West Foundation, 1980); D. Smiley and R. Watts, *Intrastate Federalism in Canada* (Toronto: University of Toronto Press,1985), 113-14; J.V. Clyne, "Electoral Reform," Address to the Chilliwack Rotary Club, 16 January 1976.

37 Proponents include: C. Boyle, "Home Rule for Women: Power-Sharing Between Men and Women," *The Dalhousie Law Journal* (October 1983), vol. 7, no. 3 (Halifax: Dalhousie Press); C. Maille, "Primed for Power: Women in Canadian Politics" (Ottawa: Canadian Advisory Council on the Status of Women,1990); L. Young, "Electoral Systems and Representative Legislatures: Consideration of Alternative Electoral Systems" (Ottawa: Canadian Advisory Council on the Status of Women, July 1994); L. Marchand, "Proportional Representation for the Native Peoples," *Canadian Parliamentary Review* (Ottawa: vol. 13, no. 3, 1990), 9-11.

38 Consensus Report on the Constitution (Ottawa: Minister of Supply and Services Canada, August, 1992).

39 V. Bogdanor, *The People and the Party System* (Cambridge: Cambridge University Press, 1981), 67.

APPENDIX A

SUGGESTED VOTING DISTRICTS FOR BRITISH COLUMBIA
USING THE SINGLE TRANSFERABLE VOTE (STV) ELECTORAL
SYSTEM IN COMPARISON WITH THE EXISTING SINGLE
MEMBER PLURALITY (SMP) ELECTORAL SYSTEM

Existing Districts	Population (1991)[1]	STV Districts and number of seats[2]	Population per MLA	Deviation in %[3]
Esquimalt-Metchosin	49,920			
Oak Bay-GordonHead	45,750			
Saanich North/Islands	46,395			
Saanich South	44,005			
Victoria-Beacon Hill	42,095			
Victoria-Hillside	48,040			
		Victoria (6)	46,034	8.8
Alberni	31,090			(-26.5)
Comox Valley	54,585			(+29)
Cowichan-Ladysmith	46,025			
Malahat-Juan De Fuca	40,115			
Nanaimo	52,470			
North Island	43,710			
Parksville-Qualicum	46,825			
		Paradise (7)	44,940	6.2
Vancouver-Burrard	45,130			
Vancouver-Fraserview	47,655			
Vancouver-Hastings	49,570			
Vancouver-Kensington	51,600			
Vancouver-Kingsway	46,275			
Vancouver-Langara	48,070			
Vancouver-Little Mnt.	47,875			
Vancouver-Mnt. Pleasant	48,875			
Vancouver-Point Grey	47,035			
Vancouver-Quilchena	45,465			
		Vancouver (10)	47,755	12.8

Existing Districts	Population (1991)[1]	STV Districts and number of seats[2]	Population per MLA	Deviation in %[3]
North Vanc.-Lonsdale	43,070			
North Vanc.-Seymour	48,355			
Powell River-Sunshine	38,940			
West Vanc.-Capilano	45,165			
West Vanc.-Garibaldi	40,225			
		North Shore (5)	43,151	1.9
Delta North	46,755			
Delta South	42,680			
Richmond Centre	43,175			
Richmond East	42,925			
Richmond Steveston	40,475			
		Delta (5)	43,202	2
Surrey-Cloverdale	54,275			(+28.2)
Surrey-Green Timbers	50,765			(+51.4)
Surrey-Newton	64,080			
Surrey-Whalley	40,835			
Surrey-White Rock	51,830			
		Surrey (5)	52,557	24.2
Burnaby-Edmonds	47,115			
Burnaby-North	44,945			
Burnaby-Willingdon	49,195			
New Westminster	43,535			
Port Moody-Burnaby Mtn.	47,915			
		Eastside (5)	46,541	9.9
Coquitlam-Maillardville	51,540			
Maple Ridge-Pitt Meadow	36,880			
Mission-Kent	39,075			
Port Coquitlam	57,895			
		Fraser Valley North (4)	46,347	9.5
Abbotsford	43,745			
Chilliwack	48,890			
Fort Langley-Aldergrove	44.625			
Langley	41,980			
Matsqui	49,405			
		Fraser Valley South (5)	45,657	7.9
Kelowna East	52,245			
Kelowna West	55,270			(+30.6)
Okanagan-Boundary	37,070			
Okanagan-Penticton	44,400			
Okanagan-Vernon	48,750			

Existing Districts	Population (1991)[1]	STV Districts and number of seats[2]	Population per MLA	Deviation in %[3]
		Okanagan (5)	45,694	7.9
Kamloops	43,695			
Kamloops-North Thomp.	36,290			
Shuswap	44,266			
Yale-Lillooet	33,630			
		Kamloops (4)	39,470	-6.7
Columbia River-Revelsto.	31,025			(-26.6)
Kootenay	36,510			
Nelson-Creston	37,525			
Rossland-Trail	33,510			
		Kootenays (4)	34,642	-18.1
Cariboo North	30,215			(-26.2)
Cariboo South	32,420			
Prince George-Mt. Robs.	31,075			(-26.5)
		New Caledonia (3)	31,236	(-26.1)
Peace River North	30,025			(-29)
Peace River South	34,040			
Prince George North	29,380			
		Peace River (3)	31,148	(-26.3)
North Coast	37,355			
Prince George-Omenica	39,315			
Skeena	54,275			(28.2)
		Bulkley (3)	36,351	-14

Note: Vancouver could easily be split into two 5-seat districts without significantly affecting proportionality, but that might not be necessary. As experience has shown, under STV, local or neighbourhood interests will attract candidates who specialize in representing those interests. STV allows for representation of both political ideology and neighbourhood, but if there is to be a choice between those two, the choice is made by the voter.

A second reason for objecting to a 10-seat district relates to the length of the ballot paper. However, it would be no longer than those currently used in civic elections.

Notes

1   Prepared by CSB, Government Services, Victoria, using Statistics Canada data, and aggregated by provincial electoral district.

2   The larger the district size, the easier it is for minorities or minority opinions to be represented. In a 3-seat district it takes 25 percent to obtain a seat, and in a 9-seat district just 10 percent.

3   Percentage deviation from the provincial average or quota. Judge Thomas
     Fisher in his Report of the Royal Commission on Electoral Boundaries for
     British Columbia, December 1988, recommended a deviation in district popu-
     lation no greater than 25 percent plus or minus the provincial average. The
     legislature adopted the Report in time for the 1991 general election, but inter-
     vening population shifts meant 10 districts exceeded the permitted deviation
     at the time the election was held. Bracketed percentages indicate which dis-
     tricts exceed the permitted deviation, and by how much, using 1991 census
     data. The 15 STV districts proposed here meet the 25 percent rule, except for
     2 which are fractionally over.

APPENDIX B

Table 1: CLASSIFYING COUNTRIES BY ELECTORAL SYSTEMS

CLASSIFYING VOTING SYSTEMS is almost impossible since there are so many possibilities, permutations and mixtures. Different studies use different categories; for example, some classify STV as a proportional system, others as a mixed system.

The following countries are categorized in the generally accepted broad categories of PR, Mixed, and SMP. The latter, it will be noted, are mostly countries that are or have been part of the British Commonwealth. To claim that most countries use PR would be false; to claim that most people live under PR is also false. It seems true that most democracies use PR. Such questions cannot even be approximated without rigid operational definitions of terms such as "country", "PR" and "democracy." The following list is not precise or exhaustive, merely suggestive.

PR	MIXED	SMP
Angola	Chile	Bangladesh
Australia (Senate)	Croatia	Canada
Austria	Georgia	Congo
Belgium	Germany	Great Britain
Brazil	Hungary	India
Columbia	Italy	Jamaica
Costa Rica	Japan	Jordan
Cyprus	Lithuania	Kenya
Czechoslovakia	Mexico	Latvia
Denmark	New Zealand	Malaysia
Dominican Republic	Republic of Korea	Nigeria
Estonia	Venezuela	Pakistan
Finland	Yugoslavia	Philippines
Greece		United States
Guatemala		
Honduras		
Iceland		
Indonesia		

Ireland
Israel
Lebanon
Malta
Netherlands
Nicaragua
Norway
Poland
Portugal
South Africa
Spain
Sweden
Switzerland
Turkey

Table 2: COMPARISON OF ACTUAL 1991 BC ELECTION RESULTS UNDER SMP TO PROJECTED RESULTS USING 15 STV DISTRICTS

		SMP	STV
No. of registered voters		1,989,054	1,989,054
No. of voters who voted		1,493,200	1,652,307[1]
% of voters who voted		75.0	83.07
No. of voters who elected their choice		666,713[2]	1,384,627[3]
% of voters who elected their choice		44.65	83.8
No. of voters who did not elect their choice		826,487	267,680
% of voters who did not elect their choice		55.35	16.2
% of popular vote	NDP	40.71	40.71[4]
	Lib.	33.25	33.25
	SC	24.05	24.05
No. and (%) of seats	NDP	51 (68)	36 (48)
	Lib.	17 (22.6)	26 (34.6)
	SC	7 (9.3)	13 (17.3)
Index of disproportionality, in %[5]	NDP	13.6	3.6
	Lib.	5.3	.67
	SC	7.3	3.3
Index of proportionality[6]	NDP	86	96
(Range is 0 - 100)	Lib.	94	99
	SC	92	96

Table 3: COMPARISON OF ACTUAL 1996 BC ELECTION RESULTS UNDER SMP TO PROJECTED RESULTS USING PR

		SMP	PR
No. of registered voters		2,107,676	2,107,676
No. of voters who voted		1,582,701	1,751,267[7]
% of voters who voted		75.09	83.09
No. of voters who elected their choice		761,469[8]	1,467,561[9]
% of voters who elected their choice		48.11	83.8
No. of voters who did not elect their choice		821,232	283,706
% of voters who did not elect their choice		51.99	16.2
% of popular vote	NDP	39.45	39.45[10]
	Lib.	41.82	41.82
	Reform	9.27	9.27
	PDA	5.73	5.73
No. and (%) of seats	NDP	39 (52)	30 (40)[11]
	Lib	33 (44)	32 (42.6)
	Reform	2 (2.6)	7 (9.3)
	PDA	1 (1.7)	4(5.3)

TABLE 4: 1993 FEDERAL ELECTION RESULTS

	Liberal	PC	NDP	Bloc	Reform	Other	Totals
Ontario							
Vote share %	53	18	6	0	20	3	
Seat share %	99	0	0	0	1	0	
# of seats	98	0	0	0	1	0	99
Quebec							
Vote share %	33	13	2	49	0	3	
Seat share %	25	1	0	72	0	0	
# of seats	19	1	0	54	0	0	75
British Columbia							
Vote share %	28	13	15	0	36	8	
Seat share %	19	0	6	0	75	0	
# of seats	6	0	2	0	24	0	32
Alberta							
Vote share %	25	15	4	0	52	4	
Seat share %	15	0	0	0	85	0	
# of seats	4	0	0	0	22	0	24

	Liberal	PC	NDP	Bloc	Reform	Other	Totals
Manitoba							
Vote share %	45	12	17	0	22	4	
Seat share %	86	0	7	0	7	0	
# of seats	12	0	1	0	1	0	14
Saskatchewan							
Vote share %	32	11	27	0	27	3	
Seat share %	36	0	36	0	29	0	
# of seats	5	0	5	0	4	0	14
Nova Scotia							
Vote share %	52	23	7	0	13	5	
Seat share %	100	0	0	0	0	0	
# of seats	11	0	0	0	0	0	11
New Brunswick							
Vote share %	56	28	5	0	8	3	
Seat share %	90	10	0	0	0	0	
# of seats	9	1	0	0	0	0	10
Newfoundland							
Vote share %	67	27	3	0	1	2	
Seat share %	100	0	0	0	0	0	
# of seats	7	0	0	0	0	0	7
Prince Edward Island							
Vote share %	60	32	5	0	1	2	
Seat share %	100	0	0	0	0	0	
# of seats	7	0	0	0	0	0	7
Yukon/NWT							
Vote share %	49	17	21	0	10	3	
Seat share %	67	0	33	0	0	0	
# of seats	2	0	1	0	0	0	3
Canada Totals							
Vote share %	41.3	16.0	6.9	13.5	18.7	3.6	
Seat share %	60.3	0.7	3.0	18.3	17.6	0	
# of seats	178	2	9	54	52	0	295

PR DISTRIBUTION OF SEATS

	Liberal	PC	NDP	Bloc	Reform	Other
	122	47	20	40	55	10

NUMBER OF VOTES PER SEAT BY PARTY

Liberal	31,730
PC	1,093,211
NDP	104,397
Bloc	34,185
Reform	49,216

Source: Elections Canada

It is noteworthy that Reform's total vote count in Ontario is 982,691 and Reform's combined Alberta/British Columbia vote count is 1,223,001. However, Reform obtained only 1 seat in Ontario, but 46 in Alberta/British Columbia. Our electoral system does not bridge regionalism; it exacerbates regionalism.

Table 5: VOTE SHARE AND SEAT SHARE IN B.C. GENERAL ELECTIONS 1956–96[12]

Year	1956	1960	1963	1966	1969	1972	1975	1979	1983	1986	1991	1996
Total Seats	52	52	52	55	55	55	55	57	57	69	75	75
				Social Credit Party in percentages								
Of vote	**45.8**[13]	**38.8**	**40.8**	**45.6**	**46.7**	31.1	**49.2**	**48.2**	**49.7**	**49.3**	24	0.39
Gain/loss	——	-7	2	4.8	1.1	-15.6	18.1	-0.1	1.5	-0.4	-25.3	-23.6
Of seats	75	61.5	60	60	69	17.2	63.6	54.3	61.4	68	9.3	0
Gain/loss	——	-13.5	-1.5	0	9	-51.8	46.4	-9.3	7.1	6.6	-58.7	-900
				New Democratic Party in percentages								
Of vote	28.3	32.7	27.8	33.6	33.9	**39.5**	39.1	45.9	44.9	42.6	**40.7**	**39.4**
Gain/loss	——	4.4	-4.9	5.8	0.3	5.6	-0.4[14]	6.8	-1	-2.3	-1.9[15]	-1.3
Of seats	19.2	30.7	26.9	29	21.8	69	32.7	45.6	38.5	31.8	68	52
Gain/loss	——	11.5	-3.8	2.1	-7.2	47.2	-36.3	12.9	-7.1	-6.7	36.2	-23.5
				Liberal Party in percentages								
Of vote	21.7	20.9	19.9	20.2	19	16.4	7.2	0.4	2.6	6.7	33.2	41.8[16]
Gain/loss	——	-0.8	-1	0.3	-1.2	-2.6	-9.2	-6.8	2.2	4.1	26.5	8.6
Of seats	3.8	7.6	9.6	10.9	9	9	1.8	0	0	0	22.6	44
Gain/loss	——	3.8	2	1.3	-1.9	0	-7.2	-1.8	0	0	22.6	21.4

Notes

1   Blais and Carty studied voter turnout for 509 elections in 20 countries to verify whether claims of greater voter turnout under PR, made by proponents of PR such as Lakeman, are justified. Their findings confirm that voter turnout is 8 percent higher in PR systems than SMP systems, which is the number used here. Lortie places the increase at 11.4 percent. (A. Blais and K. Carty, "Does Proportional Representation Foster Voter Turnout?" *European Journal of Political Research*, Vol. 18, No. 2 [1990] Dordrecht: Kluwer Academic Publishers, 167-182; and Lortie [Royal Commission on Electoral Reform and Party Financing], vol. 1, 54.)

2   Source: *Report of the Chief Electoral Officer*, 35th Provincial General Election October 17, 1991. This is the amount of total votes cast for the 75 winning candidates.

3   This represents 83.8 percent of the total expected to vote. This percentage is the theoretical minimum number of voters who will elect the succesful candidates,

provided not more than 16.2 percent of ballot papers become non-transferable. 16.2 percent is the maximum number of votes that could be wasted, because they do not help to elect anyone, again with the same proviso. This percentage is the average of all 15 percentages determined by applying the formula (Total population, divided by N, where N equals number of seats, plus one) to each of the 15 STV districts, as per Appendix B, and expressing the resulting number as a percentage of the total population. These percentages correspond very closely to Lakeman's predictions and actual findings. (E. Lakeman, *How Democracies Vote*, London: Faber and Faber, 1974, 125-29, and Appendix II, 281.)

4   Assuming the number of parties would not increase and their vote share would remain constant.

5   Based on Lijphart's formula, which is a refinement of those used by Rae and Loosemore-Hanby. The average under STV for the 3 parties is 2.5 percent, which corresponds very closely to Lijphart's findings of 2.4 percent for Ireland. (A. Lijphart, *Democracies*, New Haven: Yale University Press, 1984, 160-65.)

6   As used by Lortie, vol. 1, p. 19.

7   Blais and Carty studied voter turnout for 509 elections in 20 countries to verify whether claims of greater voter turnout under PR, made by proponents of PR such as Lakeman, are justified. Their findings confirm that voter turnout is 8 percent higher in PR systems than SMP systems, which is the number used here. Lortie places the increase at 11.4 percent. Blais A, and Carty K, "Does Proportional Representation Foster Voter Turnout?" *European Journal of Political Research*, Vol. 18, No. 2 (1990) Dordrecht: Kluwer Academic Publishers, 167-182: and Lortie, vol. 1, 54.

8   Source: *Report of the Chief Electoral Officer*, 36th Provincial General Election May 28, 1996. This is the amountof total votes cast for the 75 winning candidates.

9   As in Table 1, this is 83.8 percent of the total expected to vote. The number of wasted votes depends on the type of PR system used. Under STV, this percentage is the maximum number of votes that may not contribute to electing any candidate, provided not more than 16.2 percent of ballots become non-transferable. Under MMP the percentage of second ballots – the ballots that select government – is not likely to exceed 15 percent depending on the threshold and the vote-share of parties under the threshold.

10   Assuming the number of parties would not increase and their vote share would remain constant.

11   This assumes almost strict proportionality. Lijphart found STV in Ireland to produce a deviation from strict proportionality of 2.4 percent. (Lijphart, *Democracies*, 160-65.) However, Ireland uses mostly three-member ridings. In practice five-member ridings will produce greater proportionality.

12   The two general elections immediately prior to 1956 used the alternative ballot, and before that the Liberal-Conservative Coalition contested elections during, and just after WWII. Therefore, to test the relationship of a party's vote-share to seat-share under Single Member Plurality (SMP), the elections between 1956 and 1996 are most useful.

13   Bold indicates the percentage of vote-share that won majority government for that year. In each of the 12 elections legislative majorities were artificially manufactured

14   The 0.4 percent loss in vote-share resulted in 36.3 percent loss in seat share. The loss in seats is 90 times greater than the loss in votes.

15   Parties can win an election while losing vote share.

16   Occasionally, SMP awards government to a party with fewer votes than its rival.

APPENDIX C

SINGLE TRANSFERABLE VOTE COUNTING PROCEDURE AS USED IN THE REPUBLIC OF IRELAND[1]

STEP 1 The ballot papers are sorted and counted according to first preferences.

STEP 2 A quota is calculated using the Droop formula: divide the number of valid ballot papers by N and add 1 (where N is equal to the number of seats to be filled, plus 1).[2] Candidates whose number of first preference ballot papers meet or exceed the quota are declared elected.

STEP 3 If no candidate is elected the candidate with the least number of first preference ballots is removed, and those ballot papers are transferred to remaining candidates according to the preference instructions the voter left on the ballot paper.

STEP 4 Whenever a candidate meets the quota, surplus ballot papers for that candidate must be transferred to remaining candidates in proportion to the support those remaining candidates received within the total number of ballot papers for the just elected candidate. The formula is as follows: the surplus number is divided by the total number for the elected candidate, the resulting fraction is multiplied by the number of ballot papers indicating a preference for the unelected candidate.

STEP 5 Steps 3 and 4 are repeated until all seats except one are filled. At that point the candidate with the highest number of ballot papers among the remaining candidates is declared elected.

Notes

1   Sources used: D.W. Rae, *The Political Consequences of Electoral Laws* (New Haven: Yale University Press, 1967) 36-7; E. Lakeman, *How Democracies Vote* (London: Faber and Faber, 1974), 146-47; 289-90; P. Hains, *Proportional Misrepresentation*, Hants., England: Wildwood House, 1986, 99-107; D.J. Amy, *Real Choices/New Voices*, New York: Columbia University Press 1993, 237-38.

2   The principle of the single transferable vote was first proposed in 1855 by Andrae in Denmark, and in 1857 by Hare in England. Hare's quota is a simple division of the number of valid ballot papers by the number of seats. Hence, the Hare quota is much larger than the Droop quota. Lakeman observes that the smaller Droop quota allows fewer votes to be surplus and thus lessens wasted votes. Also, the effect is to exclude the possibility of party manipulation. See Lakeman, *How Democracies Vote*, 113; 146-47.

BIBLIOGRAPHY

Amy, D.J. *Real Choices/New Voices*. New York: Columbia University Press, 1993.

Angus, H.F. *Citizenship in BC*. Victoria: King's Printer, 1926.

——. "Report of the Commission of Inquiry into Redefinition of Electoral Districts." Victoria: Queen's Printer, 1966.

Aiken, G. *The Backbencher*. Toronto: McClelland & Stewart, 1974.

Barber, B. *Strong Democracy*. Berkeley, Los Angeles: University of California Press, 1984

Barker, P. "Voting for Trouble." In *Contemporary Political Issues*, edited by M. Charlton and P. Barker, 2nd. ed. Scarborough: Nelson Canada, 1994.

Balinski, M., and H. P. Young. *Fair Representation*. New Haven: Yale University Press, 1982.

Birch, A.H. *Representation*. London, Pall Mall Press, 1971.

——. *Representative and Responsible Government*. London: George Allen and Unwin, 1964.

Blais, A., and K. Carty. "The Psychological Impact of Electoral Law: Measuring Duverger's Elusive Factor." *British Journal of Political Science*, 1991.

——. "Does Proportional Representation Foster Voter Turnout?" *European Journal of Political Research*. Dordrecht: Kluwer Academic Publisher, Vol. 18, No.2 (1990).

Blais, A., and E. Gidengil. *Making Representative Democracy Work*. Toronto: Dundurn Press, 1991.

——. "The Debate over Electoral Systems." *International Political Science Review*, Vol. 12, No. 3 (1991).

Blake, D.E. *Two Political Worlds*. Vancouver: UBC Press, 1985.

Blake, D.E., et al. *Grassroots Politicians: Party Activists in British Columbia*, Vancouver: UBC Press, 1991.

Bogdanor, Vernon. *The People and the Party System*. London: Cambridge University Press, 1981.

——. *What Is Proportional Representation?* Oxford: Martin Robertson, 1984.

——. *Representatives of the People?* Hants., England: Gower Publishing, 1985.

Bogdanor, Vernon, ed. *Coalition Government in Western Europe*. London: Heineman Educational Books,1983.

Bogdanor, Vernon, and D. Butler, eds. *Democracy and Elections*. Cambridge: Cambridge University, 1983.

Bowers, J.R. *Regulating the Regulators*. New York: Praeger, 1990.

Bowbrick, G. "Revisiting the Implications of Recall and Initiative and their Potential Implementation in British Columbia." Unpublished paper, University of British Columbia, Faculty of Law, 1992

Boyle, C. "Home Rule for Women: Power-Sharing between Men and Women." *The Dalhousie Law Journal*, Vol. 7 No. 3, October 1983.

Boyle, T. Patrick. *Elections British Columbia*. Vancouver: Lions Gate Press, 1982.

Boyer, P.J. *Lawmaking by the People*. Toronto: Butterworth, 1982.

——. *Direct Democracy in Canada*. Toronto: Dundurn Press, 1992.

——. *The People's Mandate*. Toronto: Dundurn Press, 1992.

British Columbia. *Electoral History of British Columbia 1871–1986*. Victoria: Elections B.C., and Legislative Library, 1988.

Cairns, A. "The Electoral System and the Party System in Canada, 1921–1965." *Canadian Journal of Political Science* 1, March 1968.

Cairns, A., and D. Wong. "Socialism, Federalism and the B.C. Party Systems 1933–1983." In *Party Politics in Canada*, edited by H.G. Thornburn, 468-506, 6th. ed. Scarborough: Prentice-Hall Canada, 1991.

Canada. Royal Commission on the Economic Union and Development Prospects for Canada, *Report*, 3 vols. V.3, part 4. Ottawa, Supply and Services Canada, 1985.

——. Royal Commission on Electoral Reform and Party Financing, *Report* Vol. 1, 2. Ottawa: Minister of Supply and Services, 1991.

Canada West Foundation. *Conference Report: Renewal of Canada — Institutional Reform*. Calgary, 1992.

Canadian Advisory Council on the Status of Women. "Women in Politics," *Issue Summary*, November 1993.

Canadian Study of Parliament Group. *A Review of the McGrath Committee Report on the Reform of the House of Commons*, 2 December 1992 (*Proceedings, Year 7*).

Carty, R.K., et al. eds. *Leaders and Parties in Canadian Politics*. Toronto: Harcourt Brace Jovanovich Canada, 1992.

——. *Party and Parish Pump*. Waterloo: Wilfrid Laurier University Press, 1981.

Cassidy, M., ed. *Democratic Rights and Electoral Reform in Canada*. Toronto: Dundurn Press, 1991.

——. *Fairness and Stability in Canadian Elections: The Case for an Alternative Electoral System*. Ottawa: Parliamentary Centre for Foreign Affairs and Foreign Trade, 1992.

Castles, F. G. "Female Legislative Representation and the Electoral System," *Polity*, November 1981.

Clarke, H.D., et al., eds. *Parliament, Policy and Representation*. Toronto: Methuen, 1980.

——. *Absent Mandate*. Toronto: Gage Educational Publishing Co., 1991.

Clyne, J.V., "Electoral Reform." Address to the Chilliwack Rotary Club, 16 January 1976.

Cohen, Carl. *Democracy*. Athens, Ga.: University of Georgia Press, 1971.

Courtney, J. C., et al., eds. *Drawing Boundaries*. Saskatoon: Fifth House Publishers, 1992.

——. "Leadership, Conventions and the Development of the National Political Community in Canada." In *National Politics and Community in Canada*, edited by K. C. Carty and P. W. Ward. Vancouver: University of British Columbia Press, 1986.

Crewe, I. "MPs and their Constituents in Britain: How Strong Are the Links?" In *Representatives of the People?* edited by V. Bogdanor. Hants., U.K.: Gower Publishing, 1985.

Cronin, T. E. *Direct Democracy: The Politics of Initiative, Referendum and Recall*. Cambridge: Harvard University Press, 1989.

Dawson, R. MacGregor, and W. F. Dawson. *Democratic Government in Canada*, 5th ed. (revised by N. Ward). Toronto: University of Toronto Press, first published 1949.

De Tocqueville, A. *Democracy in America* {1835}. New York: Washington Square Press, 1964.

Deverell, J., and G. Vezina. *Democracy, Eh?* Montreal: Robert Davies Publishing, 1993.

Dobell, Peter, and Byron Berry. "Anger at the System: Political Discontent in Canada." *Parliamentary Government* 39, January 1992. Ottawa: Parliamentary Centre for Foreign Affairs and Foreign Trade.

Dunn, C. "The Meaning of Responsible Government." *Canadian Parliamentary Review,* Vol.11, No.3, 1988: 12-13.

Duverger, M. *Political Parties.* 2nd ed. Toronto: Methuen, 1959.

Dyck, J. H. A. "Representative Recall and Initiative Legislation: Two Forms of Direct Democracy." University College of Cariboo: paper prepared for Select Standing Committee on Parliamentary Reform, 29 September 1992.

Elkins, D. J. *Manipulation and Consent.* Vancouver: University of British Columbia Press, 1993.

———. "Politics Makes Strange Bedfellows: The B.C. Party System in the 1952 and 1953 Provincial Elections."*BC Studies* 30, Summer 1976.

Elliot, D. R., and I. Miller. *Bible Bill.* Edmonton: Reidmore Books, 1987.

Elton, D. and R. Gibbens. "Electoral Reform: The Need is Pressing, the Time is Now." Calgary: Canada West Foundation, 1980.

Fishkin, James S. *Democracy and Deliberation,* New Haven: Yale University Press, 1991.

Flanagan, T. "Reform of Canada's Parliamentary Institutions." Unpublished paper for Reform Party of Canada, June, 1991.

Forsey, E. *How Canadians Govern Themselves.* Ottawa: Publication Canada, 1980.

Franks, C.E.S. *The Parliament of Canada.* Toronto: University of Toronto Press, 1987.

Freeman, Michael. *Edmund Burke and the Critique of Political Radicalism,* Chicago: University of Chicago Press, 1980

Furlong, P. "Government Stability and Electoral Systems: The Italian Example." *Parliamentary Affairs,* Vol. 44, No.1, January 1991. Oxford University Press.

Gagnon, G. and D. Rath. *Not Without Cause.* Toronto: Harper & Row, 1991.

Goddard, A.M. *Legislative Behavior in the British Columbia Legislative Assembly.* Ann Arbor: University Microfilms, 1973.

Grant, G. *Lament For A Nation.* Ottawa, Carleton University Press, 1970

Grofman, B., and A. Lijphart, eds. *Electoral Laws and Their Political Consequences.* New York: Agathon, 1986.

Grumm, J. H. "Theories of Electoral Systems." *Mid-West Journal of Political Science,* 1958.

Hains, P. *Proportional Mis-Representation.* Hants., England: Wildwood House, 1986.

Harris, J.P. "The Practical Workings of Proportional Representation in the United States and Canada." New York: National Municipal League, *Supplement to the National Municipal Review,* May 1930, Vol. XIX, No. 5.

Hermens, F. A. *Democracy or Anarchy? A Study of Proportional Representation,* New York: Johnston Reprint Corporation, 1972.

Hill, A. and A. Whichelow. *What's Wrong With Parliament.* London: Penguin Books, 1964.

Hoag, C.G., and H. Hallett. *Proportional Representation.* New York: Macmillan, 1926.

Hochin, T. A., ed. *Apex of Power.* 2nd ed. Scarborough: Prentice-Hall of Canada , 1977.

Hogg, P.W. *Constitutional Law of Canada.* 2nd ed., Toronto: Carswell Co., 1985.

Howay, F.W., and E.O.S. Scholefield. *British Columbia.* Vancouver: S.J. Clark Company, 1914 (Vol. II).

Johnston, Richard. *Public Opinion and Public Policy in Canada: Questions of Confidence.* Toronto, University of Toronto Press, 1986.

189

Jackson, Robert J., and Michael M. Atkinson. *The Canadian Legislative System: Politicians and Policymaking.* Toronto: Gage Publishing, 1980.

Johnston, D. *On the Hill.* Montreal: Optimum Publishing International, 1986.

Johnston, P.J., and H.E. Pasis. *Representation and Electoral Systems.* Scarborough: Prentice-Hall, 1990.

Irvine, W. *Does Canada Need a New Electoral System?* Kingston: Queen's University, 1979.

———. "A Review and Evaluation of Electoral Reform Proposals." In P. Aucoin, *Institutional Reforms for Representative Government.* Toronto: University of Toronto Press, 1986.

Kent, Tom. *Getting Ready For 1999.* Ottawa: The Institute for Research on Public Policy, 1989.

Keyes, J. M. *Executive Legislation.* Toronto: Butterworth, 1992.

Kilgour, D. and J. Kirsner. "Party Discipline and Canadian Democracy." *Canadian Parliamentary Review,* 1988, 11:10.

Kornberg, A. *Canadian Legislative Behavior.* New York: Holt, Rinehart, & Winston, 1967.

Kornberg, A. et al. *Representative Democracy in the Canadian Provinces.* Scarborough, Prentice-Hall Canada, 1982.

Kornberg, A., and W. Mishler. *Influence in Parliament.* Durham: Duke University Press, 1976.

Kornberg, A., and Musolf L. D. *Legislatures in Developmental Perspective.* Durham: Duke University Press, 1970.

Kristianson, G., and P. Nicholson. "Improving the Image and Operation of the British Columbia Legislature." Brief to the Standing Committee on Standing Orders and Private Bills of the Legislative Assembly of British Columbia, 1984.

———. "The Non-partisan Approach to BC Politics: The Search for a Unity Party - 1972-1975." *BC Studies* 33, Spring 1977.

Lakeman, E. *How Democracies Vote.* London: Faber and Faber, 1974.

———. *Power To Elect.* London: William Heineman, 1982.

Langstone, R. W. *Responsible Government in Canada.* London: J.M. Dent and Sons, 1931.

Laschinger, J. *Leaders and Lesser Mortals: Backroom Politics in Canada.* Toronto: Key Porter Books, 1992.

Laycock, D. "Reforming Canadian Democracy? Institutions and Ideology in the Reform Party Project."*Canadian Journal of Political Science* 27: 2 June 1994: 213–48.

Lee, R. M. *One Hundred Monkeys.* Toronto: Macfarlane Walter and Ross, 1989.

Leslie, G. *Breach of Promise.* Madeira Park: Harbour Publishing, 1991.

Lijphart, A. *Democracy in Plural Societies: A Comparative Exploration.* New Haven: Yale University Press, 1977.

———. *Democracies.* New Haven: Yale University Press, 1984.

Lijphart, A., and B. Grofman, eds. *Choosing an Electoral System.* New York Praeger, 1984.

———. *Electoral Systems and Party Systems.* New York: Oxford University Press, 1994.

Lippmann, W. *The Public Philosophy.* New York: Mentor Books, 1955.

Lipset, S. M., and S. Rokkan eds. *Party Systems and Voter Alignments: Cross-National Perspectives.* New York: The Free Press, 1967 (chapter 1).

Lipson, L. "Party Systems in the United Kingdom and the Older Commonwealth: Causes, Resemblances and Variations."*Political Studies.* 1959.

———. *The Democratic Civilization.* New York: 1964.

MacGregor, Dawson R. *Democratic Government in Canada.* Rev. ed. Toronto: University of Toronto Press, 1963.

McTeer, Maureen. *Parliament: Canada's Democracy and How It Works.* Toronto: Random House, 1987.

Maille, C. "Primed for Power: Women in Canadian Politics." Ottawa: Canadian Advisory Council on the Status of Women, 1990.

Marsh, M. "The Voters Decide? Preferential voting in European List Systems."*European Journal of Political Research* 13 (1964).

March, R.R. *The Myth of Parliament.* Scarborough: Prentice-Hall of Canada, 1974.

Matheson, W. A. *The Prime Minister and the Cabinet.* Toronto: Methuen, 1976.

McLean, Iain. "Forms of Representation and Systems of Voting." In *Political Theory Today,* edited by David Held. Cambridge: Polity Press, 1991.

McLeod, J., ed. *Agenda 1970: Proposals for a Creative Politics.* Toronto: University of Toronto Press, 1970.

MacMinn, G.E. *Parliamentary Practice in British Columbia.* 2nd ed. Victoria: B.C. Government, 1987.

Mill, J.S. *Utilitarianism, Liberty, Representative Government.* London: {1863, 1859, 1861} J.M.Dent and Sons, 1957.

Miller, W.E., and Stokes D.E. "Constituency Influence in Congress." *American Political Science Review* 57, March 1963: 45–56.

Mitchell, D.J. *W.A.C. Bennett.* Vancouver: Douglas and McIntyre, 1983.

Morley, T.J., et al. *The Reins of Power.* Vancouver: Douglas and McIntyre, 1983.

Morton, W.L. *The Progressive Party in Canada,* Toronto: University of Toronto Press, 1950.

Morton, F.L., and R. Knopff. "Does the Charter Mandate `One Person, One Vote'?" Calgary: University of Calgary, Occasional Papers Series, Research Study 7.1, 1991.

Neilson, W., and J. MacPherson, eds. *The Legislative Process in Canada: The Need for Reform.* Proceedings of Conference, March 31–April 1,1978, Victoria: University of Victoria.

Norris, P. "Women's Legislative Participation in Western Europe." *Western European Politics* 4 (1985).

Norton, P., ed. *Parliament in the 1980s.* Oxford: Blackwell, 1985.

Ornstein, N.J. *The Role of the Legislature in Western Democracies.* Washington: American Institute for Public Policy Research, 1981.

Pateman, C. *Participation and Democratic Theory.* Cambridge, 1970.

Phelps, E.M. *Selected Articles on The Recall.* New York: H.W. Wilson Co., 1915.

Philips, H. *Challenges to the Voting System in Canada, 1874-1974.* London, Ont.: University of Western Ontario, 1976.

Pitkin, F. Hanna. *The Concept of Representation.* Berkeley: University of California Press, 1967.

——. *Representation.* New York: Atherton Press, 1969.

Plant, Raymond. "Criteria for Electoral Systems: The Labour Party and Electoral Reform." *Parliamentary Affairs,* Vol. 44, No. 4, Oct. 1991. Oxford University Press.

PR Society of Canada. "The Crisis in Party Politics." Vancouver: Westminster Review Publishing Office, September 1916.

Puttick, K. *Challenging Delegated Legislation.* London: Waterlow Publishers, 1988.

Rae, D. *Political Consequences of Electoral Laws.* New Haven: Yale University Press, 1967.

Resnick, P. *Parliament vs. People.* Vancouver: New Star Books, 1984.

Rose, R. *Politics in England.* 5th ed. London: The McMillan Press, 1989.

Ruff, N.J. "Institutionalizing Populism in British Columbia," *Canadian*

Parliamentary Review, Winter 1993/94 (24-32).

Rule, W. "Electoral Systems, Contextual Factors and Women's Opportunity for Election to Parliament in Twenty-Three Democracies."*Western Political Quarterly,* Vol.40, No. 3 (1987).

Russell, B. *Power.* London: {1938}, Unwin Books, 1967.

Russell, P. "Can the Canadians Be a Sovereign People?" *Canadian Journal of Political Science,* XXIV: 4 December 1991.

Sartori, G. *The Theory of Democracy Revisited.* Chatham, New Jersey: Chatham House Publishers, 1987.

Saunders, C. "Rethinking the Parliamentary System: Contributions from the Australian Debate." *Alberta Law Review* 29 (1991), 336-50.

Schmitt, C. *The Crises of Parliamentary Democracy.* Trans. Ellen Kennedy. Cambridge, Mass.: MIT Press, 1985.

Sharman, C. "The Strange Case of a Provincial Constitution: The British Columbia Constitution Act." *Canadian Journal of Political Science,* March 1984 102-03.

Sharp, C.D. "The Case Against the Referendum." Fabian Tract No.155. London: Fabian Society, 1911.

Sigurdson, R. "Preston Manning and the Politics of Postmodernism in Canada." *Canadian Journal of Political Science,* XXVII:2, June 1994.

Smiley, D., and R. Watts. *Intrastate Federalism in Canada.* Toronto: University of Toronto Press, 1985.

Smith, L., and E. Wachtel. "A Feminist Guide to the Canadian Constitution." Ottawa: CACSW, 1992.

Steeves, D.G. *The Compassionate Rebel: E.Winch and His Times.* Vancouver: Evergreen Press, 1960.

Taagepera, R., and B. Grofman. "Rethinking Duverger's Law: Predicting the Effective Number of Parties in Plurality and PR Systems — Parties Minus Issues Equals One." *European Journal of Political Research* 13 (1985), 341-52.

Taagepera, R., and M. S. Shugart. *Seats and Votes.* New Haven: Yale University Press, 1989.

Taylor, P.J., and R. J. Johnston. *Geography of Elections.* New York: Holmes and Meier Publishers, 1979.

Thomas, D. "Turning a Blind Eye: Constitutional Abeyances and the Canadian Experience." Calgary: Mount Royal College, 1992.

Thompson, R. *The House of Minorities.* Burlington, Ont.: Welch, 1990.

Tocqueville, Alexis de. *Democracy in America.* Vol. II. Trans. H. Reeve. Boston: John Allyn Publisher, 1882,

Uhr, J. "Executive–Legislative Relations: Learning from Locke." *Canadian Parliamentary Review,* v.10:1, Spring 1987, 9-11.

Ward, N. "Confederation and Responsible Government." *Canadian Journal of Economics and Politics,* 24:1, February 1958.

Wahlke, J., et al. *The Legislative System: Explorations in Legislative Behavior.* NewYork: John Wiley and Sons, 1962.

Weller, P. and D. Jaensch, eds. *Responsible Government in Australia.* Victoria: Drummond Publishing, 1980.

Westell, A. *The New Society.* Toronto: McClelland & Stewart, 1977.

Wright, J.F.H. "An Electoral Basis for Responsible Government: The Australian Experience." In *Choosing An Electoral System,* by A. Lijphart and B. Grofman. New York: Praeger, 1984.

Young, L. "Electoral Systems and Representative Legislatures: Consideration of Alternative Electoral Systems." Ottawa: Canadian Advisory Council on the Status of Women, July, 1994.